Tough Love for Schools

For my mom and dad, who taught me the value of tough love.

Tough Love for Schools

Essays on Competition, Accountability,
and Excellence

Frederick M. Hess

The AEI Press

Publisher for the American Enterprise Institute

WASHINGTON, D.C.

Distributed to the Trade by National Book Network, 15200 NBN Way, Blue Ridge Summit, PA 17214. To order call toll free 1-800-462-6420 or 1-717-794-3800. For all other inquiries please contact the AEI Press, 1150 Seventeenth Street, NW, Washington, DC 20036 or call 1-800-862-5801.

Library of Congress Cataloging-in-Publication Data

Hess, Frederick M.
Tough love for schools : essays on competition, accountability, and excellence / Frederick M. Hess.
    p. cm.
Includes bibliographical references and index.
ISBN 0-8447-4211-2 (cloth: alk. paper)
  1. Educational accountability—Political aspects—United States.
2. Public schools—United States. I. Title.

LB2806.22.H47 2006
379.1'58—dc22

                             2005030556

11 10 09 08 07 06   1 2 3 4 5 6

Printed in the United States of America

Table of Contents

Acknowledgments

I am indebted both to those who initially edited and published the various articles here and to the talented colleagues who helped me arrange, compile, and publish this collection. I want to offer thanks and heartfelt appreciation to my invaluable assistant, Morgan Goatley, for her diligent work assembling the volume and her insightful editorial assistance.

While these articles had been previously published, it was no small job to modify, update, and compile them for this volume. The talented duo of Juliet Squire and Michael Ruderman cheerfully accomplished this work, tracking down references that had long slipped my mind and providing provocative and sophisticated feedback. Finally, Rosemary Kendrick played an important role in editing and completing the manuscript. A number of the articles now read considerably better than did the original versions, and I think that is due largely to the efforts of Morgan, Juliet, Michael, and Rosemary.

A few of the chapters are coauthored works, so I thank my friends Chester Finn, Andrew Kelly, and Patrick McGuinn for giving their permission to include them here. I'd also like to thank the various editors who massaged a number of these articles when they were published in their original form. Three to whom I am particularly indebted as I read this collection are Sally Zakariya, the editor of the *American School Board Journal*; Tyce Palmaffy, the longtime articles editor of *Education Next*; and Bruce Smith, the editor of *Phi Delta Kappan*.

As always, I want to express my particular thanks to the wonderful institution that is the American Enterprise Institute. I can think of few other places where a scholar experiences the support, the intellectual freedom, and the caliber of colleagues that I have been privileged to enjoy here. I want to offer my particular thanks to AEI's president,

Christopher DeMuth, for his unwavering support. I'd also like to offer my thanks to the redoubtable team of managers, marketers, and editors at AEI, the folks who free me and my fellow scholars to spend our time reading, musing, and writing.

Finally, I want to thank those directly involved in the production of this volume, particularly Monty Brown, Sam Thernstrom, and Lisa Ferraro Parmelee.

Introduction

In the world of K–12 schooling, you have to look long and hard to find those jaundiced enough to declare publicly that teachers are no more saintly than anyone else, that accountability systems should shutter poor schools and remove lousy teachers, that schools should be more efficient and cost-effective, that profit-driven competition might be good for public education, that teaching experience is not essential to being a school principal, or that public schools may already have all the money they need.

Well, these are the kinds of "radical" ideas you will encounter in this volume. Rather than offer a soft-shoe sales pitch, telling you that testing "demonstrates our faith in teachers" or that school vouchers are good because "every child deserves a choice," I want to talk bluntly about accountability, competition, excellence, and the public good.

Now, for many in education, this is troubling enough. That I am a former teacher and education professor who believes in frank talk and tough-minded remedies strikes them as downright perplexing. When I talk to audiences of educators, public officials, or professors, I am frequently asked some variation of the question: "Why are you so tough on public education?"

I'll tell you. I believe schooling is capable of fueling democracy and promoting human progress—and that our educational system is not answering the challenge. I reject the notion, so prevalent in contemporary education and politics, that loving something means becoming an apologist for it. The nature of tough love is that we demand *more*, not less, of the people and the things we cherish. Tough love for schooling presumes that we must ask how schools can do more, rather than how they can get more, and that we be blunt and clear-eyed in our assessments and proposals.

To prove that America's schools are vital to our nation's future, some reformers like to quote trade statistics, national growth projections, and productivity figures. After all, Americans spend more than $500 billion a year to support public K–12 schooling, which consumes the largest fraction of state and local government outlays; after health care, K–12 and higher education constitutes the largest piece of the American economy. Authors like Thomas Friedman have argued powerfully that the weakening of international barriers to trade, commerce, and communication mean that the quality of our educational system will determine our nation's course in the decades ahead.[1]

Other observers think it necessary to provide evidence demonstrating that our schools are in trouble. After all, researchers have estimated that only one-third of all eighteen-year-olds graduate from high school with basic literacy skills and the completed courses necessary to attend a four-year college.[2] In fact, the most recent national assessment of reading found that barely one-third of fourth or twelfth graders read at a "proficient" level. Meanwhile, our student performance on international assessments is mediocre, at best.[3]

At the same time, of course, the United States leads the pack when it comes to spending on education. In fact, in 2000, the most recent year for which international comparisons are available, the Organization for Economic Cooperation and Development (OECD) reported that the United States spent more than any other industrial democracy, even those famed for their generous social programs. On a per-pupil basis, the United States spent on primary education 27 percent more than Japan, 56 percent more than France, 66 percent more than Germany, 80 percent more than the United Kingdom, and 122 percent more than South Korea.[4]

Personally, I do not think litanies of statistics documenting our educational travails or the importance of education are all that essential, because most Americans do not need to be convinced that K–12 schooling is vital to our national well-being, or that our schools can and must improve. The real questions are what we should do to make them better, and how we make sure that proposals work as intended.

Going by newspaper and magazine coverage, it is easy to assume that those toughest on America's schools are critical because they have never taught, do not appreciate the challenges educators face, fail to grasp the importance of education or intellectual inquiry, or have some ideological axe to grind.

In his keynote address to the 2005 National Education Association convention, NEA president Reg Weaver, the leader of the nation's largest teachers' union, called upon delegates to "stand together [and] walk in unison" against "the negative, mean-spirited, contrived attacks aimed at undermining and derailing the great institution of public education while advancing an agenda of privatizing, charterizing, and voucherizing for personal gain."[5]

Weaver is far from alone in taking this stance. Hostility to tough love stretches far beyond the teachers, professors, and education professionals who might be expected to sympathize with his position. Parents, voters, and public officials are emotionally attached to schooling and grow wary when they hear reformers talk bluntly about incentives, sanctions, profitability, or competition. As one of the "mean-spirited" critics that Weaver has in mind, I think that's a problem. I think the faith that Americans place in teachers and schooling has been manipulated by Weaver and his allies and used to protect mediocrity and squelch reforms that threaten comfortable routines.

I find Weaver's characterization amusing, at least when I think of my own story and that of the "critics" whom I know best. I, for one, tend to be critical of education for the same reason parents are tough on their children—because we are most demanding of that which we hold most dear. It is my own intimate acquaintance with schooling and inquiry that makes mediocrity so painful to behold.

A Bit of Personal History

My own K–12 experience was both fortunate and largely wasted. I had the privilege of attending schools in Fairfax County, Virginia, long regarded as one of the finest public school districts in the nation. At the same time, I was an undisciplined, lazy, unmotivated student, taking no pride in my performance and unconcerned with my prospects. I avidly scoured the *Washington Post* from cover to classifieds each day, yet failed to complete assignments on the same questions I pursued on my own time. Later, I would often wonder about the source of this disconnect, developing a resultant fascination with matters educational.

In my junior year of college, spurred by this curiosity and needing a job to finance pizza, beer, and textbooks, I started substitute-teaching in the Waltham, Massachusetts, public schools. Somewhat to my astonishment, I found the other side of the desk an enormously engaging place—even as a warm body standing in for an absent teacher.

Upon graduation, and possibly still disoriented from my Waltham experiences, I opted to pursue a career in teaching. That fall, I headed off to one of the nation's citadels of teacher training, the Harvard University Graduate School of Education. At Harvard, I received a master's of education in teaching and curriculum and, presumably, learned something about teaching high school social studies (though what I learned, beyond the fact that "diversity" was the defining quality of good classroom teaching, has not always been entirely clear).

Eventually, I found myself in Baton Rouge, Louisiana, teaching social studies at a magnet high school. On the whole, the experience made teaching seem like it could be the greatest job on earth. Getting the position had been something else entirely. Knowing I'd need a job for the fall, I had mailed about a hundred and twenty letters of inquiry to school districts across the nation the previous January and February. I assumed that a handful of academic honors and an A average at Harvard would attract intimations of interest, even in a slow job market.

Boy, was I wrong. I didn't hear a peep. I didn't receive a single letter of interest, acknowledgment, or even rejection. There was nothing; just a non-response that was pretty impressive in its scope. In spring 1990, I was offered a position by the East Baton Rouge Parish school district at a cattle-call job fair in Boston, when a human resources director noticed "Harvard University" on my name tag. After fifteen minutes of conversation, she pushed a contract in front of me. Five months later, in August 1990, I found myself living in a one-bedroom apartment in Louisiana.

In all my time in Baton Rouge, as in the time I have since spent observing classrooms across the country, I do not believe I ever saw anyone with a sinister agenda or anyone simply unconcerned with the welfare of the kids. What I saw was an organization filled with typical people—some well-meaning, some hardworking, most just trying to juggle all the obligations and pressures of life—that did not seek out talent, reward performance, or have any clear sense of what it was supposed to be doing. As a result, these people behaved like people typically behave when mediocrity is accepted, excellence is not rewarded, effort is not demanded, and expectations are ambiguous. At the time, I thought this might be an unusual situation. More than a decade later, I realize the situation was just as typical as the employees who worked in it.

What I found was what so many teachers learn: Within my classroom, with my door closed, the job was a joy. Like so many of the teachers I have admired most, I delighted in the teaching, in the subject matter, in designing lesson plans, in crafting simulations. I loved lecturing, working with groups, and engaging in debates. I loved coaching the Quiz Bowl team, women's soccer, debate, and whatever else I got myself into. Even for a callous guy like me, getting to teach, know, and mentor a hundred and forty students was a heartwarming privilege.

What I didn't love was the bureaucracy, an evaluation system that took pro forma assessment to a new level, the utter disinterest of colleagues in what others were doing, or the need to use textbooks that were more than fifteen years out of date. I often suspect I would still be happily ensconced in my classroom if there had been support for individual initiative, if I had sensed that excellence would be rewarded, if I had seen a career path based on something other than accrued seniority, and if I had felt part of an organization that demanded my best. Dazed and more than a little confused by the lethargy I experienced in Baton Rouge, I quickly became frustrated with the school, the district, and the general state of my job. I figured it made sense to go somewhere where I could try to understand how so many well-intentioned people could create such a morass.

I left Baton Rouge to pursue a PhD at Harvard, fully intending to return to K–12 schooling. I told myself, over and over, that pursuing a doctorate was just a pit stop. Shortly after I departed the confines of my classroom, however, the frustrations, impediments, and culture that I had taken for granted started to look a lot less benign and a lot more peculiar. With that subtle change in perspective, my scholarly inquiries acquired a very personal motivation. Suspecting that the problems I saw were widespread, systemic, and institutional, I parted ways with the teachings of leading educational thinkers. While most of their work focused on dynamic teachers, effective classrooms, and what good schools should look like, I found myself instead wondering about how we could foster initiative, competence, and rigor.

At Harvard, I pursued a PhD in government in the graduate school of arts and sciences. I studied political science, supervised student teachers and taught introductory seminars, read widely in education and politics, and tried to make sense of what I had seen. Spurred by my experiences in the classroom, I set out to write a doctoral dissertation investigating the plight of urban school reform efforts. Ultimately, in a study that entailed examination of reform efforts in fifty-seven districts, I concluded that political pressures on superintendents and school boards fatally wounded even the most touted effort.

That dissertation evolved into my first book, entitled *Spinning Wheels*. The volume attracted some praise and helped me land a faculty position at the University of Virginia's Curry School of Education. In an interesting bit of foreshadowing, the book was published by the Washington, D.C.-based Brookings Institution only after several education professors who were asked by Brookings, Harvard University Press, and Teachers College Press to review the manuscript strongly urged that it not be published—arguing variously that reform could not be studied in such a systemic fashion; that I failed to appreciate fully the unique, subtle, and intricate nature of various reforms; and that discussions of political motivations and incentives were unhelpful and inappropriate in thinking about reform strategies.

The dissonance between my worldview and that of colleagues in the education community became increasingly evident in the five years I taught at the University of Virginia. When it came to issues like teacher quality, charter schooling, school vouchers, educational accountability, and school board governance, I repeatedly found myself crossing swords with peers in the education community. Eventually, I departed the university for the American Enterprise Institute, where I happily reside as director of education policy studies. The pieces you are about to read were written during my tenure at the University of Virginia or in my time here at AEI, but all of them have been revised, to varying degrees, for this volume.

Embracing Systemic Reform

Why have I dragged you through this tedious thumbnail biography? As I have noted, much of my own research, analysis, and argument has been shaped by my experiences in teacher preparation, high school teaching, doctoral training, and teaching in a school of education. I have never forgotten the inane process of applying for the teaching job, or the chilly reception so much of my work received in schools of education.

My gut concern is that our system of schooling has evolved into one that smothers good educators and clear thinking. One of my earliest experiences with this dynamic was when I offered to launch an advanced-placement economics class at my school by teaching an extra period a day. I encountered a Kafkaesque series of obstacles, concluding in a stern reprimand from an assistant superintendent for having contacted the central office supervisor at my principal's direction. Over the years, I have learned how typical my experiences were, and how unrelenting is the gauntlet that entrepreneurial educators are expected to run.

The more I have studied these questions, the more I have understood that we ask educators to operate in an anachronistic system that smothers initiative and frustrates competence. These are issues we don't discuss much. They get lost amid self-congratulatory declarations about our love for the children, saccharine encomiums to teachers, and vague calls for more money and favored programs. But the truth is that tapping our national genius for initiative, entrepreneurship, and reinvention will go a long way in determining our shared fate in this new century.

The challenge is that even those open to entrepreneurship often seem to imagine that harnessing this power is a matter of identifying a handful of "entrepreneurs," like Teach For America founder Wendy Kopp or KIPP Academy cofounders Mike Feinberg and David Levin, and then lionizing and mimicking them. Meanwhile, the establishment initially approaches such programs with deep skepticism, only to embrace them once they demonstrate that they are tame, well-behaved, and willing to coexist with the established order.

In the end, both reformers and defenders of the status quo sink into debates about inspirational personalities, boutique programs, and feel-good reforms—with little attention to what it would take to actually upend the established order. Establishment voices spend their time demanding more money. Critics who fancy themselves "radical" champions of market-based reforms engage in paeans to the wonders of giving new choices to poor parents, while avoiding frank talk about the tough steps needed to make educational markets actually work.

I don't want to talk about happy stories or airy promises. I want to discuss how we can build a system that fosters these ventures, acknowledges that most will fail, weeds out the failures, fertilizes the successes, and attracts talent and ingenuity. The point is not to come up with a few pat solutions or a new conventional wisdom, but to launch a wave of fresh thinking and innovative problem-solving.

Politics and School Reform

Of course, such considerations launch us into politics and public policy—topics from which many educators recoil in distaste. This shouldn't come as a surprise. In a democratic nation, public schooling is inextricably bound up with politics. Whatever their particular merits, reforms like charter schooling, class-size reduction, school vouchers, performance-based pay, and any number of other measures are a product of political deliberations and public decisions. They are championed by interest groups, subjected to log-rolling, advanced through compromise, and implemented by public agencies. The notion that schools or school reform ever could be or should be above politics is foolishness. When we are debating measures that will affect our children and alter common institutions, the debate is, by its very nature, political. Visible in disputes ranging from charter-school regulation to the crafting of history standards is the ancient democratic tension between the passionate desires of a small number of citizens and the more diffuse demands of the larger community.

In the end, reforms almost never look in practice like they do on paper. This is hardly a surprise; the more complicated the design of a government program, the more likely its components will be awkward. These frustrating realities have undermined the ability of school choice to promote competition, undercut attempts to establish rigorous curricular standards, and created serious tensions for the No Child Left Behind

Act. This is why a whole generation of social critics that came of age in the 1960s and '70s, cutting its teeth on the results of Lyndon Johnson's "Great Society," grew up with a healthy skepticism toward grandiose governmental solutions. These thinkers have fueled the drive in recent decades to prune back government, promote market competition, embrace innovation, and look beyond good intentions. Unfortunately, sentimentality has too often squelched these sensible impulses when it comes to schooling.

The overlap of politics and schooling would seem an opportunity for political scientists. Unfortunately, for contemporary academics, such "applied" questions are dismissed as small potatoes unworthy of serious attention. Much of the research that does get done focuses not on the big questions of how politics and policy interact, but on minute questions of ethnicity, gender, and the proper use of jargon. I guess there's not too much harm in education policy professors amusing themselves by writing articles like "Lived Experience of an Aboriginal Feminist Transforming the Curriculum," "Bad, Mad and Sad: Developing a Methodology of Inclusion and a Pedagogy for Researching Students with Intellectual Disabilities," or "A Vygotskian Perspective on Teacher Education." However, there is a pressing need for thinkers willing to look past trivia and talk bluntly and boldly about the educational choices confronting parents, practitioners, and policymakers.

Unfortunately, at the moment when this kind of insight could prove particularly useful, even the limited number of interested scholars has retreated from the big questions to join the ranks of "evaluators" intent on measuring particular initiatives. This retreat has been most evident among political scientists, who might be expected to tackle the key questions. Those who have eluded the disciplinary pressures to move to "weightier" considerations and have maintained an interest in substantive education policy have found themselves spending much of their time evaluating and debating school voucher programs. This development is due largely to the enormous success of the 1990 volume, *Politics, Markets, and America's Schools*, coauthored by Stanford political scientists John Chubb and Terry Moe.[6] Chubb and Moe's compelling, data-driven argument for school vouchers altered the debate and pushed research on the effects of school choice to the center of political science.

While this research has advanced our understanding of school vouchers and provided a laudable model of rigorous education research, it has also resulted in a lack of attention to the political tensions that shape school reform. Simply put, Americans will not endorse radical educational change merely because social scientists believe they have found it has a positive effect on reading and math achievement for some students. Instead, the public will quite rightly make such decisions based on a web of factors. In the case of school vouchers or charter schooling, for instance, individuals will also consider whether they trust nontraditional schools, whether the policy changes open up the system to promising innovations, whether the new arrangements seem to invite too many fly-by-night operations, whether they believe democratic values are being advanced, and so on. The public will rightly and inevitably care about the initial measurable impact on student achievement in reading and math, but this will be only one factor among many. In fact, this reflects great wisdom on the public's part, because even straightforward results produced by early experiments may or may not hold up as programs are expanded, new schools open up, and the entire shape of public schooling begins to change.

When engaging in politics and policymaking, there's a natural desire to appeal to "science" and "expertise." Such appeals promise to sidestep all the frustrating ambiguities, convoluted realities, and fundamental disagreements that typically characterize policy debates. The appeal to science can foster either a healthy respect for evidence and hard truths or an unwillingness to take responsibility to wrestle with complexity and accept the inevitability that policy may necessarily be imperfect and uncertain. In fact, when it comes to the questions that matter most—like whether competition is good for schooling, what we think kids need to know, whether teachers should be paid based on the quality of their work, or what kinds of expertise principals should have—even high-quality research is not going to settle the issue. No research design (for the reasons I discuss in chapter 18, "Science and Nonscience") is going to be able to parse carefully the various hypotheses and test them in a manner that settles the issue. Rather, these questions will continue to turn on common sense, judgment, and our own particular understanding of the world.

Education reform will play out as it should play out in a democratic nation—through public reasoning, public argument, and public policy. American education is not going to be reinvented by the scientists who venture into their dark laboratories to devise increasingly sophisticated techniques for analyzing data or testing interventions. Their services are a welcome contribution, and of much value, but they are limited. Schools will be reinvented by entrepreneurs able to fashion more productive management models, those who use advances in technology and knowledge to improve educational quality and efficiency, those who devise strategies to lure new talent into the field, those who provide the resources necessary to sustain these efforts, and those who change policies so that these efforts will flourish and proliferate.

The role of the educational scholar, then, is not merely to refine research methodologies or find a tiny niche in which to specialize, but to clarify reform strategies, bluntly consider the costs and benefits, and assess challenges and opportunities that confront reformers. To be useful, these efforts should not serve a partisan agenda or some personal cause; rather, they should provide a metric against which agendas and crusades can be measured and judged. Unfortunately, the nature of the contemporary academy and of today's polarized public debate has diminished the appetite for pointed but politically independent analysis and argument. In lieu of strongly framed, reasoned, tough-minded debate on proposed reforms, magazines and newspapers are too often filled with political cant, treacle, and tedious appeals to partisans.

What's Ahead in This Volume

That, then, is the justification for this volume. You hold a collection of my efforts to reason about the challenges posed by school reform and educational politics. This is not a volume of research. In fact, you will have to look pretty hard to find writing that contemporary academics would deem "scholarly." These essays are written for parents, policymakers, practitioners, and students of education.

The volume is organized in five parts, each drawing on a strand of my work. The first part looks at a few essential, linked topics: the relationship of presidential leadership and education reform, the role of philanthropic leaders in reforming public education, and the seminal question of what public education really means. The second part addresses questions of competition and accountability. The third focuses on the politics of school reform. The fourth takes up the critical but narrower question of how we determine who becomes teachers and principals. And the final section offers a collection of pieces considering some of the major questions looming on the road we travel in pursuing twenty-first–century school reform.

I hope you enjoy reading this collection as much as I have enjoyed pulling it together. For me, it's been a pleasure to go back, look over these essays, and revisit the issues. Whether you deem the pieces convincing, I hope you will find them provocative and useful in furthering honest, reasoned, and constructive debate about how to prepare America for the rigors of the twenty-first century.

PART I

Public Leadership and Public Schooling

Introduction

We begin with a look at how the acts of private and public leaders and popular understanding of public schooling shape the reform agenda. The first two essays in this section examine the role of political leaders and philanthropists in crafting the reform agenda and how education, in turn, influences policy debates. The latter two point out that the fate of a reform is highly dependent on whether popular thinking deems it inconsistent with "public education."

The first essay is probably the most scholarly piece in the collection (so, if you find it a little slow, don't be thrown). I have long thought one of the great fallacies of the education debate was the notion that education politics was largely distinct or removed from national politics. In fact, "Seeking the Mantle of Opportunity," first published in *Educational Policy*, argues that in recent decades education policy has reflected and profoundly influenced the shape of national political debates. The essay examines the relationship of presidential politics to K–12 reform in the past four decades, arguing that school reform has—very much contrary to popular belief—been interwoven with the key pivots that have taken place in the years since Lyndon Johnson launched the Great Society.

The second piece strikes a somewhat different note, turning from political leadership to consider the way in which business and philanthropic leaders shape school reform. I became interested in the role of the private sector while writing *Common Sense School Reform*. In concluding that book and explaining why reform efforts so often miss the mark, I opined, "I am always amazed at the number of tough-minded business executives who have fallen prey to the promises and pieties of the status quo reformers. Leaders who demand bottom line results from their own employees accept excuses and banalities from school reformers that they would find laughable in their own firms."[1]

The sentiment drew on personal experience, but the topic was one I had never examined in any depth. Curious, I began to look much more carefully at the role of philanthropic leadership in shaping reform. One early result was the article "Retooling K–12 Education," which appeared in a 2004 issue of *Philanthropy* magazine. The piece prompted Vartan Gregorian, former president of Brown University and the current head of the Carnegie Corporation, to write, "Hess's comments do a disservice to the many long-time reformers who put their best efforts into bringing about real change in America's K–12 public education."[2] I'll invite you to judge the merits of Gregorian's comments for yourself.

The final two pieces frame the rest of the volume. My work is shaped by two complementary impulses: a respect for the essence of public education, and a conviction that much of the existing institutional apparatus of public schooling is anachronistic and no longer faithful to its mission. Most of the essays in this book deal with the substance and politics of retooling these institutions for the twenty-first century. In this first section, however, "Making Sense of the 'Public' in 'Public Education'" and "What Is a 'Public' School?" try to explain those things we need to preserve as we reform public schooling. This somewhat professorial exercise is necessary in order to anticipate complaints that many of the reforms I will discuss later represent a "betrayal" of public education.

"Making Sense of the 'Public' in 'Public Education'" was first published by the Progressive Policy Institute in 2002. It challenges easy claims that such reforms as school vouchers or charter schooling are at odds with "public schooling" and sketches five key questions to guide our thinking on just what public education really requires. "What Is a 'Public' School?" was written at the request of the popular education journal *Phi Delta Kappan* and sought to answer the questions posed in the previous essay. *Phi Delta Kappan* used the follow-up as a forum on the direction of public schooling that included four pretty provocative (and generally critical) commentaries, and then my rejoinder. If you find the essay interesting, the exchange may be worth reading in full.[3]

At the end of the day, I see the emergence of for-profit schooling, charter schooling, or school vouchers not as threats to public education, but as efforts to update an anachronistic system. While it is hard for many in the education establishment to fathom, I suspect that entrepreneurship, for-profit operators, and wide-open competition will ultimately be better able to serve our kids, advance our common values, and prepare America for the twenty-first century than our wheezing, hidebound system of public education.

1

Seeking the Mantle of "Opportunity": Presidential Politics and the Educational Metaphor

with Patrick McGuinn

Despite the tendency of analysts to accord educational questions only a minor role in understanding presidential elections, the reality is that questions of public schooling have been symbolically and substantively intertwined with the key political developments of recent decades. In fact, the national politics of education anticipate and reflect larger developments, as Democrats and Republicans have discovered that education provides a way to tap the American commitment to both opportunity and individual responsibility.

That education has come to play an important symbolic and substantive role in national politics should not be surprising. Political thinkers from Plato to Rousseau to Thomas Jefferson to John Dewey have seized upon the revolutionary capacity of schooling to reshape societal arrangements without requiring states to coerce adult citizens. From Plato's "republic" to Dewey's "lab school," philosophers have understood that society could use schooling to forge ideal citizens. In the contemporary American context, there resides the hope that schools can shape skilled, responsible, and self-sufficient citizens, strengthening the nation and alleviating any further need for government assistance.

In exploring the relationship between education and presidential politics, it's important to recognize that the federal government has historically played a very limited role in schooling.[1] Before the 1960s, the federal role in K–12 education was minimal, and, even after the 1965 passage of the Elementary and Secondary Education Act (ESEA), the federal government generally contributed less than 10 percent of total education spending. It was not until the 1990s that education emerged as a major issue in national elections. The political significance of education, however, has far exceeded the direct federal role.[2]

Education's rising profile is made clear by public opinion polls conducted in recent decades. In 1973, the National Opinion Research Center at the University of Chicago began asking in its General Social Survey (GSS) a battery of questions that asked whether respondents thought the nation needed to spend more money on eleven social priorities. The relative importance the public attaches to various issues can be assessed by comparing the percentage of respondents who said the government was spending "too little" money tackling each problem.

In 1973, education ranked fifth out of eleven areas the public thought deserving of more funding. By 2004, education ranked second (see table 1). Perhaps more telling than the rise in rank was the increase in emphasis. In 1973, 49 percent of respondents said too little was being spent on education (while 44 percent said spending was about right). By 2004, 73 percent of respondents thought too little was being spent on schooling while just 22 percent said spending was about right.

Central to the strategic vision of both major parties in recent decades has been the desire of Republicans and Democrats to position themselves as defenders of an "opportunity society," consistent with a culture committed to both individual responsibility and the promise of equal opportunity. In the 1960s, established Republican doctrine embraced individualism and localism, flatly rejecting any government role in proactively seeking to extend opportunity. In 1964, however, a new strain of Republicanism emerged. It offered a sunnier conservatism, suffused with the implicit assurance that opportunity was the birthright of every American. While this new conservatism would prove politically potent, it would eventually be caught between its promise to democratize opportunity in a society pocked by inequality and its philosophical hostility toward activist federal government.

Historically, the Democrats, with a base of minority, urban, and disadvantaged voters, were inclined to promote a more activist social agenda. However, growing middle-class disenchantment with redistributive social programs made it necessary to find another way to promote government

TABLE 1

EDUCATION AS A SPENDING PRIORITY, 1973 AND 2004

Question: *We are faced with many problems in this country, none of which can be solved easily or inexpensively. I'm going to name some of these problems, and for each one I'd like you to tell me whether you think we're spending too much money on it, too little money, or about the right amount. Are we spending too much, too little, or about the right amount on . . . ?*

Percent responding "too little money"

1973		2004	
. . . dealing with drug addiction	66%	. . . improving and protecting the nation's health	78%
. . . halting the rising crime rate	65%		
. . . improving and protecting the nation's health	61%	**. . . improving the nation's education system**	**73%**
. . . improving and protecting the environment	61%	. . . improving and protecting the environment	63%
. . . improving the nation's education system	**49%**	. . . halting the rising crime rate	56%
		. . . dealing with drug addiction	53%
. . . solving the problems of the big cities	48%	. . . solving the problems of the big cities	39%
. . . improving the conditions of blacks	33%	. . . the military, armaments, and defense	34%
. . . welfare	20%	. . . improving the conditions of blacks	32%
. . . the military, armaments, and defense	11%		
		. . . welfare	23%
. . . the space exploration program	7%	. . . the space exploration program	14%
. . . foreign aid	4%	. . . foreign aid	10%

SOURCE: Surveys by National Opinion Research Center, University of Chicago, February 1973 and August 18, 2004–January 4, 2005, iPOLL Databank, The Roper Center for Public Opinion Research, University of Connecticut, http://www.ropercenter.uconn.edu/ipoll.html (accessed November 1, 2005).

activism. Education provided Democrats, as it would Republicans, with an alluring synthesis of equity and opportunity. On the one hand, education escaped the moral-hazard dilemmas associated with the troubled politics of welfare, since no critics would argue that school spending would undermine the work ethic or self-reliance of children. On the other hand, education offered Democrats a way to direct resources toward the disadvantaged.

Of course, any effort to provide a brief, stylized political discussion of the kind presented here will leave out much that is important. Education is only one thread in a complex tapestry, and to try to weave the tale of decades of politics with that lone thread inevitably requires some questionable leaps. With that caution in mind, let's leap.

The Federal Role before 1964

Before the 1950s, federal involvement in education was almost nonexistent, and questions of schooling rarely emerged in national political campaigns. The Constitution is silent on education, and the issue was historically deemed the province of state and local government. It was not until 1867 that a tiny, four-person U.S. Office of Education was established, and it was another five decades before the federal government first provided an annual appropriation for K–12 schooling. Education played a minor role in the political affairs of a nation where, in 1930, less than a fifth of adults over twenty-five had completed high school, and where Progressives had fought to convince the public that schooling ought to be entrusted to the educational experts.[3] When it finally emerged as an issue, it was typically due to religious and ethnic tensions rather than concerns about school quality.

Education gained new prominence after World War II, as high school completion became the norm and the GI Bill spurred a dramatic spike in college enrollment. Whereas in 1940 just 38.1 percent of twenty-five- to twenty-nine-year-olds had graduated high school, and just 5.9 percent had completed four years of college, by 1970 75.4 percent had finished high school and 16.4 percent had four years of college.[4] For the first time, education became part of the lexicon of the working-class American and a key to economic and social mobility.[5]

After the Supreme Court's 1954 *Brown v. Board of Education* ruling on school segregation and the Soviet Union's launch of Sputnik in 1957, education raced up the national agenda. The Supreme Court's powerful statement in *Brown* on the importance of equal educational opportunity, along with the civil rights struggles of the following decade, gave rise to a public conception of education as the birthright of a free citizenry. Educational opportunity was increasingly considered vital to ensuring all Americans the chance to better their circumstances.

Sputnik recast education as a matter of national security. Republican president Dwight Eisenhower responded to the fear that the United States had fallen behind its Cold War rival by championing the 1958 National Defense Education Act, which significantly increased federal support for education. Given the demands of the Cold War, a commitment to education meshed neatly with the perceived demands of national security. After Sputnik and *Brown*, a conviction took root that education was not just a local or familial concern, but a matter of social justice and national need.

Through the end of the 1950s, education remained a minor issue for presidents and for voters in national elections. Eisenhower, for example, referred to education in his public speeches and papers less than a hundred times a year during his eight years in office (see table 2 on the following page). In the 1960s, although federal education activity attracted more attention, it remained a minor component of a broad Democratic commitment to the disadvantaged. Republicans opposed federal involvement in schooling as one more manifestation of intrusive government. Both stances meshed with the parties' larger agendas and appealed to their traditional constituencies.

While foreign policy and economic concerns would continue to dominate national elections, and though education remained peripheral to the government's activity in areas like social insurance and welfare, the late 1950s marked a watershed. Subsequently, presidents and presidential aspirants could no longer simply ignore education and had to begin devoting increasing attention to the issue. John F. Kennedy mentioned education an average of 259 times a year during his time in office; in the wake of the launch of the Great Society campaign, Lyndon Johnson mentioned it an average of 621 times a year (see table 2).

TABLE 2

PRESIDENTIAL ATTENTION TO EDUCATION

Years	President	Total Mentions of Education in Presidential Public Papers	Average Mentions per Year
1789–1913	Washington–Taft	226	2
1929–33	Hoover	148	37
1933–45	Roosevelt	382	29
1945–53	Truman	667	74
1953–61	Eisenhower	771	96
1961–63	Kennedy	777	259
1963–69	Johnson	3,104	621
1969–74	Nixon	1,428	238
1974–77	Ford	830	277
1977–81	Carter	2,055	514
1981–89	Reagan	2,497	312
1989–92	Bush	2,657	664

NOTE: Table tallies the total mentions of the word "education" in the public papers of U.S. presidents through 1992. Compiled by author from archives of presidential papers, http://www.gpoaccess.gov/pubpapers/index.html (accessed April 14, 2001).

From the Great Society to the Conservative Moment: 1964–80

The first development to elevate the federal role in education had its roots in an ideological transformation that reshaped the post-1964 Republican Party. For decades, the party had been dominated by a midwestern, fiscally prudent, localist, incrementalist, isolationist conservatism that rejected any federal responsibility for promoting an active economic or social agenda. This conservatism translated easily into education, where concerns about quality or equality were readily labeled the province of state and local governments.

In 1964, a radically different conservatism would come to the fore, championed by Republican presidential nominee (and Arizona senator) Barry Goldwater. This new conservatism rejected stodgy traditional conservatism in favor of a frontier-accented doctrine of individualism, self-reliance, economic liberty, social mobility, and entrepreneurship. Goldwater would go down to crushing defeat in 1964, but his new conservatism would reshape the Republican Party and emerge triumphant with the 1980 election of Ronald Reagan.

The latent conflict between Goldwater-style radical individualism and conventional Republican localism has often been misunderstood, especially in the realm of education. On the one hand, the Goldwaterite commitment to opportunity and individual responsibility resonated with suburban and southern voters concerned with the welfare state. On the other, Americans exhibited an abiding belief that the playing field ought to be level—that everyone deserves a chance to succeed. Without a visible commitment to increasing opportunities for the disadvantaged, Goldwaterism risked appearing merely as an excuse for injustice. However, federal efforts to combat social and economic inequality would contradict a Republican heritage of decentralization, small government, minimal redistribution, and the centrality of the family. Henceforth, Republicans would struggle to reconcile plausibly a commitment to equal opportunity with a desire to minimize wealth redistribution and maximize local control.

Unlike the Republicans, Democratic leaders were comfortable with active federal involvement in education. After defeating Goldwater in 1964, Lyndon Johnson continued to push an expansive social agenda, including the 1965 Elementary and Secondary Education Act, the first comprehensive package of federal aid to education. An aggressive federal educational role fit neatly with the New Deal paradigm of an activist government, public investment, and social insurance. The Democratic stance on education also appealed to the urban, black, labor, and intellectual components of the party's New Deal coalition. Support for national control and desegregation caused consternation, however, among southern Democrats. In part due to educational tensions, the ties binding them to the New Deal coalition began to unravel.

During the next four years, the federal courts required a number of northern cities to engage in extensive busing programs designed to overcome public school segregation. Reviled by working-class white voters, busing helped undermine support for activist government and threw

Democrats on the defensive. Nixon's massive 1972 presidential election victory demonstrated that Republicans could capitalize on this discontent. Highlighting the more redistributive and race-conscious elements of Johnson's Great Society and the cultural radicalism of the student left, Republicans successfully depicted the Democrats as having abandoned mainstream America. The 1972 Democratic nominee, George McGovern, a diffident South Dakotan, was effectively tagged the candidate of "amnesty, acid, and abortion."

The challenge for the Democratic leadership would be maintaining the party's commitment to the disadvantaged while countering the notion that support for civil rights and redistribution made them the party of the handout. The problem receded in the 1976 election, when former Georgia governor Jimmy Carter eked out a victory on the basis of his moderate positions and popular revulsion over the Watergate scandal.

In the 1976 election, both the National Education Association (NEA) and the American Federation of Teachers (AFT) endorsed a presidential candidate for the first time, throwing their support behind Carter. This alliance would lend the Democrats useful political muscle and give them enhanced credibility on education, but it would simultaneously bind the Democratic stance on education to the preferences of the nation's public school teachers. In winning the support of the NEA, Carter pledged that he would establish a cabinet-level Department of Education. Created in 1979, by 1980 the department administered approximately five hundred federal education programs.

During the Nixon years, Republicans began to dream of winning over enough disaffected Democrats to construct a new national majority. Republican opposition to busing and support for local schooling had a powerful appeal for working-class, white, urban, and suburban Democrats. These efforts, along with growing Republican strength in the South, would mark the end of the New Deal coalition.

In the late 1970s, the nascent campaign of Ronald Reagan targeted the nation's fifty million Catholics, an historically Democratic group that had grown disenchanted with the party's cultural liberalism. Cultivating Catholic support, Reagan voiced his opposition to abortion, argued for permitting prayer in schools, and called for school vouchers that would permit public funds to support parochial school tuition.

The period 1965–80 yielded three key changes in the national political dynamic. First, the Republicans learned they could effectively attack traditional liberal largesse. Second, the Democratic majority unraveled, as racial and cultural tensions weakened support among southerners, working-class whites, Catholics, and suburban voters. Third, the Democrats established themselves as the party of education, largely by embracing the nation's public school teachers and advocating steady increases in federal education spending. Meanwhile, the Republican stance on education became characterized by opposition to federal spending and criticism of many public school practices.

The Triumph of an Opportunity-Based Conservatism: 1980–92

In 1980, Carter was challenged by Goldwater heir Ronald Reagan, who attacked Carter for being weak on the Soviets abroad and for supporting an intrusive and stifling welfare state at home. Reagan argued that Democrats had abandoned equality of opportunity in favor of equality of results, and this shift was to blame for the nation's stagnant economy and general malaise. Reagan's message resonated with voters seeking to find a scapegoat for the environment of high unemployment, high inflation, and low growth. His call for slashing taxes and government spending enjoyed wide support, with polling in 1980 suggesting that 71 percent of respondents wanted to cut government spending, and just 19 percent opposed cuts.[6] As part of this general attack on government, the 1980 Republican platform called for "deregulation by the federal government of public education and . . . the elimination of the federal Department of Education." The platform fretted that "parents are losing control of their children's schooling" and that Democratic education policy had produced "huge new bureaucracies to misspend our taxes."[7]

Reagan offered a domestic policy agenda that satisfied his Goldwaterite allies, traditional conservatives, and disaffected Democrats by promising to roll back the federal government while still providing opportunity to the disadvantaged. Proposing to accomplish this through his "New Federalism" initiative, he managed to call for less government while appearing sensitive to the need for a level playing field by arguing that the federal government obstructed social and economic progress, and that the states were better equipped to safeguard opportunity for all. For instance, Reagan was able to call for abolishing the new Department of Education without being seen as hostile to public schools. Though generally supportive of the department, voters backed Reagan's proposal to transfer federal education programs to the local level by a 62 percent to 21 percent margin.[8] Overall, though, Reagan operated at a disadvantage on education. Democrats enjoyed a fifteen-point advantage over Republicans on the issue in 1981, with 32 percent of the American people expressing faith in the ability of Democrats to address education while only 17 percent thought the Republicans would be better able to do so (see table 3). The point was of little significance, however, given the strength of the president's broader appeal.

In 1981, Reagan reformed many of the provisions of ESEA when he won passage of the Education Consolidation and Improvement Act (ECIA). The changes reduced federal funding for education by almost 20 percent and increased the flexibility of states in the use of federal education funds. The reduction in federal funding and control, however, would be used by Democrats to question the depth of the Republican commitment to equal opportunity. Also in 1981, Reagan named a high-profile commission to produce a report on the state of American education. The commission's widely publicized 1983 report, *A Nation at Risk*, painted a dire portrait of American schooling and argued that the failure of the United States to keep pace with the educational system of Japan—whose economy had become the envy of the world—was putting its future in jeopardy.

The Reagan administration's opposition to activist social policy meant that the reforms prompted by the report emerged at the state level. Foreshadowing changes to come, many of the leaders of these reform efforts were moderate, southern Democratic governors such as Charles Robb of Virginia, Bill Clinton of Arkansas, and Bob Graham of Florida. In some ways, the surge of state activity bolstered Reagan's argument that the states were the appropriate forum for tackling education reform. In fact, even after the issuance of *A Nation at Risk*, the 1984 Republican platform would assert that, "From 1965 to 1980 the U.S. indulged in a disastrous experiment with centralized direction of our schools."[9]

TABLE 3

PUBLIC ATTITUDES TOWARD THE ABILITY OF THE MAJOR PARTIES TO
ADDRESS EDUCATION, 1981–2000

Questions: *Do you feel that the Democratic Party or the Republican Party can do a better job in making sure our children get a better education, or don't you think there's any real difference between them?* (1981)

Please tell me whether you feel the Republican Party or the Democratic Party would do a better job of handling [the following issue], or don't you think there is any real difference between them? Providing quality education. (1984)

When it comes to dealing with education, which party do you think would do a better job—the Democratic Party, the Republican Party, both about the same, or neither? (1989, 1992, 1996, 2000)

Year	Democrats	Republicans	Advantage
1981	32%	17%	Dem +15
1984	37%	19%	Dem +18
1989	30%	15%	Dem +15
1992	42%	17%	Dem +25
1996	40%	24%	Dem +16
2000	35%	23%	Dem +12

SOURCE: Surveys by *Time*/Yankelovich, Skelly, and White, May 4–12, 1981, and January 31–February 2, 1984; NBC News/*Wall Street Journal*, November 4–7, 1989, July 5–7, 1992, May 10–14, 1996, and March 2–5, 2000, iPOLL Databank, The Roper Center for Public Opinion Research, University of Connecticut, http://www.ropercenter.uconn.edu/ipoll.html (accessed November 1, 2005). All surveys used national registered voter samples except for the 2000 poll, which surveyed national adults.

During the 1984 campaign, Reagan attacked his Democratic opponent, Walter Mondale—formerly vice president under Carter—as another apologist for welfarism. Against a backdrop of economic growth, confidence in American foreign policy, and affection for Reagan, Mondale's attacks on the president gained little traction. Reagan crushed Mondale in a forty-nine state landslide. Even at the height of his popularity, however,

Reagan could not shake the public perception that Democrats were more concerned with ensuring opportunity for all. When a 1984 poll asked voters which candidate would better ensure that government "policies are fair to all people," respondents preferred Mondale over Reagan by 53 percent to 40 percent.[10]

In 1985, after Reagan's second victory, southern governors and other moderates who felt threatened by the liberalism of the national party formed the centrist Democratic Leadership Council. Offering a vision of limited government, public investment, and fiscal prudence, the DLC leadership—including such rising figures as Arkansas governor Bill Clinton and Tennessee senator Al Gore—sought to refashion the New Deal–era Democratic commitment to redistribution. Focused on finding a new way to balance responsibility and opportunity, the "New Democrats" found education and welfare reform to be areas of pressing interest.

In the presidential election of 1988, Reagan's vice president, George H. W. Bush, was challenged by Michael Dukakis, the three-term governor of Massachusetts. Given continuing skepticism with increased federal activity, Dukakis took care to avoid overtly liberal themes and tried to focus the campaign on "competence" rather than "ideology." This marked the first time a Democratic presidential nominee had explicitly sought to distance himself from the party's activist legacy. The Bush campaign, however, succeeded in depicting Dukakis as a "tax and spend" liberal in the mold of McGovern, Carter, and Mondale, reversing Dukakis's early lead and yielding a sizable Bush victory.

A Nation at Risk had put education on the national agenda. In particular, there was ongoing public agreement that standards ought to be raised. For instance, a 1987 Gallup poll found that 84 percent of Americans thought the federal government should require state and local educational authorities to meet minimum national standards.[11] Both wings of the Republican Party, however, were opposed to such a federal intrusion into the prerogatives of local government. Republican opposition to standards and to Democratic calls for more federal education spending left the Republicans in a very vulnerable position. In 1984, the Democrats had enjoyed an 18 point lead over Republicans when the public was asked which party would do a better job of improving education (see table 3).

TABLE 4

PUBLIC ATTITUDES TOWARD THE MAJOR PARTY CANDIDATES ON
EDUCATION, 1984–2000

Year	Democrat (%)	Republican (%)	Advantage
1984	39 (Mondale)	43 (Reagan)	Republican +4
1988	51 (Dukakis)	34 (Bush)	Democrat +17
1992	55 (Clinton)	35 (Bush)	Democrat +20
1996*	57 (Clinton)	27 (Dole)	Democrat +30
2000	46 (Gore)	45 (Bush)	Democrat +1

SOURCE: Surveys by Gallup/Newsweek, October 22–24, 1984; ABC News/Washington Post, September 14–19, 1988; and Gallup/CNN/USA Today, August 31–September 2, 1992, August 5–7, 1996, and October 23–25, 2000, iPOLL Databank, The Roper Center for Public Opinion Research, University of Connecticut, http://www.ropercenter.uconn.edu/ipoll.html (accessed November 1, 2005). Samples were of national registered voters. Question wording varied somewhat, but respondents were asked a variation of "Which candidate do you think would better handle the issue of education?"
* In 1996, Perot was listed as third choice for respondents, thus lowering the totals for each of the candidates for the two major parties.

Seeking to address this weakness, Bush campaigned by declaring his intention to govern a "kinder, gentler nation" and to be "the education president." The 1988 Republican platform took a slightly softer tone than the 1984 platform, acknowledging the case for a limited federal role but declaring that "parents have the primary right and responsibility for education."[12] Nonetheless, in the election, Democratic nominee Michael Dukakis beat Bush by 17 points on the issue of education (see table 4). The campaign marked the first of three consecutive elections in which the Democratic nominee would soundly thrash the Republican on the education question.

One significant development in the campaign was the shifting Republican approach to school choice. Reagan's choice rhetoric had focused on appealing to disaffected Catholics, but in 1988, Republicans began a tentative effort to use school choice as a way to neutralize the party's weakness on education and the fairness issue. In particular, the Republican platform voiced its support for federal school vouchers as a way to "empower [low-income families] to choose quality . . . schooling." School choice held a natural attraction for the Republicans by promising a way to address educational concerns without expanding the role of the federal government.

Republican efforts to wield school choice effectively, both during the Bush administration and throughout the 1990s, would be hobbled by the party's inability to convince voters of its commitment to serving the disadvantaged. In particular, Republicans tried to portray school choice as a civil rights issue—focusing on the ability of school vouchers and charter schools to help African-American and urban youths trapped in inferior schools. They sought to use growing national support for school choice—especially among African-Americans and urban residents—to dispel the perception that the Republican Party was unconcerned with the plight of the disadvantaged. For a variety of reasons, however, including the frosty reception of the established civil rights leadership, minority skepticism of Republican intentions, and successful Democratic efforts to paint Reagan-Goldwater Republicanism as callous, Republicans had little success in using this tack to broaden their support among either minorities or swing voters (points that will be discussed more fully in chapter 10, "'Trust Us,' They Explained").

Unable to make headway on school choice and reluctant to mount a potentially damaging fight, but recognizing the salience of education and the need to do something, the Bush administration opted for a largely rhetorical push that featured a historic gathering of the nation's governors in 1989. From it emerged six educational goals that would form the crux of the symbolically potent America 2000 reform plan that Bush would offer with much fanfare. Though Bush did not call for any substantive increase in federal involvement, his support for standards and testing marked a significant break with Republican tradition and was seen by congressional leadership as an effort to nationalize education. (Of course, today, after the passage of No Child Left Behind at the behest of a Republican White House, such concerns appear almost quaint.)

During the 1980s, presidential elections turned on foreign policy and Republican critiques of Great Society–style social welfare policies. By forcing Democratic nominees to defend an increasingly costly and unpopular federal welfare state, neither Reagan nor Bush had to offer much more than a general rejection of Great Society–style liberalism. However, as Bush's 1988 pledge to be "the education president" hinted, growing public attention to education and emerging concern with the Republican commitment to equal opportunity would eventually force the Republicans to develop a more substantive response.

The "New Democrats" Strike Back: 1992–2000

The end of the Cold War changed the dynamic of presidential elections— in particular, it elevated the profile of domestic policy. In 1992, the Democrats would capitalize in dramatic fashion. Amid the string of defeats in the 1980s, moderate Democrats had argued that the party needed to win back swing voters by shedding its "tax-and-spend" reputation. At the same time, it could not afford to alienate its core urban and minority supporters. Seeking to negotiate this tension, the "New Democrats" pioneered a rhetoric that emphasized expanding opportunity and shared responsibility, arguing that a skill- and knowledge-based economy required the workers' party to shift from a redistributive model toward one that fostered societal investment in workers.

The 1964 revolution had left Republicans vulnerable on the issues of fairness and opportunity, should the Democrats ever escape the "big government" label. In 1992, the Democrats slipped that noose, as nominee Bill Clinton jettisoned the rhetoric of redistribution and offered instead a call for investment and equal opportunity. Rather than defending the welfare state against charges of indulgence or irresponsibility, he charged that the Republicans had not kept their promise to give all Americans the chance to succeed. Polls showed that voters thought Clinton better able than Bush to improve public education—by a 55 percent to 35 percent margin. That year, the Democrats also enjoyed a massive 25 point advantage over Republicans on education. In the fall of 1992, Clinton unseated President Bush on the strength of the "New Democratic" platform. The Democrats' effort to reposition themselves was evident in the party's 1992 platform, which proclaimed, "Rather than throwing money at obsolete programs, we will eliminate unnecessary layers of management [and] cut administrative costs." On education, the platform argued, "Governments must end the inequalities that create educational ghettos among school districts and provide equal educational opportunity for all," but also charged that schools must be held accountable to "high standards of educational attainment."[13]

This rhetoric put the Republicans on the defensive, exposing the tension between the party's commitment to individual opportunity and its rejection of activist social policy. Seeking to honor both imperatives, Bush was forced either to deny the existence of social and economic inequities, or deny there was anything government could or should do to help. In the face of public discontent stirred by a recession, Bush's stance made him appear ineffectual and out of touch. The Democrats had finally found a way to exploit the latent conflict between the Republican promise of an opportunity society and the party's rejection of government activism as a means to that end.

During and after the 1992 election, the Republicans struggled to answer the challenge posed by the New Democrats. Two responses were available; both were by now familiar. One called for Republicans to more aggressively advocate choice-based reforms, such as public school choice, charter schooling, and school vouchers. In 1990 and 1991, charter schooling and school vouchers had enjoyed their first state-level legislative successes. The second response endorsed the national standards and increased accountability that Bush had first proposed in 1989. In the words of the 1992 platform, "The critical public mission in education is to set tough, clear standards of achievement and ensure that those who educate our children are accountable for meeting them."[14] This approach had the advantage of demonstrating a clear commitment to ensuring that all students were educated effectively, of holding the public education establishment's feet to the fire, and of offering a basis for increasing the academic rigor of K–12 curricula.

The problem with the standards-based approach for Republicans was that it represented the first step on a slippery slope toward nationalizing curricula and schooling. This was the concern that had sunk Bush's America 2000 plan, and it would cause the Republicans, in the end, to shy away from any national system of accountability during most of the 1990s. In fact, congressional Republicans would attack Clinton's Goals 2000 plan for its proposal that the federal government encourage the development of national standards and play an active role in coordinating and supporting state testing.

Republicans made historic gains in the 1994 midterm elections. Riding a backlash against Clinton's ambitious health-care proposal—which brought back memories of Democratic "big government"—the Republican leadership launched a determined effort to roll back the federal government and abolish several cabinet agencies. They handed Clinton a significant political opportunity when they called for the abolition of the Department of Education, however. The public rejected Republican proposals to cut spending for the Department of Education, by 79 percent to 15 percent, and to eliminate the department altogether, by 80 percent to 15 percent.[15] The proposals permitted Democrats to depict the Republicans as hostile to education.

In 1996, Senate Majority Leader Robert Dole, a bastion of the party's traditional wing, was the Republican presidential nominee. Dole fared no better than Bush had at countering the New Democrat credo, and Clinton beat him by 30 points, 57 to 27, on the question of which candidate would better handle education (see table 4). Dole's proposed 15 percent tax cut and his attacks on the Clinton administration withered under Democratic claims that the Republicans were the party of the rich. Like Bush, Dole sought to counter Democratic appeals by arguing that federal involvement was counterproductive. Dole attacked the teachers' unions as emblems of the Democratic attachment to big government and bureaucracy, again arguing that school vouchers could provide a coherent response to concerns about educational quality. While choice-based reforms enjoyed significant support among minority and urban voters, Dole's efforts fell flat and Clinton again massively outpaced his Republican opponent on the education question. Reflecting the heightened profile of education, 86 percent of registered voters indicated in 1996 that the candidates' education policies were either extremely or very important in determining their presidential vote.[16]

More significant than the particulars of the education debate in 1996 was the fact that Clinton, after the 1994 health-care debacle, reestablished the party's New Democrat credentials. Attacks on the Democrats as permissive and indulgent no longer possessed the razor teeth they once had. Both parties now offered visions of an America characterized by opportunity and self-reliance. Particularly useful for the Democrats was that the terms of the debate now enabled them again to champion federal activism, so long as their rhetoric favored equal opportunity rather than equal results. This allowed centrists to cater to the party's base while crafting an appeal more amenable to suburbanites and southerners.

Convergence—Opportunity through Accountability: The 2000 Election

Education allowed the New Democrats to repackage government activism as an effort to ensure that all Americans have the opportunity to succeed. To answer this challenge, the Republicans would need to find a way to repackage the party's opposition to expansive federal activity. Republican policymakers had long hoped that the party's support for choice-based reforms would solve this problem, but, after nearly a decade, its efforts on that front continued to yield almost no electoral gains. In fact, critics such as the NEA and the National Association for the Advancement of Colored People (NAACP) enjoyed substantial success in depicting school choice as segregationist and wielding it against the Republicans.

In 2000, the Republicans nominated Texas governor George W. Bush, son of the former president, as their presidential candidate. Bush trumpeted a "compassionate conservatism," arguing that government could play a constructive role, but that individuals and communities ultimately had to be responsible for themselves. Pivotal to Bush's vision was his emphasis on education, and the promise that "no child would be left behind." Bush's vision was spelled out most clearly in his widely discussed "duty of hope" speech, delivered in Indianapolis on July 22, 1999, which offered a proactive Republican program for democratizing opportunity while rejecting Great Society–style liberalism. Bush proclaimed that his would "not be the failed compassion of towering, distant bureaucracies," but also pointedly criticized conservatives who denied that the federal government could play a constructive role in addressing social problems.[17] He dismissed those with "a destructive mindset: the idea that if government would only get out of the way, all our problems would be solved."[18] Bush's rhetoric implied that a conservative government could help promote opportunity, and that schooling would be central to that vision.

As governor of Texas, Bush had championed the state's stringent accountability plan as a means to ensure that all children—especially Hispanic and black children, and those in urban areas—were receiving an adequate education. The credibility he had earned with his staunch support of accountability and successful efforts to reach out to minority communities permitted candidate Bush to advocate school choice, oppose significant increases in educational expenditures, and criticize the public school establishment. Where previous Republicans had been attacked as hostile toward education when they took similar stands, Bush's educational credibility allowed him to argue that he was proschooling, even when he criticized the existing public school system.

During the 2000 campaign, Bush touted his educational agenda as evidence of his compassion. He would effectively resurrect the Reagan argument that the Republicans wanted to help the disadvantaged, and the best way to do so was to provide opportunity. However, where Reagan had promised that expanding opportunity required getting liberal government out of the way, Bush argued that it required government to ensure that the liberal education and social welfare establishment was being held accountable for serving disadvantaged children and citizens in need. The Bush appeal served to put the onus for social problems implicitly on ineffective public agencies and employees—in the case of schooling, on school districts and teachers—and enabled him to end the longstanding Republican deficit on education by achieving near-parity with his Democratic opponent on the question of educational leadership. In 2000, a week before the election, 46 percent of Americans favored Democrats on education, while a nearly identical 45 percent favored Republicans (see table 4).

Vice President Al Gore, the Democratic nominee, echoed Clinton's 1992 and 1996 strategy, proposing significantly more spending than Bush, supporting public school choice, and calling for the federal government to provide special assistance to improve low-performing schools. Where Clinton had enjoyed great success with that approach, however, Bush's strong stance on accountability and his support for a handful of targeted programs permitted him to parry Gore's attacks by painting Gore as a captive of the public school establishment. For the first time in more than two decades, the Republicans were able to battle the Democrats to a near standstill on the education question. Bush's performance proved crucial when voters ranked education the nation's most important issue, and Bush eked out an electoral college victory.

The problem for Republicans was that the triumph of "compassionate conservatism" came at a cost. In countering the Democratic accusations of callousness, it implied a commitment to an expanded federal role in education. Meaningful national accountability required that Washington become proactive in the selection and implementation of accountability systems. Moreover, having positioned himself as a champion of education, Bush would find it awkward to challenge Democratic calls to increase federal education spending, leading to unprecedented growth in outlays during Bush's first term.

In office, Bush moved immediately to promote ambitious federal legislation on educational accountability, teacher quality, and testing. Bush's landmark No Child Left Behind Act, which would prove to be the signature domestic accomplishment of his first term, would pass with widespread bipartisan support, but eventually prove immensely troubling to the localist wing of the Republican Party.

This story is one that is still being written, so we will leave off here and resume the tale at another time. For those readers curious about the next chapter in this saga, however, the design, passage, and politics of No Child Left Behind are discussed at length in chapter 20, the essay that bookends this volume.

2

Retooling K–12 Giving

Philanthropy plays a peculiar role in contemporary American education. In sheer size, K–12 philanthropy is dwarfed by state, local, and federal expenditure on public schooling. In 2004–5, U.S. taxpayers spent upwards of $500 billion on K–12 education. Meanwhile, in 2002, philanthropic foundations reported giving just $4.2 billion to educational institutions and activities of all kinds, with most giving directed at higher education and only about $1 billion explicitly targeted to K–12 schooling.[1] In fact, even by the most generous estimate, no more than about 40 percent of the $4.2 billion in total giving can even be loosely linked to K–12 schooling (with the rest going to higher education, adult education, and so on).

Dan Fallon is chair of the education division of the Carnegie Corporation, which gave away $26 million in education support in 2004. He observes, "No one should be under the illusion that a foundation is going to create something remarkable in the shadow of a $440 billion enterprise. Our task is to help get good ideas into the marketplace so that society has good alternatives from which to choose."[2]

While it is vital to recognize how limited are foundation resources compared with the vast governmental expenditures on K–12 schooling, it would be a mistake to assume that education philanthropy is not influential. Given that the vast majority of education spending is tied up in personnel costs, schools and school districts actually control remarkably little discretionary revenue for substantial or sustained efforts to find new and better ways of educating. In this realm—promoting, piloting, and supporting change—even small grants can enjoy powerful leverage.

Education philanthropy plays out against a broader shift in school reform that has occurred in the two decades since the 1983 release of

A Nation at Risk, the famed federal report that lambasted the state of K–12 schooling. Early reform efforts that attended to class scheduling, site-based councils, and course requirements have been superseded or abandoned in recent years as policymakers have focused increasingly on broader questions of accountability, governance, choice-based reform, expanding the talent pool of educators and administrators, and rethinking compensation.

The Annenberg Challenge

The most famous philanthropic effort to improve K–12 schooling serves today as a cautionary tale. In December 1993, at a White House ceremony, Walter Annenberg, former ambassador to Great Britain, pledged $500 million over five years to help improve the nation's most troubled public school systems. The grant represented the single largest gift ever made to American public schooling and would support reform efforts in eighteen communities, including New York, Chicago, Philadelphia, Houston, and Los Angeles. Participating districts were required to secure matching funds, which ended up generating more than $600 million in additional giving.[3]

While philanthropy constitutes only a fraction of 1 percent of total K–12 spending in the United States, the realities of school budgeting and public policy mean that this money can have a vastly disproportionate impact on the direction of America's schools. At the launch, Annenberg explained, "I felt I had to drop a bomb on the situation to show the public what needs to be done."[4] Vartan Gregorian, then president of Brown University, home to the "Annenberg Challenge," declared that the gift would help "rekindle the notion of school reform."[5] The scope, high visibility, and broad ambition of Annenberg's bold effort to radically improve urban schooling across the nation set a new standard for givers.

Gail Levin, executive director of the Annenberg Foundation, recalls, "The Challenge's approach was to support local innovation and ideas . . . [especially] teacher professional development."[6] Annenberg funds also supported community partnerships and leadership, new assessments and benchmarks, and enhanced curricula and instruction. In short, Levin notes, the grant funded professional development, community involvement, and similar exercises in "capacity building"—efforts to enhance the "capacity" of the district to improve teaching and learning.

A decade later, this ambitious effort has largely disappointed, casting a harsh light on conventional philanthropic efforts to improve schooling. Michael Casserly, executive director of the Council of Great City Schools, observes, "The best I can say about Annenberg was that it provided us a terrific bad example. The grants were poorly conceived, poorly managed, and . . . disconnected from any ability to drive any broader policy changes. The lesson is: Don't do that again."[7] An independent evaluation of Annenberg Challenge efforts in New York, Philadelphia, and Chicago noted that local politics, resistance from teacher unions, overgrown bureaucracy, fragmentary implementation, and a misplaced reliance on professional development and community building undermined the reforms and meant that "Ambassador Annenberg didn't get much for his money." The analysis concluded that "good intentions and a generous checkbook are clearly not enough to transform American education."[8]

Gail Levin acknowledges that, in many sites, "The Challenge seriously underestimated district-level resistance to reform . . . [and] the depth of resistance from tough-minded, contract-dependent teachers' unions and principal associations in the largest urban districts."[9] Vartan Gregorian, however, points out that bleak assessments underestimate the degree to which the Annenberg Challenge succeeded at "raising expectations for educational excellence, promoting the idea that communities do not have to tolerate failing schools, [and showing] that dogma could be replaced with solutions."[10] In doing so, despite its disappointments, the Challenge set out important markers for the next generation of reform.

Challenging the Status Quo

The Annenberg experience put an exclamation point on longstanding frustrations over the results of philanthropic giving to public schooling, and its disappointing conclusion heralded the entry of a new generation of funders eager to try another tack. Bill Porter, executive director of Grantmakers for Education, says,

I think the whole understanding of the challenge has shifted. What we're learning is that changing education systems is a lot harder than folks expected. These systems are largely driven by policy, politics, and public funding, so it's not an area where you can wade in, make a few grants, and hope to change the world. Hoping to change public systems has been a knottier, thornier problem than funders expected even ten years ago.[11]

The transition has, in some ways, been sudden and dramatic. In 1998, the fifth anniversary of the launch of the Annenberg Challenge, the four foundations awarding the most grant money for elementary and secondary education were the Annenberg Foundation, the Lilly Endowment, the David and Lucile Packard Foundation, and the W. K. Kellogg Foundation. Emphasizing conventional school and district improvement, these four foundations accounted for about 30 percent of the money granted by the top fifty givers to education. And in the same year, four of the top five grant recipients were Annenberg Challenge affiliates, according to Foundation Center data.[12]

Just four years later, in 2002, the top two givers were the Bill and Melinda Gates Foundation and the Walton Family Foundation. These two foundations gave $196 million to K–12 efforts, accounting for about 25 percent of all grant money given by the top fifty education funders. In 2002, the top recipient of foundation-giving in K–12 philanthropy was the Children's Scholarship Fund, an organization that helps provide private school tuition to low-income children.[13]

Two things are notable about this shift. One is its abruptness. In 1998, Gates was not among the top fifty givers to K–12 education, and Walton ranked twenty-sixth among education funders, giving less than $5 million. The other is that these foundations—launched by men who made their fortunes as entrepreneurs and hands-on corporate leaders in the new economy—adopted a "muscular philanthropy" that promotes a focused vision of school reform and uses the foundation's resources to promote it. Gates targets its money heavily on high school reform, especially on efforts to shape smaller and more intimate high schools. Walton has given extensively to private K–12 scholarship programs and to supporting and promoting school choice.

Bruno Manno, senior program associate at the Annie E. Casey Foundation, muses about this changing of the guard:

> I think the change has been driven by people's dissatisfaction with what their money has gotten them. If a foundation hopes it can just keep giving money to a district for professional development and produce improvement, and after ten or fifteen years things look pretty much as they did before, frustration can lead them to try something else.[14]

A "New" Education Philanthropy?

The foundations that fueled education reform for much of the twentieth century—names like Carnegie, Ford, and Annenberg—have tended to invest in enhancing curriculum, instruction, and professional development, and tweaking school-site governance or the school schedule. This kind of "capacity-building" presumes that the stumbling blocks to improvement stem from a lack of expertise or resources. The lessons of recent decades, especially the Annenberg experience, highlight the limits of this giving strategy in a field where foundation efforts are only a tiny fraction of spending in troubled, stagnant systems.

Two distinctions are important when discussing the "new" education philanthropy. The first recognizes the manner in which the focused and entrepreneurial bent of foundations like Walton and Gates contrasts with traditional education giving. The second recognizes that within the larger community of focused, "new" philanthropists, there is a critical difference between those givers who focus on driving structural change that will radically overhaul the provision of schooling and those who seek to promote a particular school environment or model of instruction.

In sorting through these two strands of the "new" giving, Chester E. Finn Jr., president of the Thomas B. Fordham Foundation, explains,

> There is a distinction between helping the system try to improve and paying to either force the system to improve

against its will or to give people alternatives to the system. Funding the current system or the experts working with the system is the old education philanthropy. On the other hand, giving to the standards movement or to choice—measures that don't trust the existing system—creates pressure on the system or supports mechanisms to help kids escape it.[15]

There is a split, in other words, between those who would first focus on professional development, tweaking curricula, and refining instructional delivery and those who want to reimagine public schooling more fundamentally. In my 2004 book *Common Sense School Reform* I termed this a conflict between "status-quo" and "common-sense" reformers. Status-quo reformers advocate providing more money, expertise, training, and support but steer away from radical changes in job security, accountability, compensation, or work conditions. Unwilling to consider fundamental change, they allow the status quo to define what is possible.

Common-sense reformers see a more profound need to overhaul and update the arrangements of public schooling by seeking out new talent and rewarding excellence, purging ineffective educators and shuttering ineffective schools, supporting entrepreneurship, harnessing competition and accountability, and insisting management be guided by clear goals and reliable data. They recognize the merit of many status-quo suggestions, but believe that these are mostly distractions from the larger tasks at hand.

The New Givers

The new education givers have increasingly adopted a hands-on approach in which foundation personnel develop a well-defined theory of change and tend to regard grant recipients more as partners or investments. Most, such as the four discussed below, have targeted particular niches where they believe they can make a difference. The new givers share a common commitment to entrepreneurial and focused social philanthropy. The larger question is whether even the most innovative "new" givers will prove willing fundamentally to challenge a status quo that is resistant to competition, performance-based pay, educational leaders with new skill sets, and an emphasis on efficiency and productivity.

The Bill and Melinda Gates Foundation has lumbered into education as the proverbial eight-hundred-pound gorilla, and its largesse has rapidly made its emphasis on high school improvement and the need for smaller schools an organizing principle of school reform in districts across the nation. Tom Vander Ark, the foundation's executive director for education, has consistently pointed out that the foundation does not see small schools as a silver bullet, but simply as one piece of school improvement. For instance, the Gates Foundation has taken care to explicate some common-sense steps that make successful high school reform possible, officially proclaiming that "certain 'omission critical' policy conditions must be in place for large-scale success: standards and assessments, accountability, need-based funding, school choice, college access."[16] Still, the foundation's emphasis on school size and on increasing the number of small schools has sometimes overshadowed the reality that today's small schools are frequently successful as boutique institutions that (a) have students and faculty who have chosen to be there, and (b) receive extensive exemptions from onerous regulations and staffing rules.

The Walton Family Foundation is unapologetic about its emphasis on expanding parental choice and competition, though it is more circumspect about what "competition" entails. In 2003, nearly 60 percent of Walton grants for K–12 education went to charter schools, scholarship programs, or advocacy related to choice issues. That year, the foundation's biggest single grant was to the Children's Scholarship Fund, which provides financial support to help poor children attend private schools, and its second largest grant was to the Children's Educational Opportunity Foundation of America, which funds local scholarship programs across the country. These two grants alone accounted for 25 percent of the foundation's total giving in 2003.[17] The late John Walton explained, "We have enthusiastically supported the charter movement—as well as vouchers and scholarships to private schools—because we believe empowering parents to choose among competing schools will catalyze improvement across the entire K–12 education system."[18] The foundation's emphasis on supporting school choice typically leaves unaddressed just how increased opportunities for private school attendance, unaccompanied by changes in how public schools are funded or regulated, will compel public schools to improve.

The Milken Family Foundation, launched by Lowell and Michael Milken in 1982, has focused its efforts on the area of teacher quality and the pioneering of new models of teacher pay and evaluation. The foundation has sought to establish schools that employ market-sensitive pay scales and offer teachers career advancement options that keep them in the classroom, out of administration, and paid according to performance rather than the traditional, seniority-driven, district salary scale. Its signature Teacher Advancement Program (TAP), launched in four Arizona schools in 2000, provided a $100,000 grant to each participating school on the condition that districts introduce merit pay and performance-based accountability for teachers in participating schools.[19] At the time the program was launched, Pennsylvania's then-secretary of education, Eugene Hickok, said the foundation's plans to soon introduce a version of the TAP program in eight states were "really a chance to redefine the profession."[20] By summer 2004, the program had been instituted in over seventy schools across eight states.[21]

TAP achieved this growth in large part, however, by compromising on the principle of radically overhauling compensation and evaluation, instead settling for having the program play the role of a performance-linked bonus. As Lew Solmon, senior vice president of the Milken Family Foundation, explains,

> For the performance rewards, we originally had hoped it would become part of the salary schedule and replace the standard salary schedule. It's not happening like that except in one place [Eagle, Colorado]. It's not happening because it was more politically viable to sell the performance-based bonuses. So, because TAP is an add-on, nobody does worse.[22]

The Broad Foundation first got involved in K–12 education in 1992. In 2003, the foundation pledged $18 million in grants to K–12 schooling. About 10 percent of the giving was directed to accountability, another 10 percent to choice-based reform, and 55 percent to district governance and management.[23] The foundation has focused on helping promote the ability of education leaders to make decisions based on performance. Broad's efforts have been particularly focused on bringing new leaders into districts, improving board governance, and highlighting systemic excellence. Broad Foundation founder Eli Broad explains, "Ninety-eight percent of superintendents are trained as teachers—not managers," and they typically have little background in complex financial, labor relations, system management, personnel, and capital resource decision-making.[24] It follows that the infusion of a new generation of leadership from outside the overly bureaucratic environment of public schools will bring marked improvement in student achievement. Consequently, the Broad Urban Superintendents Academy and the Broad Institute for Schools Boards are intended to help attract talent, build a critical mass of understanding that extends beyond the narrow confines of school governance or administration, and disseminate the material. Significantly, these Broad efforts are providing reformers and policymakers with entrepreneurs, programs, and successes to highlight and emulate. A critical challenge, however, is whether Broad will promote these programs as boutique efforts relevant only for hand-picked, specially trained cohorts, or as models of a more flexible approach to solving systemic problems.

The Temptations of the Status Quo

Philanthropists give to K–12 education for the best of reasons: to be good citizens and to give our children a more promising future. For many givers, the last thing they want such efforts to do is provoke controversy. The frequent result is that most have deferred over time to status quo experts full of expertise, good intentions, and promise, and shied away from edgy measures.

The mere act of giving large sums can raise concerns among vocal elements of the community, and the stakes rise even higher when one is giving to support reforms like accountability, nontraditional educators, or choice-based reform. The public relations perils for foundations committed to change-focused giving were made clear in a 1999 *Chronicle of Philanthropy* article by Barbara Dudley, former executive director of Greenpeace USA. Dudley attacked the Gates Foundation's education efforts, complaining, "What offends is the fact that [Gates] gets to decide what the schools' priorities should be without having to churn his billions through a democratic process the way the rest of us churn our thousands."[25] Faced with the possibility that they will be assaulted for their civic efforts, it is easy for philanthropies to soft-pedal their efforts to promote significant change in the public schools or to give in conventional, inconspicuous, educator-directed ways that don't provoke criticism.

This has resulted in what Robin Pasquarella, president and CEO of the Seattle Alliance for Education, has called "Band-Aid giving." Referring to efforts to patch a broken system or make feel-good contributions of computers even though teachers may not use them effectively, Pasquarella has observed, "They're random acts of kindness. There's nothing wrong with that. . . . It just doesn't change anything."[26]

These Band-Aids can sometimes prove worse than pointless; they can drain energy from more useful efforts, allow leaders to hold off on tough-minded measures, or undermine coherence and focus. Michael Casserly of the Council for Great City Schools believes "the Annenberg effort set back reform in the [participating] systems . . . it stalled the effort to build districts and sent the instructional programs into a place that was so fractured and incoherent that it may have done as much harm as good."[27]

Schoolhouse Lessons

The philanthropic community is in the midst of a slow, difficult evolution from the earnest efforts epitomized by the Annenberg Challenge to a savvier, more politically aware approach. As Raymond Domanico, author of the Fordham Foundation study of the Annenberg Challenge effort in New York, concluded, "This was a non-confrontational approach to reform. The Annenberg Challenge was not set up to challenge the status quo; rather it relied upon much the same set of relationships and processes that had yielded the status quo in large public school systems."[28] In the end, public educators are hesitant to accept the risks needed to produce real change—and public officials are reluctant to urge them to do so.

Critically, the new givers—including those discussed above—have learned the importance of focus and attending to the sustained, lasting results of their generosity. Bill Porter of Grantmakers for Education points out that high-impact givers are starting to focus upon

> using the resources at your disposal to build the public will for change and the will to sustain the change. The sustainability issue is: Once your grant dollars are done how do you sustain the change? Whose dollars are going to fill the vacuum—other funders, public dollars, a partner who's going to redirect support? The ultimate in sustainability is changing the policy. We can build some interesting teacher training programs, for instance, or we can try to change licensing programs for all teachers in the state.[29]

Or, in the words of Dan Fallon of the Carnegie Corporation, "We're an incubator and not an oxygen tent. At some point the market has to take over and these organizations have to find a way to support themselves. We know we cannot provide support indefinitely."[30]

First, we need to recognize that there are three keys to driving sustained improvement: programs, people, and policy. Because policymakers and officials have trouble imagining that which they have never seen and are understandably hesitant to advocate for brand-new measures, foundations can play the critical role of modeling programs that would otherwise remain unexplored. And it's vital to bring new and entrepreneurial individuals into school improvement. But these people and programs risk dying like beached whales if the larger environment isn't changed.

Second, it's crucial that education philanthropists understand the difference between focused, sustained efforts that fundamentally challenge or overhaul a lethargic, outdated system, and those that merely represent one more attempt to help the status quo limp along. There is an enormous difference between simply being focused versus being focused on levers that will change behaviors so as to drive systemic improvement. Questions about the Gates Foundation's efforts to promote small schools or the Walton Foundation's efforts to expand parental choice, for example, are not about the admirable focus of these foundations, but about whether these reforms will drive systemic excellence.

A final caution is that increasingly hands-on and focused givers may be tempted to dismiss as naysayers those critics who point out potential flaws in their theory of action. Barbara Kibbe, former program director at the David and Lucile Packard Foundation, notes, "Holding on to your humility when you occupy a grantmaker's chair takes ongoing effort because there is a real power differential. . . . It is a rare grantee who will give a funder honest feedback."[31] Foundation staff are routinely courted by those seeking funds and may find that potential skeptics are hesitant to speak up for fear of offending a large and influential source of support, so it is imperative that those funders interested in high-impact giving invite cold-eyed appraisals of their efforts to leverage sustained improvement.

Ultimately, education philanthropy drives broader change by modeling new paths and convincing private actors or public officials to change policies or leverage larger resources. Whereas the old model of giving did little along these lines, and instead focused on pouring resources into the maw of enormous public systems, the new model has taken pains to highlight practices such as the establishment of small schools, school choice, or the recruitment of nontraditional leaders. In a sector where even the most generous gifts are no match for the money routinely spent on outdated and outmoded systems, the "new" education philanthropy's influence will ultimately turn on its ability to change politics and policy.

Gisele Huff of the Jaquelin Hume Foundation, where the emphasis is on supporting high-impact policy research and advocacy, explains,

> No matter how much philanthropists are willing to invest in programs that skirt the major issues of education reform, they will never be able to compete with the public sector's spending. The only way philanthropists can leverage their investment is to tackle public policy directly, bringing about meaningful change at the core rather than on the edges.[32]

For taking bold steps in areas where school districts are ill-equipped to lead and where caution stays the hand of public officials, the new givers are to be lauded. But the lessons they take from their efforts, and the policies they then champion, may matter more than the programs themselves.

The new philanthropists have a choice as to what message they wish to send. In the short term, they may find it politically advantageous to play down the degree to which their efforts imply a radical rethinking of the status quo or threaten comfortable routines. In the long term, however, rhetoric matters. If public officials and private citizens are allowed to imagine that a small coterie of nontraditional superintendents, smaller schools, pay-for-performance systems, or limited-choice programs alone will yield dramatic improvement, and the promised results don't materialize, then even the most muscular of philanthropists may find that they have wedged themselves into a box that they are too weak to escape.

3

Making Sense of the "Public" in Public Education

What is a "public" school? That question looms large over the national debate about school reform. In light of the Supreme Court's 2002 *Zelman v. Simmons-Harris* decision ruling that school vouchers are constitutional, the No Child Left Behind Act's provisions mandating public choice and after-school tutoring options for children in low-performing schools, the proliferation of charter schooling and tuition tax-credit plans, and the phenomenon of for-profit companies like Edison Schools running public district schools and public charter schools, it is past time to rethink the bounds of the public and private in education.

Historically, defenders of the public purpose in education have offhandedly labeled their opponents or proposed reforms as "anti–public education." While this tactic has long been used as a blanket defense for the status quo, it is becoming less relevant to teaching or learning and serves primarily to stifle practical discussion about how to balance the community, familial, and national interests in improving schooling for all our children. Amidst widespread support for public school choice plans, explosive growth in charter schooling, and the Supreme Court's ruling that voucher programs pass constitutional muster, there is growing recognition that it may be possible to serve public purposes and cultivate civic virtues in places other than conventional state-run schools.[1] As we tackle today's educational challenges, we need to rethink how we provide schooling in a rapidly changing world while remaining true to our shared heritage of liberty and community.[2]

The Public and the Private in Schooling

The debate over charter schools is an example of both critics and proponents seeking the high ground by defining themselves as defenders of public education. Charter schooling is a process by which the state permits a variety of individuals to open state-funded schools. Unlike traditional public schools, which are managed by districts responsible for all schools in a given geographic area, charter schools are chartered by state-approved entities, such as school districts, state school boards, museums, city governments, and universities. Charters are managed independently from the school district and are run by individuals, local organizations, nonprofit and for-profit educational management organizations (EMOs), and various other operators. Because their existence depends on state grants, charter schools are regarded as public schools subject to conventional regulations and constraints. However, their charters can free them from many of the regulations, requirements, and contractual restrictions that apply to district schools.

With regard to charters, our traditional definitions are all over the map. For instance, I was prompted to write this chapter initially when three conversations elicited three wildly varying assessments of whether charter schools are "public" schools. One Department of Education official told me that charter schools are unique among forms of school choice because "they are public schools." A superintendent worried that charter schools are "a greater threat to public schooling than are school vouchers" because "charter schoolers are having success passing their private schools off as public schools." A few days later, a respected scholar offhandedly said that she would find charter schooling acceptable so long as it "fostered the values of public education."

Such statements reveal a lack of clarity in our thinking about K–12 education. The result is that debates over educational choice and privatization tend to devolve into arguments about whether various proposals are consistent with "public schooling" instead of focusing on the questions of what our children require and how we can best meet their needs.

When we say "public schools," we generally mean state-sponsored schools characterized by a reliance on public funds and by formal state oversight. In common usage, however, the phrase "public schooling" implies much more. It resonates with vague notions of democracy, legitimacy, equal opportunity, nondiscrimination, and shared values. We forget that these notions are not always implicit in government-run schools, a fact readily illustrated by state-run schools in totalitarian states or those that operated under Jim Crow laws in the American South. In the case of the contemporary United States, some researchers have argued that private schools may do a better job than public schools of embodying and promoting public values such as tolerance and civic virtue.[3] Others have pointed out that our public schools have been, and continue to be, characterized by inequities in funding and service provisions and by how students are assigned to programs like special or gifted education.[4]

In fact, we too often turn a blind eye when the practices of traditional public schools do not comport with the proclaimed public interest. At the same time, we are wary of schools that do not fit neatly into our traditional conception of public schooling, whether or not they educate and socialize children in ways we find desirable. The case of charter school enrollment can help illustrate this point.

Advocates of charter schools frequently argue that these schools are not allowed to choose among applicants and must admit students based on a lottery if they are oversubscribed. They trumpet this point because they know selective enrollment policies would attract accusations of discriminatory intent. However, the contention that this restriction ensures the public character of charter schools is flawed on two counts.

First, charter schools can significantly shape their student bodies—for reasons both good and bad—through selective recruiting, targeted advertising, and gentle suasion. Whether we deem charter schools public is pretty much irrelevant to whether they should be permitted to engage in such behavior. What matters is determining how much of it is acceptable and under what circumstances, and how to ensure that schools don't overstep those boundaries.

Second, and much more significant, the standard these proponents are attempting to meet is a mythical one. Conventional public schools do not equably teach whoever shows up, and do not offer all students equal access to opportunities or programs. For example, students labeled as gifted are enrolled in some special programs and classes, while students labeled with special needs are placed in others; advanced-placement and international baccalaureate students have their own courses, while low-performing students are often steered into vocational or bottom-track classes. Moreover, the fact that public school enrollment is driven by geographical residence ensures significant race- and class-based segregation. To condemn charter schooling for failing to meet a mythical standard poses the risk that we could condemn a promising alternative and opt for an inferior status quo, merely because we are judging the two with different rulers.

Double-standards of this kind make no sense. After all, John Dewey, philosopher and champion of public education, observed nearly a century ago that private institutions may serve public ends, and that public institutions may fail to do so.[5]

The Shared Notion of the Public Good

Defenders of the status quo are often able to successfully attack choice-based reforms as "anti–public education" because Americans by and large believe the public has some legitimate responsibility to ensure that all children receive an adequate and appropriate education. Even such noted public critics as libertarians John Stuart Mill and Milton Friedman have always conceded that there is some component of public good to education, and have argued for state funding and/or monitoring of educational mastery to ensure that all children are adequately served.[6]

However, this agreement poses a new challenge by demanding that we first determine what constitutes an adequate education and then consider, separately, how it ought to be provided. It is important to recognize that, in multiple sectors, legislators routinely craft policies intended to address public needs, but then rely upon a variety of public agencies and private firms to execute these policies. As in the case of allowing a private vendor to provide community bus services, we typically regard the service as public without worrying much about the nature of the service provider. Simpleminded proclamations regarding what makes schools "public" have encouraged would-be reformers and their opponents to squabble myopically over the symbolic banner of "public education" while overlooking the bigger questions of how we can provide all children with the opportunity for an excellent education.[7]

Three Conceptions of "Public"

There are three useful ways to understand what it means for educational services to be public—we'll call them the procedural, the input, and the outcome approaches. None of these is perfect, and each poses particular issues, but there are grave weaknesses with our rhetorical reliance on the procedural approach. Thinking more carefully about the input and outcome approaches will help provide a more useful frame for policy.

Traditionally, we call public schools those in which policymaking and oversight are the responsibility of governmental bodies. Nongovernmental providers of educational services, such as independent schools, EMOs, and home-schoolers tend to be labeled as nonpublic. Looked at this way, the only question is whether a formal political body is making decisions regarding service provision.

There are two problems with relying on this seemingly straightforward definition. First, exactly how hands-on must the government be for a service to be deemed publicly provided? After all, the Department of Defense, NASA, the Environmental Protection Agency, the Department of Education, and nearly every other state, federal, or local government agency contracts with for-profit firms to support, provide, and evaluate service delivery. In the course of their work for public agencies, these private firms are required to make decisions that influence the distribution of publicly provided goods and services. These services are still typically regarded as public, however, because they are authorized by public officials, paid for out of the public treasury, and serve community ends. In short, it is not clear when a government-directed activity ceases to be public. For instance, in the case of education, why should one not regard a for-profit voucher school that provides a high-quality education as a contracted provider of a public service—just like the for-profit textbook-maker, curriculum-provider, or consultant that public school districts already use?

This procedural approach pays no heed to content or outcomes. It makes no allowance for the possibility that public agencies may make decisions that are discriminatory or repressive, or that otherwise fail to serve the public interest. It is crucial to recognize that being government-run does not necessarily equate to serving the public good. Such has been our experience with segregated schools, many housing redevelopment projects, and oversight bodies that tolerate self-serving behavior.

A second approach to defining "public" is to focus on inputs. By this metric, any activity that involves money collected by the government should be deemed public because it involves the collection and expenditure of tax dollars. However, this is a far more nebulous distinction than we sometimes suppose. Schools in the Milwaukee school voucher program receive funding from the state of Wisconsin. Does this mean that perhaps they ought to be regarded as de facto public schools on that basis alone? Similarly, many Wisconsin dairy farmers receive federal subsidies. Does this mean they ought to be regarded as public enterprises? Or, recognizing that Wisconsin public school districts and public universities seek millions of dollars in private contributions on an annual basis, should we perhaps regard these as private institutions?

A particular complication is the often unrecognized fact that many traditional public schools currently charge families money. Although hard figures are notoriously difficult to gather, tens of thousands of families across the nation pay thousands of dollars in tuition each year to enroll their children in public schools in other districts. For instance, in fall 2002, the families of more than 2,300 Indiana public school students were paying fees of up to $6,000 or more for this purpose.[8] Public schools and districts routinely charge tuition or fees of families who wish to participate in interdistrict public choice plans, or who have children participating in a variety of extracurricular or academic activities. Do these charges mean these schools or districts are no longer public, or that they are somewhat less so than public schools without such fees? If district schools are collecting tuition or accepting private donations from families, it can become difficult to draw a sharp distinction between public and private funding.

Tax credits may further blur the line between taxation and privately directed contributions. For instance, cities routinely offer tax abatements in order to lure private businesses. Does this public support mean these businesses are somehow less private? Arizona, Pennsylvania, and Florida have adopted ambitious tax-credit plans that permit taxpayers to direct their tax dollars to scholarship funds for vouchers for low-income children. Essentially, taxpayers can choose to direct some percentage of public resources to private schools.

At that point, should we regard the money as public or not? The point is that we're not really consistent about deciding when the receipt of public money means an enterprise is public.

A third approach to understanding "public" focuses on whether an organization seeks to fulfill a public purpose, regardless of how the service is paid for or whether it is provided by a governmental body. Private charities such as the Red Cross or the Salvation Army seek to advance public ends by working to alleviate community poverty, hunger, illiteracy, and other ills. These efforts are public in the sense that they benefit the broader community, even when conducted by private groups or individuals unaccountable to formal public bodies.

Today, an array of nonprofit entities routinely serves public needs, while for-profit entities are necessarily taken with private concerns. With traditional public schools increasingly relying on for-profit vendors to provide meals, run buses, perform maintenance, and even run educational programs, debates about the ethics of for-profit providers have become heated. Somewhat lost in these disputes is the fact that public schools have always done business with for-profit providers of textbooks and teaching supplies, bought buses and janitorial supplies from for-profit providers, and hired for-profit builders to construct facilities.

New proposals for privatization bring profit-seeking vendors closer to the teaching and learning core, and in some cases permit them to assume control of that core. This development raises important questions about where the public sphere ends and the private one begins. For-profit firms such as Edison Schools are now managing scores of traditional public schools across the nation. Does this make these schools somehow "less public"? By what metric should we determine whether these schools are more or less public than local nonprofit Catholic schools?

Which Community Is "the Public"?

Opponents of private-school vouchers, charter schools, or home school-ing often argue that these educational approaches are too focused on the narrow needs of self-selected groups of children and families rather than the broader public interests. By design, though, our federal system calls for decisions to be made at various levels—from the highly localized to the national. It's not self-evident that education is well-served by trans-ferring decisions from self-selected school communities to larger, more formalized political bodies like school districts or state legislatures.

In recent years, policy decisions have shifted a growing amount of control to the states and the federal government. Moving decision-making to a higher level enhances the array of interests reflected. How-ever, it is not clear that the decision-making process at one level or another ought to be considered more public. To make that claim would be to suggest that mayoral elections or town meetings are less public than presidential elections or state legislative debates.

It's true that there will almost always be greater homogeneity in self-selected communities, like charter, magnet, and private schools, since they generally attract educators and families who share certain beliefs and views regarding education. This means that school-level decisions over policy and practice will represent only one segment of the community. Some might suggest this makes schools of choice—whether private, charter, or public choice schools—less democratic and less public.[9] On the other hand, schools of choice enjoy noticeably higher rates of support and participation among families, and frequently among neighborhood groups that constitute the school community.[10] Such involvement could readily lead us to regard these schools as more democratic and more public.

In truth, even ardent proponents of democratic participation do not suggest that every voice needs or deserves input into every decision. Local decision-making, school-site councils, and decentralization are premised on the notion that children benefit when parents and educators are given more say in shaping their community schools. Both progressive and con-servative education reformers have argued that largely autonomous schools where faculty and students can forge a shared local vision are more educationally effective than schools governed by more traditional bureaucratic oversight. To the extent that we deem these concerns vital, it seems clear they should apply equally to all schools—whether run by government or otherwise.

Making Sense of "Public Education"

Assuredly, I am not providing here a "correct" definition of public schooling or seeking to instruct policymakers as to the merits of charter schooling or tuition tax credits. My aim is more modest. It is to bring coherence and consistent judgment to our discussions about school reform. The question asked of reform proposals should not be: "Does this fit our traditional conception of how schools operate?" We should instead ask: "Given our shared objectives, what will help educate our children—as individuals and as citizens—most effectively?"

The current confusion can play a pernicious role in policymaking. More than one legislator has supported charter schooling because "they're public schools" or opposed it because "those schools are basically private schools." This type of distinction is unhelpful and stifles discussion of larger and more important questions. Children would be better served if discourse focused more on what we want schools to do and how best to achieve those goals, and less on jostling to be on the side of public education. There are five key questions, or sets of questions, that can help guide our thinking and that may help us focus on the questions we care about:

- *What goals are we pursuing? Why do we want children to attend schools? To what extent do we want to insist upon a common educational purpose for all children?* Many of the current conflicts are the result of fundamental disagreements about what schools should do, and it is utopian to imagine that policymakers will ever settle, once and for all, precisely what the public purposes of schooling ought to be. Children will be better served if we understand and debate these differences openly, rather than trying to finesse them by creating institutional structures that stagger under the burden of a multitude of covert compromises.

- *How should we apportion responsibility for each child's education between the state and the family?* There can be fundamental tensions between familial rights and the claims of the state. Some choice schemes dramatically tilt this balance in favor of the parents; others propose a much more measured shift. Some curricular and pedagogical reforms advocated by professional educators would greatly strengthen the hand of school personnel, while home-schooling proposals flatly reject such an approach.

- *Who should be permitted to provide schooling? How actively should the state regulate providers? Will profit-seeking individuals and firms be permitted to run schools or to manage schools for others?* In theory, one extreme option is to require absolute standardization and ensure a public purpose by requiring that all children attend state-run public schools.[11] The alternative at the opposite end of the continuum is to provide little or no supervision, perhaps permitting the state to ensure that students have developed certain specific competencies but to play no other role.

- *What obligations should schools have to ensure opportunity to all students?* Are schools obliged to treat all students equally—regardless of aptitude or interest—or are they permitted to enroll and/or sort students as they see fit? If we seek a middle ground between these two extremes, how do we wish to define it? It is important that we not romanticize or demonize certain kinds of schools. For instance, some magnet schools sort students by performance characteristics correlated with race and class, while many comprehensive public high schools aggressively track students. To suggest that all students are treated identically in these settings is incorrect. The more significant question is whether we really want schools to treat all students identically. In fact, the existence of such services as special education and gifted programs suggests that we do not—that we actually want schools to treat each child in a way that is appropriate for his needs. But that implies another dilemma.

How much leeway should schools and/or parents have to decide
what is appropriate for each child? And how obligated are they
to consider the larger social implications of their decisions?

- *What components of schooling should we consider to be public?*
  There is relatively little opposition to schools buying textbooks
  and bus tires from profit-seeking vendors, or hiring profit-
  seeking consultants to lead workshops for teachers. Meanwhile,
  there is some concern about whether schools should hire
  vendors to provide school lunches, and fierce opposition to
  bringing profit-seeking vendors into the core functions of
  teaching and learning. Do we want to consider everything that
  goes on in a school building a public service? If not, how do we
  want to distinguish those activities that are public from those
  that are not?

Focusing on these questions will silence some of the easy claims and
broad generalizations that have marked the policy debates, and make it
easier to converse thoughtfully from shared purposes. We may find that
the opposite sides are not so far apart as they are sometimes imagined to
be once we move past the slogans and focus the conversation on how best
to serve all of America's children.

4

What Is a "Public School"?
Principles for a New Century

As discussed in the previous chapter, the phrase "public schooling" has become more a rhetorical device than a useful guide to policy. As our world evolves, so, too, must our conception of what "public" means—a point eloquently made more than two decades ago by famed University of Chicago sociologist James Coleman.[1]

In a world where charter schooling, distance education, tuition tax credits, and other developments no longer fit neatly into our conventional mental boxes, it is clearly time for such an effort. Nonetheless, rather than receiving the requisite consideration, "public schooling" has primarily served as a pennant around which critics of these various reforms have rallied. It is because the phrase resonates so powerfully that critics of proposals like charter schooling, voucher programs, and the rethinking of teacher licensure have at times abandoned substantive debate in order to attack such measures as "anti–public schooling."

Those committed to the promise of public education are obliged to see that the ideal does not become a tool of vested interests. The perception that public schooling has strayed from its purpose and been captured by self-interested parties has fueled lacerating critiques in recent years. Such critics as Andrew Coulson and Douglas Dewey find a growing audience when they suggest that the ideal of public schooling itself is nothing more than a call to subsidize publicly the private agendas of bureaucrats, education-school professors, union officials, and ideological leftist activists.[2] While I believe such attacks are misguided, answering them requires more than sputtering outrage—it demands that we discern what it is that truly makes schooling public, and then welcome diverse arrangements consistent with those tenets. Otherwise, growing numbers of reformers may come to regard our system of public schooling as a politicized obstacle rather than a shared ideal.

I do not here attempt to answer with any precision what public schooling should mean in the early twenty-first century, but I do move significantly beyond the open-ended questions I posed in the previous chapter. I argue that public schools are broadly defined by their commitment to preparing students to be productive members of a social order, aware of their societal responsibilities, and respectful of constitutional strictures; that such schools cannot deny access to students for reasons unrelated to their educational focus; and that the system of public schools available in any community must provide an appropriate placement for each student. In brief, it is appropriate to adopt a much more expansive notion of public schooling than the one that has traditionally held sway in the education community.

What Isn't Public?

As we have seen, "public schools" are routinely deemed to be those directly accountable to elected officials or funded by tax dollars. As a practical matter, such definitions are not very useful, largely because there are conventional "public" schools that do not fit within them, and "private" providers that do. I will not here rehash the problems with our traditional definitions—readers should refer to the previous chapter for that discussion.

An effort to tackle the "What is public?" question can most usefully build from the paradigm advanced by John Dewey, the esteemed champion of public education of the early twentieth century, who recognized that private institutions may serve public ends, and that public institutions may fail to do so.[3] A useful approach to tackling this issue is to consider that public schools might be those that serve public ends, regardless of how they are funded, operated, or monitored. The critical challenge for such a tack, of course, is that we disagree about appropriate public purposes.

What Is Public Schooling?

In the last chapter, I posed five questions to guide our efforts to bring more precision to our understanding of "public schooling." Here, I'll try to use those questions as a starting point in sketching some more durable, useful principles for reform.

What are the purposes of public schooling? Schooling serves both public and private purposes, though we often fail to note the degree to which the private benefits may serve the public interest. In particular, academic learning serves the needs of both the individual and the state. Successful democratic communities require a high level of literacy and numeracy and are anchored by the knowledge and good sense of the population. Citizens who lack these skills are less likely to contribute effectively to the well-being of their communities and more likely to be a drain on public resources. Therefore, in a real sense, any school that helps children master reading, writing, mathematics, and other essential content is already advancing some significant public purposes.[4] It is troubling that some widely quoted contemporary education thinkers, including Frank Smith, Susan Ohanian, Nel Noddings, Deborah Meier, and Alfie Kohn, have rejected this fundamental premise and encouraged public schools to promote social values while deriding the relevance of conventional metrics of academic mastery.[5]

More fundamentally, there are two distinct ways to comprehend the larger public purposes of education. One suggests that schools serve a public interest that transcends the needs of individuals. This line of thought, understood by Rousseau as the "general will," can be traced to Plato's conviction that a nation needs a farsighted leader to determine its true interests, despite the shortsighted preferences of the mob. A second way of thinking about the public purposes of education accepts the classically "liberal" understanding of the public interest as the sum of the interests of individual citizens, and rejects the idea of a transcendent general will. This pragmatic stance helped shape American public institutions that protect citizens from tyrannical majorities and overreaching public officials.

While neither perspective is necessarily "correct," our government of limited powers and separate branches leans heavily toward the more modest dictates of liberalism. Despite our tendency to suffuse education with the sweeping rhetoric of a disembodied national interest, our freedoms are secured by a system designed to resist such imperial visions.

The "public" components of schooling include the responsibility for teaching the principles, habits, and obligations of citizenship. While schools of education typically interpret this to mean that educators should preach "tolerance" or affirm "diversity," a firmer foundation for citizenship education would focus on respect for law, process, and individual rights. The problem with phrases like "tolerance" and "diversity" is that they are umbrella terms that can be interpreted in many ways, often in the service of particular political agendas. When we try to define these terms more precisely—in policy or in practice—it quickly becomes clear that we must privilege some values at the expense of others. For instance, one can plausibly argue that tolerant citizens should respectfully hear out a radical Muslim calling for jihad against the United States, or that tolerance extends only to legalistic protection and leaves one free to express social opprobrium. If educators promote the former, as their professional community generally advises, they have adopted a particular normative view that is at odds with that held by a large segment of the public.

Promoting any one particular conception of tolerance does not make schools more "public." In a liberal society, uniformly teaching students to accept teen pregnancy or homosexuality as normal and morally unobjectionable represents a jarring absolutism amid profound moral disagreement.

Nonetheless, many traditional "public" schools (such as members of the Coalition of Essential Schools) today explicitly promote a particular worldview and endorse a particular social ethos. In advancing "meaningful questions," for instance, faculty members at these schools often promote partisan attitudes toward American foreign policy, the propriety of affirmative action, or the morality of redistributive social policies. These teachers can protest that they have no agenda other than cultivating critical inquiry, but observation of classrooms or perusal of curricular materials makes clear that most of these schools are not neutral on the larger substantive questions. This poses an ethical problem in a pluralist society where the parents of many students may reject the public educators' beliefs and where the educators have never been clearly empowered to stamp out "improper" thoughts.

Public schools should teach children the essential skills and knowledge that will make them productive citizens, teach them to respect our constitutional order, and instruct them in the framework of rights and obligations that secure our democracy and protect our liberty. Any school that does so should be regarded as serving public purposes.

How should we apportion responsibility between families and public schools? The notion that schools can or should serve as a "corrective" against the family was first promulgated in the early nineteenth century by reformers who viewed the influx of immigrants as a threat to democratic processes and American norms. In the years since, educational thinkers, embracing an intellectual tradition that has roots in the thinking of Plato, Jean-Jacques Rousseau, and John Dewey, have unapologetically called for schooling to free students from the yoke of their families' provincial understandings.

The problem is that this conception of the "public interest" rests uneasily alongside America's pluralist traditions. American political thought, dating back to James Madison's pragmatic discourse on the virtues of "faction" in *Federalist No. 10*, has presumed that our various prejudices and biases can constructively counter one another, so long as the larger constitutional order and its attendant protections check our worst impulses.

The notion that schools are more "public" when they work harder to stamp out familial views and impress children with socially approved beliefs is one that ought to give pause to any civil libertarian or pluralist. Such schools are more attuned to the public purposes of a totalitarian regime than those of a democratic one. While a democratic nation can reasonably settle upon a range of state/family relationships, there is no reason to imagine that a regime that more heavily privileges the state is more "public." The relative "public-ness" of education is not enhanced by having schools intrude more forcefully into the familial sphere.

Who should be permitted to provide public schooling? Given publicly determined purposes, it is not clear that public schooling needs to impose restrictions on who may provide services. There is no reason why for-profit or religious providers, in particular, ought to be regarded as suspect.

While traditional public schools have always dealt with for-profit providers of textbooks, teaching supplies, professional development, and so on, profit-seeking ventures have recently emerged as increasingly significant players in reform efforts. For instance, the for-profit, publicly held company Edison Schools is today managing scores of traditional schools in districts across the nation. Yet these are still regarded by policymakers, educators, and parents as "public" schools.

Such arrangements seem to run afoul of our conventional use of the term "public," but the conflict is readily resolved when we recognize that all public agencies, including hospitals and transit systems, routinely harness the services of for-profit firms. Just as a public university is not thought to lose its public status merely because portions of it enter into for-profit ventures with regard to patents or athletics, so the entry of for-profit providers into a K–12 public school does not necessarily change the institution's fundamental nature. What matters in public higher education is whether the for-profit unit is controlled and overseen by those entrusted with the university's larger public mission. What matters in public schooling is whether profit-seekers are hired to serve public ends and are monitored by public officials.

The status of religious providers has raised great concern among such groups as People for the American Way and the Center on Education Policy. However, the nation's early efforts to provide public education relied heavily upon local church officials to manage public funds, provide a school facility, and arrange the logistics of local schooling. It was not until the anti-Catholic fervor of the mid- to late-nineteenth century that states distanced themselves from religious schooling. It was not until the mid-twentieth century that advocacy groups such as the American Civil Liberties Union pushed the remnants of religion out of state-run schools.

In recent decades, the U.S. Supreme Court has made clear that the push for a "wall of separation" had overreached and run afoul of First Amendment language protecting the "free exercise" of religion.[6] Moreover, contemporary America has continued to evolve since the anti-Catholic zeal of the nineteenth century and the antireligious intellectualism of the mid-twentieth century. Those conflicts were of a particular time and place. Today, as church officials are more integrated into secular society, they have less local sway and lack the unquestioned authority they once held. Just as some one-time opponents of single-sex schools can now, because of changes in the larger social order, imagine such schools serving the public interest, so, too, we should not reflexively shrink from viewing religious schools in a similar light. In most industrial democracies, including such nations as Canada, France, and the Netherlands, religious schools operate as part of the public system and are funded and regulated accordingly.

What obligations should public schools have to ensure opportunity for all students? We have never imagined that providing opportunity to all students means treating all students identically. The existence of magnet schools, special education, gifted classes, and "exam schools" that admit applicants based in large part on how they fare on an entrance test, makes it clear that we deem it appropriate for schools to select some children and exclude others in order to provide desirable academic environments. Our traditional school districts have never sought to ensure that every school or classroom should serve a random cross-section of children, only that the systems as a whole should appropriately serve all children.

Given the tension between families who want their children schooled in an optimal environment and public officials who must construct systems that address competing needs, the principle that individual schools can exclude children but that systems cannot is both sensible and morally sound. That said, this principle does mean that some children will not attend school with the peers their parents might prefer.

The dilemma this presents is that no solitary good school can serve all the children who might wish to attend, and that randomly admitting students may impede a school's effectiveness. Demanding that a science magnet school accept students with minimal science accomplishments or that any traditional school accept a habitually violent student threatens the ability of each school to accomplish its basic purposes. This is clearly not in the public interest. The same is true when a constructivist school is required to admit students from families who staunchly prefer back-to-basics instruction and will agitate for the curricula and pedagogy they prefer. In such cases, allowing schools to admit students selectively is consistent with the public interest—so long as the process furthers a legitimate educational purpose and the student has access to an appropriate alternative setting. Such publicly acceptable exclusion must be pursued for some reasonable educational purpose, and this creates a gray area that must be monitored. However, the need to patrol this area does not require that the practice be preemptively prohibited.

Moreover, self-selected or homogeneous communities are not necessarily less public than others. For instance, no one suggests that the University of Wyoming is less public than the University of Texas, though it is less geographically and ethnically representative of the nation. It has never been suggested that elections in San Francisco or Gopher Springs, West Virginia, would be more public if the communities included more residents who had not chosen to live there or whose views better reflected national norms. Nor has it been suggested that selective public institutions, such as the University of Michigan or the University of Texas, both of which turn away many applicants, are less public than are community colleges. Moreover, there is always greater homogeneity in self-selected communities, such as magnet schools or elite public universities, which attract educators, students, and families who frequently share certain values and views. None of this has been thought to undermine their essential "public-ness."

Even champions of "public education," such as Deborah Meier and Ted Sizer, argue that this shared sense of commitment helps cultivate a participatory and democratic ethos in self-selected schools. In other words, heightened familial involvement tends to make self-selected schools more participatory and democratic. Kneeling before the false gods of heterogeneity or nonselectivity undermines our ability to forge participatory or effective schools without making schools commensurately more "public."

Nowhere, after all, does the availability of a "public service" imply that we get to choose our fellow users. In every field—whether public medicine, public transportation, or public higher education—the term "public" implies our right to a service, not our right to have buses serve a particular route or to have a university cohort configured to our preferences. Even though such considerations influence the quality of the service, the need for public providers to juggle the requirements of all the individuals they must serve necessarily means that each member of the public cannot necessarily receive the service in the manner he or she would ultimately prefer. "Public schooling" implies an obligation to ensure that all students are appropriately served, not that every school is open to all comers.

What parts of public schooling are public? Debates about "public-ness" focus on the classroom teaching and learning that are central to all schools. Maintenance, accounting, payroll, and food services are quite removed from the public purposes of education discussed above. Even though these peripheral services may take place in the same facility as teaching and learning, their execution does not meaningfully affect the "public-ness" of schooling. Rather, we understand that it is sufficient to have ancillary services provided in a manner consistent with the wishes of a public education provider. For example, federal courts and state legislatures are indisputably public institutions, yet they frequently procure supplies, services, and personnel from privately run, for-profit enterprises. We properly regard these institutions as public because of their core purposes, not because of the manner in which they arrange their logistics.

Today's "Public" Schools Often Aren't

Given the incoherent conception of public schooling that predominates today, it comes as little surprise that we offer contemporary educators little guidance in serving the public interest. This poses obvious problems, given that employment as an educator doesn't necessarily grant enhanced moral wisdom or personal virtue. If schools are to serve as places where educators advance purposes and cultivate virtues they happen to prefer, it is not clear in what sense schools are serving "public purposes."

Blindly hoping that educators have internalized shared public purposes, we empower individuals to proselytize under the banner of "public schooling." This state of affairs has long been endorsed by a lineage of educational theorists including George Counts, Paulo Freire, and Henry Giroux, all of whom argued that teachers have a charge to use their classrooms to promote personal visions of social change, regardless of the broader public's beliefs. For these thinkers, "public schooling" ironically implies a community obligation to support schools for the private purposes of educators. The problem is that public institutions are not personal playthings. Just as it is unethical for a judge to disregard the law and instead rule on the basis of personal whimsy, so it is inappropriate for public school teachers to use their offices to impose personal views upon a captive audience.

One appropriate public response is to specify public purposes and demand that teachers reflect them, though we are reasonably cautious about adopting such an intrusive course. To the extent that explicit direction is absent, however, educators are left to their own devices. In such a case, our liberal tradition would recommend that we not subject children to the views of educators at an assigned school, but allow families to avail themselves of a range of schools with diverse perspectives, so long as each teaches respect for our democratic and liberal tradition.

Conclusion

Today's system of "public schooling" does little to ensure that our schools serve public purposes, while permitting some educators to use a publicly provided forum to promote their personal beliefs. Meanwhile, hiding behind the phrase's hallowed skirts are partisans who furiously attack any innovation that threatens their interests or beliefs.

There are many ways to provide legitimate public education. A restrictive state might tightly regulate school assignment, operations, and content, while another state might impose little regulation. However, there is no reason to regard the schools in the one state as more "public" than those in the other. The "public-ness" of a school does not depend on class size, the use of certified teachers, rules governing employee termination, or the rest of the procedural apparatus that ensnares traditional district schools. The fact that public officials have the right to require public schools to comply with certain standards does not mean that schools subjected to more intrusive standards are somehow more public. The inclusion of religious schools in European systems, for instance, has been accompanied by intensive regulation of curricula and policy. Regulation on that order is not desirable, nor is it necessary for schools to operate as part of a public system; it is merely an operational choice made by officials in these relatively bureaucratic nations.

As opportunities to deliver, structure, and practice education evolve, it is periodically necessary to revisit assumptions about what constitutes public schooling. The ideology and institutional self-interest that infuse the dominant current conception have fueled withering attacks on the very legitimacy of public schooling itself. Failure to address this impoverished status quo will increasingly offer critics cause to challenge the purpose and justification of public education. Maintaining and strengthening our commitment to public schooling requires that we rededicate ourselves to essential principles of opportunity, liberal democracy, and public benefit, while freeing ourselves from political demands and historical happenstance.

In an age when social and technological change have made possible new approaches to teaching and learning, pinched renderings of "public schooling" have grown untenable and counterproductive. They stifle creative efforts, confuse debates, and divert attention from more useful questions. A more expansive conception is truer to our traditions, more likely to foster shared values, and better suited to the challenges of the new century.

PART II

Competition and Accountability

Introduction

Job one in school reform, as in anything else, is quality control. There are three ways to hold organizations accountable for performance: regulation, monitoring of outcomes, and competition. As much as we would like to find a fourth way, these alone are our choices—and all we can do is choose from them or think up new ways to combine them.

Traditionally, schools have leaned heavily on regulation. School districts, states, and federal government officials set strict rules for how schools should operate and require educators to document compliance. Officials decree that a classroom can have no more than twenty-two students, that a teacher must have a particular license, that new history materials must be bought every five or six years, and so on. All of this ensures a minimal level of service. The problem with this approach, of course, is that we cannot ensure that these things do any good.

The two alternatives to this kind of regulation each focus on results rather than rules. Simply put, one requires that educators be held responsible for producing certain required results, and the other empowers individual families to judge quality and make decisions for themselves.

Performance-based accountability requires public officials to set clear goals for schools, explain how performance will be measured, and prescribe consequences for success and failure. If students are performing acceptably, the educators are deemed effective; if they are not, compliance is deemed beside the point. This kind of accountability requires a lot of political will, as elected officials are asked to stand firm even when the consequences start to pinch individual teachers and students.

With competition, accountability is a product of families seeking out good schools and leaving ineffective ones. Such a system presumes that parents can and will make judgments in the best interests of their children. These atomized decisions hold schools accountable by increasing the attendance at the good ones and emptying out the bad. Pure competition is largely agnostic about what constitutes a "bad" school, leaving consumers free to decide in the same way they judge whether a quiet vegetarian sandwich shop or a smoky barbecue joint is "better." Of course, this market-driven approach raises concerns about social fragmentation and the possibility that some parents may be unwary or negligent.

Neither results-based approach is an ideal solution. Both invite real risks, just as the regulatory model does. Both can be designed in ways sensible or silly. Ultimately, however, both rest on a logic that requires officials to make tough decisions to ensure that mediocrity has consequences, excellence is rewarded, poor-performing schools are shuttered, and competition rewards the winners while punishing the losers.

Unfortunately, the norm has been for policymakers to talk in gaudy terms about the promise of accountability or competition, then shy away from the decisions required to make these policies effective. Particularly troubling is the manner in which far too many market proponents casually turn a blind eye to the fact that markets require incentives, consequences, and rules that ensure rigorous, responsible competition. If policymakers lack the will to ensure that failure is punished and opportunities are created for new competitors to emerge, then their talk of reform amounts to little more than hollow posturing. To date, the truth is that even self-professed champions of accountability and competition have shown a lot more interest in scoring rhetorical points than in fighting for policies that will withstand the acid test.

The essays in this section consider what it takes to make education markets into real markets, ensure that test-based accountability works as intended, and deliver on the promise of charter school accountability. "The Case for Being Mean," first published in *Educational Leadership*, explains the virtues of hard-nosed accountability, why it is so hard to keep accountability systems from going soft, and why it is essential to do so. "The Political Challenge of Charter School Regulation," first published in *Phi Delta Kappan*, similarly explains why it has been so difficult to hold charter schools accountable for academic performance, and offers four institutional reforms that can make it easier for states to do so.

The final two pieces, "The Work Ahead" and "Choice Is Not Enough," first published in *Education Next* and *The Weekly Standard*, respectively, draw on my research into how competition from voucher and charter schools affects public school systems. That research, presented most fully in my 2002 book *Revolution at the Margins*, and to a lesser degree in the collaborative 1999 work *School Choice in the Real World*, examined the impact of "competition" on traditional school districts. It concluded that the effects were limited—not because competition won't work in education, but because these choice arrangements are being introduced into systems currently too insulated and too calcified to respond in a meaningful fashion.

I argue that "school choice" proponents have thus far been either unclear as to what meaningful market competition requires or unwilling to acknowledge it. This line of analysis—endorsing the promise of educational competition, while rebuking school choice advocates for being insufficiently thoughtful—has not been one of my more popular efforts. This is probably no surprise. Choice proponents have dismissed such arguments as hostile toward choice-based reforms, while choice critics have termed my blunt discussions of educational markets as mean-spirited, "deeply disturbing," and at odds with "the covenant to provide quality education to all participants in our society." This kind of split probably signals that I am either speaking hard truths or utter rubbish. You have the chance to read the pieces and make up your own mind.

5

The Case for Being Mean

The enactment of the federal No Child Left Behind Act in January 2002 made performance-based education accountability a federal mandate. The legislation followed a decade of concerted activity across the states that produced an array of high-stakes accountability systems. Those state systems have already come under fire. In such places as Nevada, Florida, and Massachusetts, where thousands of high school seniors were at risk of being denied diplomas in 2004, angry parents protested, civil rights groups threatened boycotts over the high rates of failing minority students, and educators worried that their schools would be targeted by state education agencies as low-performing or inadequate.

The allure of performance-based accountability is its promise to ensure that all students, even the most disadvantaged, will master crucial knowledge and skills. An overwhelming percentage of adults, often 90 percent or higher, supports accountability in the abstract, recognizing the appropriateness of holding public educators responsible for teaching essential material instead of permitting them to use public classrooms as personal forums.[1] Aside from a few ideological critics, even most educators are sympathetic to the goals of performance-based accountability. The important split is not between those who support and those who oppose accountability, but between those who support tough-minded accountability, despite all its warts, and those who like the ideal of accountability but shrink from its reality.

Nice versus Mean Accountability

Simply put, there are two kinds of accountability: suggestive and coercive, or, to put it more plainly, "nice" and "mean."

77

Advocates of nice accountability presume that the key to school improvement is to provide educators with more resources, expertise, training, support, and "capacity." They view accountability as a helpful tool that seeks to improve schooling by developing standards, applying informal social pressures, using testing as a diagnostic device, increasing coordination across schools and classrooms, and making more efficient use of school resources through standardization. The educational benefits produced by nice accountability depend on individual volition.

Mean accountability, on the other hand, uses coercive measures—incentives and sanctions—to ensure that educators teach and students master specific content. Students must demonstrate their mastery of essential knowledge and skills in the areas of math, writing, reading, and perhaps core disciplines at certain key points and before graduating from high school. Educators are expected to do what is necessary to ensure that they no longer pass students unequipped for the most fundamental requirements of further education, work, or good citizenship.

In such a system, school performance no longer rests on fond wishes and good intentions. Instead, such levers as diplomas and job security are used to compel students and teachers to cooperate. Mean accountability seeks to harness the self-interest of students and educators to refocus schools and redefine the expectations of teachers and learners.

For educators, mean accountability offers many benefits nice accountability does not. Unlike its nicer variant, mean accountability gives school and district leaders personal incentives to seek out and cultivate excellence. It enables policymakers to roll back regulations designed to control quality by means of micromanaging procedures. It builds popular support for education by providing state officials and voters with hard evidence on school performance. And, in well-run schools and districts, mean accountability gives effective teachers new freedom to teach as they see fit and with the materials they deem appropriate, as long as their students master essential skills.

Advocates of mean accountability agree that nice accountability yields real benefits, but they point out that these benefits have been only modest and uneven. In 2003, the National Assessment of Educational Progress reported that just 30 percent of U.S. fourth graders and 30 percent of eighth graders scored at least at the "proficient" level in reading; 38 percent of fourth graders and 28 percent of eighth graders scored "below basic." The results for urban communities were far worse, with 52 percent of fourth graders in the nation's cities scoring "below basic" in reading.[2]

The split between those who insist on mean accountability and the gentler souls comes down to whether one agrees with nice-accountability proponents that educators are doing all they can, that student failure is caused largely by factors outside the control of teachers or administrators, and that incentives will not productively alter educators' behavior.

Proponents of coercive accountability reject such claims. Common sense tells us that people work more effectively when they are held accountable for performance, rewarded for excellence, and given opportunities to devise new paths to success. Left to their own devices, most employees in any line of work will resist changes that require them to take on more responsibility, disrupt their routines, or threaten their jobs or wages. To overcome that resistance to disruptive change or new efficiencies, it is essential to make inaction more painful than action. In education, this means making a lack of improvement so unpleasant for local officials and educators that they are willing to reconsider work rules, require teachers to change routines, assign teachers to classes and schools in more effective ways, increase required homework, fire ineffective teachers, and otherwise take those painful steps that are regarded as "unrealistic" most of the time.

The notion is not simply to place more weight on the shoulders of teachers or principals or push them to work longer hours. The challenge is more fundamental. In any line of work, decision-makers want to avoid unpopular decisions. But sometimes school officials have to make painful choices: to drop a popular reading program that isn't working; to cut elective choices if students haven't mastered the basics; to fire a well-liked principal who isn't achieving results. In each case, the easiest course is to not act. The way we force people to make unpleasant choices is by pressing them to do so—even if it angers employees or constituents. Coercive accountability provides the best, most straightforward way to bring that pressure to bear in support of core academic subjects.

Rethinking Systems and Practices

For decades, U.S. schools have been constantly reforming without ever really changing. As long as we give veto power over change to those who will endure its costs, we will continue to shy away from reinventing schools as more efficient and effective organizations. We will not force painful improvement by convincing those who bear the costs of change that it really is a good idea. We must leave them no choice in the matter.

It's not just a question of making people work harder; it's about forcing managers and leaders to rethink systems and practices. Take the Detroit automakers who fell upon hard times in the late 1970s. They were producing oversized and poorly designed cars, had gotten lazy about quality control, had permitted costs and union contracts to spiral out of hand, and had added layer upon layer of middle management. The emergence of fierce foreign competition and a dramatic loss of market share shocked these firms into action. Energetic new leadership rethought the product line, redesigned quality control, slashed middle management, renegotiated contracts, and cut costs. The transformation was not about berating workers; it was about forcing those in charge to focus on high performance and make painful decisions to achieve it.

Today, district and school leaders spend their time pleading with their subordinates to cooperate because they can imagine no other ways to drive change. They are mistaken. We can drive change by requiring educators to meet clear performance goals and attaching rewards to success and consequences to failure.

Ambivalence about Being Tough

Although public officials and educators are sympathetic to the notion of accountability, they are often squeamish about the demands of coercive accountability. The benefits of accountability—a more rigorous and focused school system—are broad, widely dispersed, and often hard to isolate, whereas the costs are borne by visible students and teachers, many of whom can inevitably point to various extenuating circumstances. A Texas principal, after affirming that she believed in rigorous standards for student learning, expressed the ambivalence felt by many:

> Last year I had to tell a student that she didn't pass the "last chance" TAAS [Texas Assessment of Academic Skills] exam

administered in May of her senior year. I do not even want to imagine the heartbreak that she and her family felt. I've only had to do this once, but it was one time too many, and I don't know that I have it in me to do it again.[3]

Accountability requires education officials to make five politically sensitive sets of decisions. First, they must designate a prescribed body of content and objectives to be tested. Such a course necessarily marginalizes some other goals, objectives, content, and skills. Second, they must impose assessments that accurately measure whether or not students have mastered the requisite skills and content. Third, they must specify what constitutes mastery. Fourth, they must decide what to do with students who fail to demonstrate mastery. Finally, for accountability to alter education programs and practices significantly, the system must reward or sanction educators on the basis of student performance.

Each decision tends to produce passionate opposition among those who bear the costs. Opponents of coercive accountability seize upon the arbitrary nature of many of these decisions, demanding modifications that will increase test validity and reduce any inequities or pernicious effects produced by misuse of assessments.

Proponents of coercive accountability often have trouble holding the line against the appeals of aggrieved constituencies. In the face of heated opposition, they often agree to a series of compromises on program design and implementation that eventually undercut the coercive promise of accountability.

For example, although most states have adopted mandatory graduation exams, and about half offer school incentives linked to test scores, phase-in periods and implementation delays mean that graduation requirements and performance-based incentives for educators have taken effect in only a few states. Delays and adjustments may provide time to refine tests and curricula and potential penalties, but they also conveniently push substantive challenges into the future.

To date, most states that have actually started to approach deadlines have blinked and delayed the implementation of sanctions. A 2004 study found that at least one-third of the states that had adopted high-stakes accountability systems had slowed or scaled back their original efforts.[4]

In Arizona, for instance, 78 percent of tenth graders failed the state math test in the fall of 2004.[5] The effects of testing were pushed back from affecting the class of 2002 to the class of 2006,[6] and a proposal that would allow students in the classes of 2006 and 2007 to offset failing the exam with a good transcript is currently on the table.[7] In recent years, other states—including Alabama, Alaska, California, Delaware, Maryland, North Carolina, and Wyoming—scaled back testing programs or postponed their effects.

If policymakers don't delay implementation, they often soften accountability in various other ways. While they can be justified on educational grounds, each of these common compromises also serves to dull the mean edge of accountability:

- Lowering the stakes of the tests for students, educators, or both. Weak or nonexistent sanctions offer little incentive for teachers, low-performing students, or anyone else to worry much about test results.

- Making tests easier by lowering content standards, adopting easier questions, or reducing the cutoff scores for satisfactory performance.

- Offering lots of second chances. Giving students a number of retests or teachers several years to boost student performance means that the law of averages will help a number of moderately low performers to clear the bar.

- Permitting some students or educators to sidestep the required assessment—for example, by issuing a "basic" diploma in lieu of a standard diploma, or exempting teachers who teach specialized classes from evaluation.

The Temptations of Compromise

From the inception of high-stakes testing, proponents have tended to laud the requisite tests and accompanying systems as clear, scientifically defensible, manageable, and concise. Critics typically attack them as unreliable, simplistic, overly focused on trivia, or lacking the necessary curricular and pedagogical support. They argue that linking teacher incentives or student advancement to anything so crude will pose inevitable perils. In truth, both sides are correct.

The details of accountability—the content to be tested, the assessments to use, the definition of minimum competency, and the means of addressing the performance of educators or students—are inherently arbitrary. The closer one gets to crafting and enforcing standards, the less defensible specific program elements can appear.

Determining what students need to know, when they need to know it, and how well they need to know it is an ambiguous and value-laden exercise. Neither developmental psychologists nor psychometricians can "prove" the necessity of teaching specified content at a particular grade level. Such decisions are imperfect judgments about students' needs and capacities.

Proponents of accountability have difficulty standing firm on program details precisely because decisions regarding what students need to know, when they need to know it, and how well they need to know it are only reasonable approximations. No amount of tweaking will yield a perfect instrument.

Loath to concede that graduation testing is inevitably flawed, proponents try to placate critics with one "refinement" after another. They soften sanctions, adjust passing scores, offer exemptions, fiddle with school performance targets, delay implementation, and take other similar steps as they seek to discover just the right balance. Unfortunately, the painless, happy medium is fundamentally at odds with the purpose of coercive accountability. This series of compromises may preserve the facade of accountability, but they will eventually strip it of its power.

The Importance of Being Mean

The challenge for proponents of coercive accountability is to acknowledge the localized pain and dislocation they intend to visit upon some educators and students as the price of a system that will ensure educators are serving all of our nation's students. The challenge for those enamored of nice accountability is to explain how they plan to ensure that schools prepare all students for their adult lives. Although their caveats about inequalities in home environments and natural student abilities have merit, surely it is not overly ambitious to demand that educators find a way to teach all students the essentials of reading, writing, math, and the other key disciplines before sending them into the world.

Most accountability programs begin with at least a rhetorical commitment to the transformative ideal. Over time, critics weaken them, often while espousing their support for the principle of accountability. These critics trace their opposition to the specifics of existing arrangements, stating that they will support transformative accountability only if it is stripped of its motivating power.

The choice is between an imperfect accountability system and none at all. In the absence of coercive accountability, it is easy to graduate ill-equipped students and excuse inadequate school performance—especially among the most disadvantaged students. In the end, standards are a useful and essential artifice. Along with the accountability systems they support, they must be defended as such.

If accountability finally becomes part of the "grammar of schooling" for parents, voters, and educators, then its performance benchmarks for ensuring that students are learning, teachers are teaching, and schools are serving their public purpose will become accepted practice. State and federal officials now face a question: Will accountability fulfill this potential or become another hollow rite of spring?

6

The Political Challenge of Charter School Regulation

In the era of No Child Left Behind (NCLB), charter schooling holds out the promise of meaningful accountability without the heavy hand of standardized accountability discussed in the previous chapter. As an alternative to a reliance on uniform statewide testing, school charters can provide more nuanced accountability models that address particular issues raised by a school's mission, the nature of its student population, and so on.

One of the great ironies of contemporary education reform is that many critics of standardized accountability also oppose choice-based reforms, even though sensibly designed charter or voucher programs have the potential to address public demand for accountability without leading to the standardization of test-based statewide systems.

Recognizing the promise of the charter school model, many charter proponents have laudably sought to refine its accountability mechanisms. However, the largest hurdle in holding charter schools accountable for performance relates not to technical issues of contracting, but to the political challenges of quality control implied in the very design of charter schooling. Given that charter schools are publicly funded institutions created by legislative statute and are ultimately accountable to public entities, the political tensions are unavoidable. For all that, they have too rarely been given their due consideration. Consequently, the current system for shuttering ineffective charter schools is compelling in theory but uneven in practice, and most proposed remedies do not address the root problem.[1]

Charter schooling faces challenges to effective accountability on both the "front end"—the authorization of schools—and the "back end"—the closure of ineffective schools. This discussion focuses entirely on the "back end," which poses the toughest political problems (for reasons that will shortly become evident).

Charter schooling is based on the notion that schools can be freed from many of the rules and regulations endured by traditional district schools if they are instead held accountable for their performance.[2] This is nothing more than a simple application of modern management theory. Those schools that fail to produce the results promised in their charters or fail to uphold applicable state and local laws are to be closed by their authorizing bodies.[3] In practice, charter school authorizers sign contracts that stipulate performance expectations and empower the authorizers to shutter schools if they don't deliver. As the Center for Education Reform has explained, charter "closures provide real contractual accountability, a feature that too often is missing at many traditional public schools."[4]

Two Visions of Charter School Accountability

To date, the reality has not lived up to the theory. The most recent figures show that charter school accountability is primarily about shuttering schools with low enrollment, facility problems, financial improprieties, or mismanagement, rather than about monitoring or ensuring adequate academic performance. As of early 2004, 252 (8.4 percent) of the 2,996 charter schools that had ever opened had been closed, but just 1/100 of 1 percent had been closed for reasons related to academic performance.[5] In California, where the law requires that students attending charter schools meet the same standards as those attending regular public schools, just one of twenty-seven charter school closures has been attributed to academic performance.[6] If charter accountability is to provide a viable long-term alternative to state assessment systems, this kind of performance just won't do.

Why haven't existing accountability provisions led to more aggressive enforcement? What would it take to fulfill the promise of charter school accountability? Clearly, part of the answer is technical—many of today's authorizers lack expertise, information, and solid accountability metrics. Improving and expanding the tools, capacity, and expertise of oversight bodies, and becoming more thoughtful about collecting and analyzing data, will help. A greater challenge, however, is that charter schooling is currently working its way through a tug of war between two competing visions of accountability: the "market model" and the "regulatory model."

The market model presumes that families will hold charter schools accountable by fleeing bad schools. Such a model is agnostic about what constitutes a "bad" school, leaving consumers free to decide in the same way they judge whether a gourmet vegetarian bistro or a renowned steakhouse is "better." In such a system, schools are free to operate in any fashion, take on any mission, and measure their performance in any manner, just so long as they are able to attract and retain a sufficient number of students.

The regulatory approach is a response to two democratic concerns.[7] First, the public fears that some families may prefer schools that violate shared norms regarding the need to teach certain content, perform at a certain level of competence, or cultivate moral or ethical norms deemed threatening to the public weal. Second, the public worries that some families are too incompetent or ill-informed to make choices in their children's best interest. By shutting down schools that are deemed unacceptable, public regulation is intended to make sure that all families make "appropriate" choices.

Regulatory accountability, in setting out to tell parents which schools they may or may not send their children to, requires the broader community to do two things that strike at the heart of the market model. First, the community must agree on standards—academic, procedural, moral, what have you—against which schools will be judged. These standards can include graduation rates, student test performance, teacher certification, curricular elements, or any number of things.

Second, regulatory accountability requires the community to close charter schools that fail to meet these standards—even if families choose to continue sending their children to them. If all parents chose their children's schools in an acceptable manner, such regulation would be unnecessary; so the basic assumption of the regulatory model is that regulators will countermand the choices of some families.

The problem is that we all tend to care more strongly about what is best for our own children than what is best for the anonymous masses.

Although the vast majority of Americans support the regulation of charter schools in the abstract, attempts to hold a particular charter school accountable pit the marginally concerned general public against the intensely concerned families who have chosen to send their children to that school. The tension is analogous to that which we will shortly discuss regarding multicultural curricula in chapter 9, "Inclusive Ambiguity." When an oversight board decides to close or not renew the charter of an existing school, it must enforce the abstract preferences of an inattentive majority against the wishes of families who have decided that the school is both satisfactory and desirable.

The Challenge of Regulatory Accountability

The challenge of charter school regulation is obvious once we see it as a political, and not simply an educational, question. It is the age-old difficulty of serving the collective but dispersed interest of the inattentive, disorganized broader community in the face of intense interest from a relatively concentrated charter school community. What are the advantages enjoyed by a given charter school community?

Children are enrolled in a charter school because their families have chosen that school. Parents who seek out, apply to, and transport their children to a charter school obviously regard it as superior to their local public school. Moreover, even if parents did not strongly believe this prior to enrolling their child, it is likely that they will come to view the school positively over time, if only to justify their decision and subsequent efforts.

A charter school community is a self selected and easily organized group. Charter school families share a common concern, are in repeated contact, and have an organizational link that can facilitate communication and the dissemination of information. Similarly, charter school teachers have chosen to become faculty members of the school, are in daily contact with each other, and find it a simple matter to share information with one another and the parents of their students.

Meanwhile, members of the broader community have no particular stake in a charter school their children do not attend. Consequently, the inattentive broader community is unlikely to get exercised enough to want to close a school, unless a situation arises that is so egregious as to command public attention. For instance, when a school is preaching racist doctrines or engaging in financial improprieties, the violation of agreed-upon norms is clear enough that the broader community will endorse intervention to prohibit families from "wrongly" choosing the school. This helps explain why the vast majority of shuttered charter schools are closed for reasons relating to finances, facilities, or misman-agement. Such cases, however, say little about our ability to shut down academically mediocre but otherwise inoffensive charter schools.

The influence of charter school constituents is strengthened by our sys-tem of government. Actions of legislators and public administrators can be readily monitored by those who have the incentive to do so, enabling con-cerned voters to identify, pressure, and punish "unfriendly" officials. Meanwhile, the democratic process pretty much assures that those with strong preferences will be active and will exert a disproportionate level of influence on public officials, while the mass of citizens who are only mar-ginally affected by the resolution of an issue will have little incentive to pay much attention or invest much energy in the process.

In the case of charter school regulation—especially given the open-ness of most charter review processes—it is a simple matter for mobilized communities to bring pressure to bear. Meanwhile, the larger public has no reason to mount a parallel effort. Because charter school regulatory boards are generally state bodies with roles and budgets shaped directly by the state legislature, they have little incentive to offend vocal con-stituencies in the name of the abstract ideal of accountability.

So long as a school is enrolling students, those students' families clearly believe the performance to be acceptable. Closing a school by fail-ing to renew its charter requires that the authorizing body tell the school's supporters that they are either ignorant (unable to judge school quality) or misguided (unconcerned with quality). When the aggrieved, emotion-ally invested, and easily organized charter school community rallies to oppose the decision, there is no similar incentive for the broader com-munity to seek enforcement. In fact, if the school in question is not break-ing laws or operating in a scandalous fashion, a push to close it raises uncomfortable questions about how to "fairly" measure school perform-ance, and when parents should be denied the right to choose a school that they deem appropriate. As a result, it will be the exceptional situation in which regulators will refuse to renew the charter of even a mediocre school, so long as it enrolls more than a handful of students and has not engaged in gross misconduct. What can be done about this?

Improving Regulatory Accountability for Charter Schools

Today, the promise of regulatory accountability in charter schooling is largely unfulfilled, permitting incompetent school operators to stay in business, weakening the cause of charter reform, and providing ammunition to critics and those who would subject charter schools to more standardized accountability regimes. Charter school proponent Bruno Manno has noted that

> some self-inflicted wounds of the charter movement have strengthened the hands of its critics and opponents. These include . . . inept operators whose schools are fiscally disastrous and academically inadequate . . . and supporters who press sponsors to leave the schools alone—even to renew their charters—notwithstanding their organizational, financial, and instructional failures.[8]

Moreover, failing to recognize the source of the problem, proponents too often exaggerate the benefits that the current system of charter school accountability is likely to deliver. Political forces will tend to render regulatory accountability ineffective unless the system is intentionally crafted to resist such pressures. A failure to address this fact will strengthen those who oppose charter schooling, and will make it more difficult for it to fulfill its promise.

There are four basic strategies that legislators and program designers might use to enhance regulatory accountability for charter schools. Because we don't live in Wonderland, none of these strategies offers an instant remedy, and each incurs real costs. However, they do provide options that may deliver on the promise of charter school accountability—if we are serious about doing so:

- *Raising the bar.* Charter school communities do not become political constituencies until the members come together over a common interest and form an organized network. So the easiest solution to the political dilemma of accountability is to prevent communities of advocates for low-performing charter schools from forming in the first place. This suggests a rigorous screening of charter schools before they are permitted to open. While current authorization processes are demanding, they tend to focus on procedural requirements rather than on evidence that the proposed school is likely to achieve its agreed-upon goals. A rigorous screening approach cannot eliminate the possibility that ineffective schools will emerge, but it can minimize the number of such schools.

    Such an approach would constrain innovation and would strongly encourage applicants to replicate models that had succeeded elsewhere. Our current approach is far more receptive to the notion that charter schooling offers the opportunity for innovative schools to form. However, it is important to recognize that the current authorization process—despite the well-intentioned efforts of screening committees and authorizing boards—inevitably helps ensure that ineffective charter schools will open. Once open, some may continue to attract students, bringing us back to the central regulatory dilemma.

- *Tying their hands.* A second approach to reducing the politicization of charter school accountability systems is to limit regulatory discretion. Rather than require regulators to make judgment calls about closures or nonrenewals, legislators can transform authorizing boards into the executors of automatic decisions. The easiest way to do this is by writing charter school contracts with clear, quantitatively measurable goals, and then making charter renewal contingent on achieving those goals. Such an automatic trigger will permit oversight boards to sympathize with sanctioned schools while pleading helplessness. Meanwhile, such a stance can be defended as reflecting an unwavering commitment to high standards.

Cities such as Chicago and Washington, D.C., have taken steps to implement such a model, but then granted regulators substantial leeway when deciding whether schools had fulfilled their contract terms. Efforts to build regulatory discretion into the evaluative process, while admirable, will inevitably undermine the effectiveness of this remedy.

The "mandatory nonrenewal" approach requires some standardization of assessment measures in order to enable regulators to determine automatically whether or not a charter school has met its goals. Theoretically, such standardization can coexist with campus flexibility—allowing schools to design an array of appropriate indicators and find creative ways to measure their goals. However, interpreting nonquantitative measurements tends to require judgment calls, while increasing the number of indicators to be considered in evaluation may result in more mixed outcomes and a less straightforward assessment of school performance. Both situations would require regulators to exercise more discretion and would put them back into a politicized environment in which aggressive regulation would be difficult. In practice, therefore, clear-cut decisions on nonrenewal of school charters are much more likely when based on a limited number of quantitative measurements.

- *The Federal Reserve model.* A third approach is a "Federal Reserve" model, in which charter oversight boards are isolated from public pressure, and are provided with significant resources and a clear sense of institutional mission. Such an approach would require extended terms for board members, a "professional" and less partisan approach to board appointments, and sufficient staffing to permit board members to analyze school performance thoroughly and independently. Insulating charter school regulators from public pressure while providing them with the reputational and organizational resources to defend their decisions would enable them to defend more effectively the diffuse "general" interest against particularistic sniping. Of course, this model runs counter to the convictions of many charter school advocates that education ought to be more democratic, that the role of professional educators should be reduced, and that public schools already suffer from excessive bureaucratization and intrusive regulation.

- *Competitive authorizers.* A final approach shifts from the explicitly regulatory focus of the first three models and relies on a quasimarket that is driven by authorizer self-interest. If charter school oversight boards have an incentive to protect and cultivate a "brand name"—either because they are competing for-profit entities or because they are nonprofit institutions (such as universities) that may suffer real costs from a loss of reputation—there is cause to presume that they will aggressively police the schools they authorize. Public regulatory boards, however, traditionally have had little cause for such concerns because, while a reputation for probity gains them little, aggressive regulation will increase the enmity of aggrieved school communities. Thus far, our very limited experience with universities charged with authorizing charter schools has provided little evidence on this matter.

Of course, a market model threatens notions of lay control, site autonomy, and community influence that have been central to the argument for charter schooling. Charter schools authorized and overseen by brand-conscious firms may be less diverse and autonomous than those under the current system, as firms seeking to enhance their market share are apt to assess performance on the basis of popular and salable measures—not necessarily those most appropriate to the school at hand.

The Promise of Charter School Accountability

The larger lesson here is twofold. First, if we are serious about charter school accountability, we have to consider which arrangements will be most effective. Thus far, policy has been marked more by high hopes and good intentions than by realistic appraisals. Second, while meaningful accountability will require us to carefully design regulatory mechanisms, we must also recognize the tradeoffs implied by the nature of charter schooling itself.

If we are to devise a more balanced and defensible system of charter school accountability, we need to take a hard look at the requirements of meaningful regulation. In the world of NCLB, if charter schooling is to provide a safe space for distinctive educational visions to demonstrate their value, powerful accountability mechanisms that can rival mandatory testing systems are imperative. To date, we have not seriously addressed this challenge. It is past time for us to get started.

7

The Work Ahead

What if Michael Dell, CEO of Dell Computers, and Michael Armstrong, CEO of AT&T, operated in a market where revenues depended hardly at all on attracting or losing customers? What if competition exerted minimal pressure, and market threats could often be trumped by successful efforts to glean government subsidies? What if they had only sparse information on the performance of personnel and could not fire or demote most employees? What if they could count on potential competitors' being deterred or eliminated by political and legal forces?

This should all sound familiar to education reformers because these are the market conditions faced by the administrators running urban schools today. For instance, since vouchers were introduced in Milwaukee in 1990, the school district's enrollment, total funding, and per-pupil funding have all grown steadily. Between 1990 and 2004, enrollment climbed from slightly under 93,000 students to more than 105,000.[1] Total spending by the district grew from just over $580 million in 1990–91 to more than $1.1 billion during the 2002–3 school year. In other words, since vouchers and charter schools came to Milwaukee, the district's budget has risen by some 97 percent, while its enrollment has grown by only 13 percent. Per-pupil spending has grown from about $6,200 to $11,700.[2]

A similar pattern prevailed in Cleveland, where vouchers were introduced during the 1995–96 school year. Enrollment in the Cleveland city school district actually decreased from slightly more than 73,800 in 1994–95 to about 69,650 in 2003–4.[3] Per-pupil spending grew from slightly more than $6,000 to more than $11,121 in 2003–4.[4] These conditions make competition more of a relief than a threat. Some educators in Milwaukee and Cleveland have even come to describe their cities' voucher programs as a "safety valve" that helps to ease the pressure of overcrowding. This puts the lie to the oft-repeated claim of critics like former National Education Association president Bob Chase that school choice is "siphoning off scarce public resources for the benefit of a few."[5] Competition in most urban districts is like a gnat to a bull—there, but barely noticed.

Nevertheless, in states like Arizona or Michigan, where charter schools are multiplying quickly, real changes in policy and behavior have emerged. And advocates of competition and school choice have been eager to parse every change for evidence that public school districts are responding to competitive threats and that markets are "working." Certainly, some districts have adopted potentially valuable policies, such as providing all-day kindergarten, adding an extra year of preschool, or opening themed schools that meet the demands of particular groups and families. However, observers rarely bother to note that such efforts tend to be superimposed on the existing dysfunctionalities. There is little evidence that districts are restructuring or are being pushed by market pressures to revisit their "business model."

Moreover, in most cases, districts' responses have primarily taken the form of changes in marketing and outreach. In Arizona, the Mesa Unified School District has tried advertising in local movie theaters and conducting customer-service training for employees. The Flagstaff district has distributed leaflets comparing its expenditures and outcomes with those of neighboring districts. Milwaukee launched a campaign called "High Standards Start Here," replete with banners for each school, and worked hard to promote former superintendent Alan Brown's 1999 guarantee that all Milwaukee students would be able to read by the end of second grade.

While much of this is welcome—anything that prompts a public school district to increase its attention to customer service clearly has value—these changes may, in fact, make the schools less productive. After all, taking money from the schools and putting it into ad campaigns does nothing to change the schools themselves. Advocates of choice have been too quick to characterize the add-ons, rhetoric, and ad campaigns as the leading edge of a business-like, performance-oriented response to competition because they have failed to recognize that these changes are the product of a market that is fundamentally different from the hyper-competitive models described in economics textbooks.

A fluid, efficient market, one that promotes "creative destruction," in Joseph Schumpeter's memorable phrase, cannot simply be wished into existence. The uneven experiences with developing free markets in Russia and Eastern Europe, and our own difficulties with deregulating sectors like air transportation, telecommunications, and energy, testify to the importance of the competitive environment.

In the school choice debate, it is easy to overlook the institutional and cultural nuances of market-based reform because economic competition in the United States, at least from a bird's-eye perspective, looks similar across broad swaths of the private sector. Executives and investors generally seek to maximize the return on their investments; employees respond to certain incentives; managers are empowered to make decisions on hiring, firing, and promotions; and so on. But these conditions are almost nonexistent in many public or charitable enterprises—especially those devoted to tending the needs of children or the disadvantaged. Making education competitive requires more than just high hopes; the very culture and rules of public schooling must be overhauled.

Mixed Metaphors

The idea that schools might be less than responsive to competitive pressures should come as no surprise to promoters of school choice. After all, the reasons for promoting choice often rest on the fact that public school systems are strangled by politics, bureaucracy, byzantine contractual rules, and licensing procedures that aggravate a shortage of high-quality employees. Economists have long known that the ability of a market to promote performance often depends on the competitive environment. Hence, it is surprising that so little attention has been devoted to the complexities of the education market in the debate over school choice.

In thinking about efforts to bring market competition to an arena funded, regulated, and operated by government, it may help to picture two fundamentally different kinds of markets. The classic image of the market is that of a bulldozer compelling firms to improve constantly—or be crushed. This is the picture that fans of choice seem to have in mind when they herald the promise of competition in education. However, a pickaxe may be a more appropriate metaphor in this sector. When the pain of competition is cushioned and competitors aren't nimble enough to respond easily to market forces, change may be haphazard, limited, and sporadic—more like the holes created by the pick's insistent tapping than the devastation wrought by the bulldozer's relentless blade. The mistake may be in seeing superficial reactions, like the launch of a pilot program, an advertising campaign, or a new public school choice plan as necessarily signaling the approach of fundamental reengineering. Putting a jingle on the radio may be the deepest change a school district is going to make.

This is not to say that schools will not respond at all to competitive pressures. It's just that the responses rarely appear to touch the core of what schools do. When there is evidence of deeper change, these changes seem to depend on two crucial factors.

First, smaller, more coherent organizations are more likely to respond to competition than are larger ones. Individual schools tend to respond more aggressively to competition than do school systems. For example, the statewide voucher program in Florida provides vouchers to students in low-performing schools. During the program's first year, only two schools had performed poorly enough for their students to be eligible for the voucher program. The principals and staff in these schools were put in a visible hot seat and thus given clear professional incentives to satisfy public demands. They were able to move their schools off the voucher list within a year. In this situation, when a scarlet letter "F" has been attached to their schools and state sanctions are imminent, principals can rally their teachers and take action.

However, it's unclear whether these schools were responding to the loss of students or to the public shame of being named the two worst schools in the state. If the state instead threatened to fire or reassign the principals and teachers at failing schools, the results would likely be the same. The point is that focusing meaningful pressure on individual schools is more likely to prompt a response than are more general efforts at promoting competition.

Second, competition is likely to improve performance on outcomes that are easily measured, while making sacrifices elsewhere. This would be fine, except that choice proponents and critics both ask schools to

expose children to many things that cannot be clearly or readily measured. It makes sense that the educators at the two failing Florida schools,
when subjected to clear and immediate sanctions, redoubled their efforts
to improve students' performance on state tests. Likewise, because test
scores are often used as a proxy for school quality, it is not so surprising to see improvements in test scores where schools are subjected to
more competition. Similar results have been found whenever states
subject schools to concerted pressure—as in the case of high-stakes testing. However, these changes do not necessarily reflect an improvement
in real school performance. Gains may be due in part to the simple
reallocation of time and effort. If the state demands higher performance
in math, schools may offer intensive math tutoring all morning, eliminating art and music classes to make the time available. While such
changes may be desirable, they should not be construed as evidence of
heightened productivity.

Straitjacketed School Systems

What can be done to make competition a more effective tool for school
reform? Let's look at five factors that constrain competition in education.

Competition is fundamentally about fear. The motivating power of
competition in education is that people fear for their investments or their
jobs. So far, however, the threat posed by voucher plans has generally
been quite mild. In Cleveland, for instance, the voucher for use at a private school has a maximum value of $3,000, less than 30 percent of what
the public schools spend per pupil.[6] In Milwaukee, the number of students using vouchers has increased sharply since 1997, growing from
nearly two thousand in 1997 to almost fourteen thousand in 2005, but
the voucher itself has been worth only $5,882, about 53 percent of per-
pupil spending in the public schools.[7] This has artificially constricted the
supply of new private schools and the number of children who can afford
to attend them.

  If the vouchers were set at a reasonable level, entrepreneurs would be
willing to open new schools, not only giving children the opportunity to

leave the public schools but also providing schools at which to spend the vouchers. Many choice programs have been crafted to minimize the monetary impact on public districts. Meanwhile, charter schools enroll 1.6 percent of the K–12 student population in just a handful of states.[8] They have also been subjected to extensive regulation and often target at-risk populations that public educators are happy to hand over. As long as choice plans are small and the financial pinch on districts is modest, it is unlikely that public school educators or policymakers will feel compelled to respond to competition.

Public educators are less sensitive to competitive threats than private-sector employers and employees. Public schools have no watchdog shareholders to monitor market share or organizational efficiency. The stakes for school board members are far more attenuated than are those for investors, while superintendents are rarely evaluated on issues like market share or cost-efficiency. Instead, as public officials, school leaders face incentives to tend to the concerns of active and politically potent constituencies—particularly the teachers' unions and civil rights groups—whatever the impact of their actions on system performance. A lack of clear outcome measures or accountability mechanisms makes it difficult to compel system officials to resist this natural impulse.

Administrators' ability to respond to competition hinges on their ability to compel their subordinates to act, but school administrators find it difficult to monitor and evaluate what their employees are doing. Teachers work largely in isolation, face uneven sets of challenges, and must respond not only to the academic needs but also to the physical and emotional needs of their students. These details complicate administrators' goals of identifying weak employees and ensuring that they improve. Moreover, teachers know they have little need to fear for their positions.

The urban areas primarily targeted by choice-based reforms are suffering through a prolonged teacher shortage. Districts like New York City scrambled to replace 10–15 percent of their teachers each year throughout the 1990s. This means that student enrollment must fall significantly, and for a sustained period, before such losses pose much of a threat to public educators. The natural growth in enrollment during the past decade meant that most large districts were much more concerned about where they would house the students who did *not* leave for a charter or private school. Schools in wealthy suburban areas, which typically have dozens if not hundreds of teachers vying for each open slot, might respond more energetically to competition, but widespread contentment among the parents in such districts has made schools of choice rare.

When administrators seek to monitor and motivate their employees, they are hindered by regulations, a professional culture, and collectively bargained contracts over which they enjoy limited control. In the private sector, employees who ignore their bosses' goals and directives will suffer financially and professionally and may even lose their jobs. Such tools of persuasion are largely denied to school administrators. They have few perks to offer and find it extraordinarily difficult to fire employees. For the most part, teachers will respond to competition only if they choose to.

The culture of teaching compounds the problem. Generally speaking, people enter the public and private sectors for substantially different reasons. Many teachers are attracted to education for its child-centered, humanistic, and autonomous character. Seniority-based wage scales and a flat career trajectory have long made public schools unreceptive to entrepreneurs. This poses obvious challenges for an employer eager to focus employees on performance or market share. Private-sector competition presumes that employees are concerned about career advancement and financial rewards. Executives at IBM, for instance, rarely need to worry about whether employees might disregard their directives as a result of their personal conception of the job.

Contemporary educators are unprepared, by temperament and training, to respond effectively to competition. Schools of education offer administrators little or no formal preparation in management or business practices. As we will later discuss in "A License to Lead?" and "Ready to Lead?" education schools may provide administrators with some training in pedagogy, curriculum, procedural routines, legal issues, and "leadership," but they offer no training in conventional business administration.

In the private sector, firms generally have access to personnel skilled in areas such as market analysis or advertising. School systems rarely enjoy such talents. Administrators aren't expected to possess even a glancing familiarity with such concerns; marketing skills are seldom a criterion for support staff positions; and school districts are usually reluctant to contract for services of this sort.

Unchaining the Bulldozer

As public pressure builds for higher performance and stricter accountability, some of these constraints will loosen of their own accord. But policymakers can do much to accelerate the process. The simplest way to strengthen competition is to make it more threatening. Employees who feel they should consistently demonstrate that they deserve their jobs, desirable assignments, or material rewards are much more likely to cooperate with efforts to respond to competition. Policymakers can intensify competition by increasing the number of choice schools, the size of these schools, or the financial hit experienced by public schools when they lose enrollment. Expanding voucher programs and charter schools will involve more than just lifting the enrollment caps on such programs; it will also require private- or public-sector efforts to create more schools of choice.

The limited ability of choice schools to take in more students severely limits the threat posed by competition. The number of charter schools has grown dramatically in recent years, but they still enroll only slightly more than 1 percent of K–12 students. Only a fraction of that number use vouchers to attend private schools.[9] Most choice schools are already operating at or close to capacity. Generating an ample amount of competitive pressure demands a substantial increase in either the size or the number of new schools. While charter schools have multiplied at an impressive rate, the size of these schools has remained rather small: an average of 269 students.[10] Assuming this trend persists, two thousand new charter schools will have to be started each year through 2015 for charter enrollment to approach 10 percent of the public school population.

Moreover, efforts to open new charter and voucher schools have relied heavily on philanthropic support. Such giving is limited and is often intended to seed model programs, so it is unclear what resources will fund a significant expansion.

The fastest and most effective source of growth may be for-profit schooling. Opening a school requires an extensive initial investment, one that nonprofit ventures rarely have the capital to make. School managers motivated by profitability are more likely to open big schools and chains of schools because they are attracted to the potential return. Encouraging for-profit operators will dramatically increase the pool of capital available to open and expand schools and will lessen reliance on philanthropic and governmental resources. In various personal conversations with me between 2001 and 2004, many conventional charter operators have reported that they would rather operate small, one-site schools than seek to create a chain of schools. It is easy to forget that many charter and private school educators entered education for the same humanistic, child-centered reasons as public educators. Running a large school or a chain of schools, with all the attendant bureaucracy, tends not to be their ambition in life.

Strengthening competition also requires giving school administrators solid information on student, teacher, and school performance, and the incentives to care about such things. Administrators also need the tools with which to reward and sanction employees through hiring, firing, promotion, and monitoring. Without such tools, administrators must rely on personal charm and informal nudges to drive improvement—a daunting task even for skilled and seasoned executives. The more discretion they have, the more influential they'll be. These changes, of course, would necessitate changes in the contracts, laws, and norms of professional education.

Finally, teachers and principals who care more about individual rewards and material incentives will be more receptive to administrative influence and will help administrators cut through the soggy resistance of the schoolhouse culture. This means attracting new kinds of teachers. Relaxing certification requirements, as we discuss later in "Tear Down This Wall," recruiting nontraditional educators more aggressively, and permitting administrators to reward teachers for performance will all help to attract more entrepreneurial personnel. Likewise, if education leaders are expected to respond to market imperatives, their training should more closely resemble that of business executives, and recruitment efforts should seek executive ability at least as much as previous experience in education.

In other words, creating a meaningful sense of competition will entail fundamentally changing the culture of public schooling. The question is whether we actually want to trade the comforts of our present system for the benefits of one more reliant on self-interest and amenable to competition. Competition is likely to make schools less hospitable to those educators who love the autonomy and insulation from supervision that characterize most contemporary public schools. Efforts to cultivate it may thus foster a culture of schooling that is alien to our educational heritage and create an incentive structure that distorts educational priorities. However, the new milieu may also prove more attractive to bright, ambitious teaching aspirants, and lead to the proliferation of focused and effective schools that potential teachers find more appealing.

It is not clear that we are serious about embracing a school system characterized by vigorous competition. Many advocates of charter schooling trumpet the freedom and innovation promoted by choice, but remain hostile to the ideas of unbridled markets and for-profit operators. This is not an untenable position—one can believe in school choice but not in an educational marketplace. However, small-scale competition is not going to unleash the market bulldozer. It is naive to pretend it will.

The essential point is that the effect of competition on public schools is inextricably intertwined with the history and culture of American schooling. Half-hearted competition will not overcome the bureaucratic and regulatory barriers woven into the education marketplace. Allowing competition to bloom and thrive necessitates shattering these constraints. Advocates of competition must accept this reality. And opponents of choice have an obligation to offer an alternative reform strategy that rests on something more solid than the high hopes and good intentions that have attended decades of failed reform efforts.

8

Choice Is Not Enough

In 2004, after acrimonious debate and years of wrangling, Congress enacted a federally funded school voucher program in Washington, D.C. Billed as a national test of school vouchers, the program commenced in fall 2004, with nearly a thousand students and fifty-three schools from the District of Columbia participating, and the students receiving vouchers worth up to $7,500 in the 2004–5 school year.[1] Thrilled to have won this high-profile victory after a decade of stop-and-start efforts in Congress, voucher proponents rendered grand pronouncements about its likely impact.

Republican representative Jeff Flake from Arizona, who introduced the D.C. voucher initiative, proclaimed, "Not only will these scholarships help students who take advantage of them, but they'll help the students who remain in the public school system by freeing up resources and creating a competitive environment where both public and private will thrive."[2] D.C. mayor Anthony Williams asserted that "introducing choice and ensuring competition" would improve the schools, though he also explained that the bill would "hold harmless the public schools."[3]

Sorry to spoil the party, but these claims smack of Great Society wishful thinking. This is not only because the program is capped at about 3 percent of public school students and sweetens the pot for public schools with an additional $13 million in new funding.[4] More fundamentally, the program—as both Representative Flake and Mayor Williams have emphasized—ensures that public schools have nothing to lose, and maybe something to gain, when students depart for private schools. The program offers choice without consequence, "competition" as a soft political slogan rather than a hard economic reality (and resembles, more than a little, the mindset that yields half-hearted efforts at charter school accountability of the kinds I alluded to in "The Political Challenge of Charter School Regulation"). Like many earlier voucher programs, including those involving larger numbers of students, the D.C. program is unlikely to force major improvements. Therein lies an important lesson for advocates of "choice" as the silver bullet of school reform.

After all, when D.C. charter school legislation passed in 1995, grand claims were made on its behalf. Proponents like Lex Towle of the Appletree Institute explained, "When you get a critical mass of good independent public schools, particularly in the inner city where they are most important, that will help create the competition that will raise the level of other public schools."[5] Critical mass we got—roughly one in five D.C. public school students was enrolled in a charter school by 2004.[6] Yet after ten years of charter "competition," the U.S. Census Bureau reported in 2005 that D.C.'s public schools were spending more than $16,000 per student while remaining among the worst-achieving in the nation, wracked by scandal, and plagued by managerial incompetence.[7]

How could this be possible? Doesn't it violate the basic tenets of market logic? Did Milton Friedman overpromise?

The Logic of Competition

To be blunt, competition works when it hurts. This is the corollary to the notion that accountability has to be mean to be meaningful, as I explained in "The Case for Being Mean." Markets matter precisely because they are neither gentle nor forgiving. This can make an unflinching embrace of markets difficult for politicians or reformers more interested in expanding parental choices than promoting systemic improvement. For many voucher or charter proponents, "competition" is more a rhetorical device than a serious tool to promote educational excellence.

In the private sector, when competition is threatening enough—as when American automakers and electronic manufacturers were almost wiped out by Japanese competitors in the 1980s—firms either reinvent themselves or yield to more productive competitors.[8] Unions make painful concessions or watch jobs vanish.

The absence of competition means that public schools, like other government agencies, typically lack this discipline. No matter how inefficient the agency, employees have little to fear. Subjecting school systems to real competition would indeed produce more disciplined, productive schools—and many other benefits as well. It would provide quality control extending beyond the basic accountability afforded by standardized testing. It would encourage flexibility by enabling entrepreneurial educators to challenge existing schools and reigning orthodoxies. It would permit effective schools to multiply and grow without waiting on political processes or resistant district leadership. But that is not, for the most part, how schools compete today when confronted with voucher and charter programs.

How Schools "Compete" Today

Research on educational competition has grown steadily in the past few years. Thoughtful scholars like Harvard economist Caroline Hoxby and Manhattan Institute fellow Jay Greene have published analyses suggesting that heightened educational competition is associated with modestly improved student achievement.[9] Other scholars, like Fordham Foundation president Chester Finn and Villanova University political scientist Robert Maranto, have noted that public systems sometimes respond to charter school competition by increasing advertising or trying to stifle their competitors.[10] This research is instructive and has highlighted several promising, if limited, developments.

Unfortunately, this scholarship has too often been trumpeted uncritically by choice proponents rather than used to encourage rigorous policy consideration. Too many advocates have closed their eyes and insisted, like Flake and Williams, that tentative choice experiments will suffice to create competition.

Imagine if a Wal-Mart store manager were told that losing customers would have no impact on her salary, evaluation, or job security—while attracting new customers would require her to hire more employees, assume greater responsibilities, and erect a trailer in the parking lot to handle the added business, all without additional compensation or recognition. In such an environment, only the clueless would care much about "competing." The sensible manager's preference would be for a stable customer population (although, truth be told, she'd probably rather lose customers than gain them).

But this is exactly how schools—even most "choice" schools—compete today. Take the principal of a typical elementary school in Washington, D.C., that was built to house four hundred students and currently enrolls three hundred and seventy-five. What happens if that principal loses seventy-five students to charter schools, or to the new voucher program?

Typically, three retiring teachers are not replaced, three classrooms are freed up, and the tiny amount of discretionary money that flowed to the school to support those students doesn't come in. In short, the principal's job gets a little easier. She earns the same salary and has the same professional prospects she would have otherwise, yet has fewer teachers to lead, fewer students to monitor, and a less-crowded school.

Take the same school and assume that the principal reacts powerfully and effectively to the incitement to increase enrollment, prompting the school to add seventy-five students. What happens? The principal takes on responsibility for three new teachers, must squeeze students into the last available classroom, adds two trailers out back to hold two additional classrooms, and crowds the school's cafeteria and corridors.

This principal is now responsible for two teachers who are not happy about teaching all day in a trailer and fifty families who feel the same way about their children's classrooms. In return for these headaches, the "successful" principal receives—what? At best, a small pool of discretionary monies, typically amounting to less than $50 a student, more responsibilities, dissatisfied constituents, and no more recognition or pay. Why would we expect these principals to compete in more than a token fashion?

From Choice to Competition

Choice-based reforms are the first step in promoting educational competition, but alone they are wildly insufficient. I want to suggest six steps for those serious about making competition work:

- The sine qua non of effective choice is that parents must be in a position to deny resources to poor schools and bestow resources on good ones. The money for educating a given student should follow that child when he or she changes schools, and the size of choice programs should not be restricted. The political conceit that choice will spur public school systems to remake themselves *even if they get more money for serving fewer students* should be squarely rejected.

- Principals whose schools attract students should be rewarded and recognized accordingly. Of course, various safeguards are appropriate—to ensure that popular schools are also producing adequate performance, and to reflect that some schools are naturally more attractive than others—but the logic of these measures is relatively straightforward.

- Principals and superintendents need to be able to hire, fire, promote, and reward employees. In the current system, when principals and district officials try to monitor and manage their employees in accordance with market imperatives, they stumble over regulations, professional norms, and contractual provisions. In the private sector, employees are compelled to accept management direction to a much greater extent, even in firms where workers are protected by strong contracts. Presently, principals aren't always prepared for these challenges, a reality that raises some additional complications to be discussed in "Ready to Lead?"

- It is necessary to overhaul rigid contractual arrangements that stifle potential entrepreneurs. Salary schedules based on seniority and pension plans based on continuous service penalize longtime educators who leave their positions for new opportunities.

- It is essential to increase the number of choice schools and the number of students these schools serve in order to make competition truly threatening. Many barriers, formal and informal, have limited the growth of choice options. The educators who traditionally open "mom and pop" charter schools or run private schools are unlikely to drive significant expansion. Why? Most like the idea of running a small, familial school and evince little interest in maximizing enrollment, running multiple schools, or managing a bureaucratic operation that separates them from the students. If they are to serve more children, these entrepreneurs need to be enticed with enough rewards—money, prestige, perks—that they are willing to trade the freedom and fun of their small enterprise for the headaches of expansion.

- Finally, it is essential to welcome for-profit operators if the supply of schools and seats is to be expanded significantly. The entry of for-profit operators can dramatically increase the pool of capital available to open and expand schools and lessen reliance upon philanthropic and government resources. Opening a school requires an extensive initial investment, one that it is often easier for profit-seeking than for nonprofit ventures to raise. School managers motivated by profitability are more likely to serve large numbers of children and have the resources required to operate a large network of schools.

Choice-based reform is a vital element of school reform, but it is not a reform strategy in and of itself. Most choice-based reforms in American education, including even ambitious voucher programs and charter school laws, fail to generate competition worthy of the name. The rules and norms governing school funding, work conditions, and employee compensation mean that neither principals nor teachers have much of a stake in whether their schools attract students.

In the 1970s, during the height of the Communist regime in the old Soviet Union, Moscow's shoppers could choose from scores of grocery stores. Nonetheless, you'd have to look long and hard to find a market proponent who would suggest that the Muscovite grocery market had benefited from competition. Why?

It's because employees' job security, compensation, and promotion were little affected by "competitive" performance—regardless of how effectively their stores competed. Transforming "choice" into competition requires making the consequences matter for individual educators. If we want vouchers or charter schooling to create competition more vibrant than that of the old Soviet groceries, choice alone is not enough.

PART III

Politics and School Reform

Introduction

One of the more troubling legacies of twentieth-century school reform was the desire to put schooling beyond politics. Embracing the Progressive Era mantra that "there's no Democratic or Republican way to pave a road," education reformers have long shied away from conflict, put their faith in "consensus" and "expertise," and avoided thinking deeply about the interaction of political currents and educational improvement. In academia, the result has been decades of impoverished thinking on education politics, with a wealth of banality and jargon punctuated only by the occasional work of significance.

Interestingly, the nationalization of education politics that has taken place in the past decade, spearheaded most aggressively by the putatively "conservative" administration of George W. Bush, has drawn increasing attention to these questions. There are glimmers to suggest that the rising generation of thinkers may move past indecipherable accounts of "micropolitics" or "gendered leadership" to provide meaningful insight into how expertise, constituent demands, collective interests, policy design, and political incentives combine to shape the agenda, implementation, and prospects of school reform.

As I suggested earlier, this kind of analysis and argument may ultimately prove more important than even the most carefully crafted experimental studies. After all, the *Federalist Papers* have probably done more to shape government in the world's new democracies than all the careful social science of the past fifty years. The simple, profound insights of the Founders have enjoyed a wider influence among democratic reformers in nations like Ukraine, Russia, Poland, and South Africa than have sophisticated examinations of political behavior. This is not to slight the invaluable contribution of scholarly research, but to recognize that public thinking is more often shaped by the concise expression of an elegant insight than by mounds of data or analysis.

In any event, as the essays in this section suggest, this is the bias that colors my political analysis. The first piece, "Inclusive Ambiguity," first published in *Educational Policy*, is by far the most academic of the four. I was curious as to why heated fights repeatedly broke out when states decided what literature and history to include in their standards, while discussions of math content seemed to proceed much more smoothly. The resulting research was revealing, but raised some real concerns about our ability to craft meaningful academic standards in the era of No Child Left Behind.

The next two essays, "'Trust Us,' They Explained" and "School Vouchers and Suburbanites," both deal with the politics of school choice, race, and the urban-suburban divide. Published in 2003, they appeared in the *American Experiment Quarterly* and *The American Enterprise*, respectively. The first piece was prompted by Trent Lott's embarrassing, racially offensive comments at a 2002 birthday party for legendary senator Strom Thurmond and his quick renunciation of long-held conservative positions on racially sensitive issues like affirmative action. The patent insincerity of Lott's reversal, and the implication that he regarded his own positions as racist rather than principled, dramatized many of the tensions I had observed in conservative efforts to make common cause with the black community on school reform.

"School Vouchers and Suburbanites" approaches the political challenge of choice-based reform from a perspective that is almost diametrically opposed to that of "'Trust Us.'" Rather than ask why conservatives are having trouble convincing black leaders to embrace vouchers, I ask why they are having trouble convincing their suburban base to do so. The answer is illuminating. Whereas urban black leaders can imagine all the ways in which the early promise of school choice might be stripped from their constituents, suburbanites simply recognize that charter and voucher programs are likely to have immediate, negative consequences for their schools and property values. Convincing these voters to welcome school choice will require more than slogans and moralizing—it will require school choice advocates to address substantive concerns.

Finally, I was prompted to pen "The Voice of the People," first published in the *American School Board Journal*, by the unrestrained eagerness too many reformers displayed in embracing mayoral control of school boards as a new, shiny, silver bullet. I do not argue that increased mayoral authority is a bad idea; and I have certainly never been particularly impressed by school board governance. As so often happens, however, there was a seeming rush to view governance reform as a quick fix—or at the least as a proposition with no downside. As with so many other seemingly cost-free political reforms, I believe more caution is warranted, and think alternative strategies deserve more consideration.

9

Inclusive Ambiguity

In any free nation with a population as diverse, independent-minded, and ornery as the American people, debates about public norms tread fine lines of cultural and ideological disagreement. This is particularly true in education, where faith in schooling as a homogenizing "melting pot" can rest uneasily aside our commitment to the cultural and religious sensibilities of families.

This tension is particularly significant when the policy preferences of the democratic majority clash with those of various cultural, ethnic, or religious communities over questions like curricular standards and school accountability.[1] After all, while much contemporary debate revolves around questions like charter schooling and school vouchers, such reforms currently enroll less than 2 percent of K–12 students, while accountability systems and curricular standards affect all of America's public school students.

As I discussed in "The Case for Being Mean," standards-based accountability systems determine what all children will be required to learn and then link judgment of teacher, school, and student performance to the mastery of that content. These performance-based accountability systems require officials to designate a prescribed body of content and objectives to be tested, necessarily excluding, and thus marginalizing, some goals, objectives, and content. They must also impose assessments that gauge whether students have mastered the requisite skills and material. These decisions tend to produce passionate opposition among those who feel that their interests, values, beliefs, or cultures are being shortchanged.

The decisions required by standards-based accountability have particularly sharpened conflicts with proponents of multicultural curricula and pedagogy. Multiculturalists believe that K–12 instruction needs to do more to include personages, content, and material that reflect groups, cultures, or sensibilities that the reformers deem to be underrepresented. Meanwhile, setting standards that all students are required to master requires agreement on a coherent, more focused set of learning objectives. The result is a tension between efforts to broaden and those to narrow the standards.

When standards are systematized in accordance with the imperatives of accountability, clashes between the majority and those whose particular concerns are marginalized are inevitable. After all, teachers and instructional materials emphasize the content for which students are held responsible.[2] If social studies test questions are based on twentieth-century social movements rather than on the Founding Fathers, instruction will reflect that. Given sharp disagreement over the merits of various curricular and pedagogical approaches, efforts to impose statewide agreement inevitably offend some constituencies.

The American political system is notoriously bad at pursuing collective goods, such as accountability, when doing so imposes concentrated costs on passionate, coherent constituencies. American government is highly permeable, making it relatively easy for passionate factions to block or soften adverse legislative or bureaucratic decisions. Aggrieved groups can seek to block these programs by delaying the implementation of accountability programs—a tack that opponents have employed with much success. If they cannot or do not wish to delay implementation of accountability—which is far more difficult since the advent of No Child Left Behind—the aggrieved can seek to win the inclusion of their preferred material, or can dilute the standards to the point that they are ambiguous enough to no longer offend.

In practice, there is a balancing flywheel that governs efforts to make standards more inclusive along the dimensions of race, ethnicity, gender, and religion. The majoritarian perspective generally enjoys vague, disinterested support, whereas the aggrieved interests are mobilized for particular concessions. When standards are drafted to reflect majoritarian beliefs, they often get watered down through a process of inclusion. On the other hand, when drafted "collaboratively," agreed-upon standards are either sufficiently vague as to be inoffensive or countermajoritarian enough to provoke traditionalist demands for revisions. Regardless, there is a tendency for the standards to teeter toward watery compromises. For example, middle school students in New York are now expected to "know the social and economic characteristics, such as customs, traditions, child-rearing practices, ways of making a living, education and socialization practices, gender roles, foods, and religious and spiritual beliefs that distinguish different cultures and civilizations."[3] Broad, airy guidelines provide little concrete direction as to what content teachers are expected to teach or students are expected to learn. The result is that impressive-sounding standards turn out to be crowd-pleasing compromises subject to various interpretations. Rather than being "standards-based," classroom teaching is then more likely to be driven by previous test questions, or by teachers favoring the material they know best or find most important—the exact situation standards were introduced to remedy.

Basically, policymakers have two available strategies for defusing opposition to standards. One approach is to add material to standards in response to particular complaints from critics. This "augmentative" strategy works reasonably well in an era of standards when there is no practical constraint on the amount of material that standards can include, but it is much less effective under "high-stakes accountability," when students and schools are held accountable for student mastery of specified content, and standards are expected to provide concrete guidance. Under high-stakes accountability, where students are expected to master specifically enumerated material, something has to come out of the standards when new material is inserted. Given the delicacy of these decisions, conflicts are often resolved by compromising on broad, ambiguous, and aspirational standards which permit all parties to read the final standards as receptive to their concerns. The hidden cost is that the lack of explicit direction in such compromises grants undue influence to test-makers, leaves students at the whims of their teachers' judgment, and fails to make clear what material students are expected to master.

The Political Fault Lines

Whatever the merits of the disputants in the larger debate, multiculturalism has played a significant role in shaping the standards underlying accountability, though not always in the intended fashion. The challenges have taken place along identifiable fault lines, the most prominent of these being race. Efforts to compensate for a history of slavery, Jim Crow, and the suppression of black culture have led reformers to infuse public school history and literature curricula with black figures, writers, and perspectives. The more radical voices "claim that schools victimize students of color by not presenting accurate images of their ancestors," and that a curriculum of inclusion can help remedy the ravages of racism.[4]

A second fault line is ethnicity and national origin, as Latinos, Asians, and Native Americans, among others, have demanded that their heritage be woven into the fabric of required content. A third is gender equity. Feminists call for greater inclusion of women in the literary canon and historical curricula, and this call has been echoed by advocates for gay and lesbian inclusion. A final area of contention is religion. Although religion has been largely removed from public education under the auspices of the First Amendment's establishment clause, religiously motivated debates about state standards have been among the most bitter.

These fault lines traverse some of the most politically sensitive territory in modern American political discourse: religious belief, racism, sexuality, discrimination, and assimilation. The multicultural challengers of the early 1990s sought to add minority works and perspectives to the existing curriculum, an approach that public officials could pursue through a strategy of augmentation—simply adding some authors, books, content, or historical figures to existing standards. The advisory nature of standards allowed this dilution to be accomplished at little cost, because it neither required that officials remove any existing material nor necessitated any change in testing or teaching.

The ascendance of high-stakes accountability regimes has changed those rules and forced officials to wrestle with more of a zero-sum situation. The reliance on tests of discrete content, and the need to develop more focused curricula to accompany the tests, bolster pressure to subtract some old content as new content is added and increase political tensions.

The fights over multicultural standards are bounded by three major sets of constraints: the nature of academic disciplines, constitutional stipulations, and the community's dominant sympathies.

Nature of the Disciplines

The nature of the academic disciplines themselves shapes the multicultural tensions that emerge. Two dimensions are especially significant: the degree to which traditionalists can appeal to a neutral authority in resisting multicultural proposals, and the ease with which curricular content can be modified or differences split.

Curricular fights are more common in the humanities and social sciences than in mathematics or science. Why have multiculturalists enjoyed greater success in the "soft" subjects? Literature and history are deemed negotiable because they lack the disembodied logic on which math and science ultimately rest. Fundamental mathematical laws and scientific facts are immutable; the area of a rectangle is always equal to its base times its height, and the force of gravity always causes earthbound objects to fall at 9.8 meters per second squared. In 2002, reflecting a pattern that has been evident since at least the 1970s, more than 90 percent of Americans expressed a fair degree of trust in the scientific community—ranking scientists near the top of all professionals in trustworthiness.[5]

Because the constructs of math and the sciences are abstract, externally defined, and largely apolitical, and because they are based on verifiable laws and theories largely independent of social constructions, attempts to infuse these subjects with a multicultural perspective have fared relatively poorly. Multicultural reformers have typically adopted one of two strategies: they either pad around the edges by including historical anecdotes about minorities or, more drastically, they revise widely accepted scientific or mathematical truths to embody a multicultural perspective. The first of these strategies, which focuses on expanding the disciplinary boundaries toward the more readily contested realm of social studies and culture, tends to produce the successes that multicultural proponents do enjoy in the areas of math and the sciences. Although multiculturalists have succeeded in adding more sidebars about ancient Egyptian mathematicians or Latino physicists in textbooks, they have enjoyed little success when it comes to reshaping curricula or content. Efforts to infuse math and science with more "diversity" have typically ended in failure and, not infrequently, ridicule.

Unlike mathematics and the hard sciences, absolutes are much more difficult to come by in history, literature, or the social sciences. The historian has a limited ability to appeal to neutral authority or abstract rules to justify assertions. The literature instructor has almost no such ability. The merits of literature, the importance of a renowned person, the lessons to be learned from a period of history—these are contested and uncertain.

Setting content standards in subjects such as math and the physical sciences is largely straightforward. Speaking generally, there is broad agreement on what students need to know and when they need to know it. For that reason, most conflict in subjects such as math and the physical sciences revolves more around how to teach than about what material is to be taught. The truth of the matter is that the famed math "wars" are typically about pedagogy (for instance, "new math" versus computation-based instruction) rather than content. The waters become murkier when it comes to social studies, literature, and history. Should the history curriculum give equal attention to the indigenous civilizations of pre-Columbian America and ancient Greece and Rome? Should children know more about Darwin in the Galapagos or the Book of Genesis? When standards are a question of which stories should be prioritized, decisions become political.

Consider the "African/African-American Baseline Essays," developed in Portland, Oregon, in the late 1980s, which famously attempted to drive multiculturalism throughout the entire curriculum. Although the sections on art, language arts, and music "treat[ed] their African American sections accurately," the science and math materials were filled with shocking examples of pseudoscience. They sought to trace all major discoveries in math, science, and technology back to Africa and to promulgate scientifically dubious, non-Western theories such as "psi psycho-energetics," "precognition," and "psychokinesis." Children were to be taught that the ancient Egyptians built full-size gliders in 2000 B.C. and used these aircraft for travel and exploration.[6]

Irving Klotz, a professor emeritus of chemistry at Northwestern University, was prompted to fume in *Phi Delta Kappan* that the materials had left him staggering "in incredulity" and that such "nonsense" would inculcate "an uncritical, superficial attitude toward science" in students.[7]

Sometimes, the infusion of additional materials or perspectives makes for obviously better history or humanities instruction. One cannot, for instance, fully consider the industrialization of America without referring to the experience of the European immigrants or the black migration to the northern urban centers. The challenge is that historical and literary "truths" are both negotiable and inherently political. When politics enters the equation, standards revision is no longer a search for "better history," but an attempt to satisfy competing constituencies.

The Constitutional Regime

At times, especially in the case of religion, multicultural conflict is framed by the constitutional regime. Clear demarcations as to what is and is not permissible can place some claimants in an untenable position by forcing them to challenge constitutional doctrine and by putting the points of contention beyond the control of compromise-minded legislators, public officials, or curriculum designers. The First Amendment's establishment clause has been interpreted to strictly regulate the role for religiosity in the public domain. In general, groups challenging curricula in response to religious concerns have found little success. The establishment clause was long read by the courts as erecting "a wall" between church and state, meaning that religious groups were prevented from playing more than a cursory role in curricular debates. Consequently, it is not surprising that religious curricular challenges have often failed to get off the ground.

In 1987, the Supreme Court declared in *Edwards v. Aguillard* that it was unconstitutional even for states to require equal treatment of evolution and creationism.[8] Even when creationist movements began to shift their emphasis from the spiritual aspect of creationism to the "science" of creationism, groups such as the American Civil Liberties Union, supported by the scientific community, threatened to bring civil rights suits against states or districts that mandated the teaching of creationism. Regardless of popular support, creationists faced a nearly insuperable opponent in the establishment clause and the barriers the courts imposed.

The more successful religious efforts to influence curricula, whether they be efforts to qualify the teaching of evolution or increase attention to Islam, have shied away from religious rhetoric and appealed instead in the name of multicultural ideals such as "inclusion" and "multiple perspectives." After repeated defeats on religious grounds, some creationists have moved from "moralism to pluralism" and started to invoke the principle of "equal time" in order to get creation science included alongside evolution in biology curricula.[9] This new tactic avoids the establishment clause by renouncing any claims of theism, calling instead for diverse explanations of human origins as a matter of cultural fairness and respect. Perhaps not surprisingly, proponents of "intelligent design" (the notion that an unspecified "intelligence" consciously designed the universe) have been surprisingly effective in recent years; in 1999, a group forced Kansas to drop evolution from its science standards for a time, and in 2002, Ohio adopted a compromise amendment that allowed teachers to discuss criticism of Darwin's theory.[10] This approach has permitted intelligent design proponents to make their case on constitutionally feasible ground.

Dominant Norms and Values

As noted, disciplinary and constitutional issues define the boundaries of multicultural conflicts over curricula. Most battles occur in social studies, history, and the humanities on issues that do not run afoul of constitutional doctrine. This is the contested terrain in the multicultural-inspired conflicts under accountability.

Within these parameters, groups considered legitimate or mainstream by the majority are far more effective than are more marginal or controversial groups. In contemporary America, where "compassionate conservatism" is the watchword of the Republican president and where a public recoils from overt displays of racism or religious intolerance, simple hostility to multiculturalism is an untenable position. Instead, members of the majority are encouraged to seek compromise with sympathetic "out" groups—even as they resist the demands of more marginal ones.

Take, for example, the controversy that surrounded the 2001 attempt of the NEA to pass a resolution encouraging teachers and schools to include curricular materials dealing with the struggles of gay, lesbian, bisexual, and transgender people. After conservative state lawmakers and Christian groups launched an outraged letter-writing campaign to local union representatives, the NEA quickly backtracked.[11] In an effort freighted with political baggage of a different stripe, the Sons of Confederate Veterans Virginia Regiment failed in 2001 to convince state officials to include in state history standards more about Virginia's role in the Civil War; their efforts were dismissed as an inappropriate celebration of the Confederacy.[12] These failures contrast with the great success of less controversial groups in appealing to the mainstream values of inclusion and pluralism. Curriculum writers have made enormous efforts to include women and African-American figures in curricula. Similarly, in states like Texas, the Latino community has been effective in convincing authorities to include Latino authors, artists, and historical figures in many district curricula.[13]

Teetering toward Ambiguity

In social studies, history, and literature, multicultural proponents typically advocate increasing attention to minority and female personages and accomplishment; emphasizing more pre-Columbian, African, Asian, Latin American, and social history; and reading more literary works authored by minorities, non-Americans, and women. Traditionalists respond by challenging such revisions as devaluing American history and the Western tradition, diluting curricula, and mounting thinly disguised attacks on the United States and its culture. Seeking to please sympathetic and active minorities without alienating traditionalists or provoking backlash, public officials pursue compromise, ultimately winding up with standards that are acceptable to all parties due to their elasticity. The progression from angry minority demands for inclusion to majoritarian backlash to hollow political compromise has played out repeatedly in recent years. Perhaps the classic example was the 1994 effort by the National Center for History in the Schools to craft national history standards.

In 1992, in conjunction with the National Endowment for the Humanities and the Office of Educational Research and Innovation of the Department of Education, the National Center for History in the Schools created the National Council for History Standards to oversee the process. Appointed with input from prominent traditionalists such as Lynne Cheney and Diane Ravitch, the council's membership was hailed for including an ideologically balanced mix of history scholars, educators, and advocates.[14] The real work of fashioning the standards, however, fell to the various historical and educational organizations, professional historians, and veteran teachers that the council consulted. These groups included the American Historical Association, the National Alliance for Black Education, the National Association for Asian and Pacific American Education, and the League of United Latin American Citizens.[15] The standards produced by these groups, released in three volumes at the end of 1994, emphasized the history of preliterate African and Mexican societies and asserted that children should be able to discuss gender roles in the early agricultural communities of the Fertile Crescent.[16] At the same time, the new standards did not include historical figures such as Paul Revere, Thomas Edison, or the Wright Brothers, focusing instead on America's warts. McCarthyism was mentioned nineteen times, the Great Depression twenty-five times, and the Ku Klux Klan was featured prominently.[17] Shortly after the standards were released, the Senate rejected them on a vote of ninety-nine to one, sending them back for revision.

The revision of the standards, based largely on the "valuable recommendations" of the conservative Council for Basic Education, was undertaken by a new group of scholars more skeptical of multiculturalism. Stephan Thernstrom, David Hollinger, and Maris Vinovskis joined Ravitch and others on the new panel. The new guidelines simply did away with the actual teaching examples, the section that had drawn the most ire from conservatives. When released, however, the revised standards were variously criticized by conservatives for "[attacking] our heritage" and "[getting] it wrong again," as well as for now being both nebulous and unrealistically ambitious.[18]

The revised standards were also attacked by multiculturalists who felt that the revisions had gone too far in reducing the prevalence of female historical figures. For instance, while the initial guidelines mentioned Harriet Tubman six times and asked children to discuss gender roles in almost every civilization and society included in the standards, these elements were missing in the second draft. Writing in *The History Teacher*, one author complained that it was "disturbing that women as a part of history were singled out for such an extensive revision."[19]

Despite the political criticism by both sides, the directors of the national standards project were satisfied. Gary Nash, codirector of the project, said he was pleased with the final product. Meanwhile, former critics also accepted the revisions; Ravitch and Schlesinger praised the new standards, as did columnist George Will, who found them "purged of partisanship."[20]

In reaching this happy agreement, however, the council had largely denuded the standards of meaning, settling instead for watery banalities. Two independent panels that were commissioned by the Council for Basic Education to appraise the revised standards asserted that the lack of specifics had succeeded in eliminating "many of the problems related to the absence or presence of individual names, since the standards themselves name relatively few historical figures." The panels went on to note, "The teaching of history within the general frame proposed by the standards will necessarily include examples of individuals with varying degrees of influence on the events of their own time. . . . But it is not the job of the standards to provide a list."[21] Thus, the panels reached agreement by approving hollow standards largely devoid of specific historical terms, figures, or places.

The final product's dominant theme was ambiguity: The "postwar extension of the New Deal" became the catchall "domestic policies after World War II"; the charge that students "demonstrate understanding of Nixon's domestic agenda and the Watergate affair" became the suggestion that "the student understands domestic politics from Nixon to Carter"; and the mandate for "examining the 'red scare' and Palmer raids as a reaction to Bolshevism" became the vague "assess the state and federal government reactions to the growth of radical political movements."[22]

No one much cared that the standards were nebulous: Minority constituencies and traditionalists could read their preferences into these broad guidelines, the general public was little interested in this arcane dispute, and nothing of consequence would be done with the standards. Even in this case of toothless guidelines, concise and meaningful standards proved elusive. As one close observer bluntly observed, "Since the standards are guidelines, those who find the changes offensive can re-edit the revised standards or insert the original versions."[23] It would be left up to each individual teacher to define which historical personages to study and how much time to devote to each.

This kind of easy compromise becomes more problematic after the introduction of meaningful accountability. Under standards-based accountability, delegating responsibility for curriculum to the classroom teacher is no longer inconsequential. Standards-based accountability transforms curricular standards from suggestions to high-stakes mandates. Because students are to be asked to master specific material, ambiguous standards leave them and their teachers responsible for an ill-defined body of content, undermining the very purpose of standards and the value and legitimacy of accountability.

Precisely when the stakes rise and the costs of ambiguity increase, however, the temptation to resolve clashes by resorting to studied ambiguity grows. Consider the 2001 fight over the high-stakes Virginia history standards. In November 2000, the board of education revised the state's history and social science standards. Caught in crossfire between various constituencies, the board stripped many specifics from the standards. Both liberals and conservatives noted the changes and complained about them. The liberal grassroots group Parents Across Virginia United to Reform [Standards of Learning] asserted that the standards were characterized by "the elimination of as many controversial or unpleasant things as possible,"[24] while John Fonte, head of the conservative Hudson Institute's Center for American Common Culture, attacked the elimination of specific historical figures and events.[25] David Warren Saxe, a professor of education at Pennsylvania State, noted that 62 percent of the ninety-five historical figures previously listed in the 1995 standards had been eliminated, including such Civil War figures as Stonewall Jackson and Robert E. Lee.[26] The old standards had asked that students discuss "the economic and philosophical differences between North and South, as exemplified by such men as Daniel Webster and John C. Calhoun," whereas the new standards stripped out the names.[27]

Consider also the challenge from determined Armenian-Americans who demanded that the Armenian Genocide of 1915–23 be included in the new standards. Twenty-six Armenians asked the state board of education to include in the revised standards mention of the 1.5 million Christian Armenians killed under the Ottoman Empire during 1915–23. Despite their small numbers, the Armenians enjoyed some initial success as the result of disciplined lobbying. The board of education agreed to include the "mass deportations and massacres of the Armenians" in the World War I standard, though it stopped short of labeling the event a *genocide*.[28]

Shortly thereafter, though, the board came under fire from the more-established Turkish community and decided to strike any specific reference to ethnic violence in the Ottoman Empire during or after World War I. The revised standard now asked students to explain "the genocide of Armenians and deportations and massacres of Turks, Kurds, and other ethnic groups," infuriating Armenians who argued there was no historical evidence that Turks had been massacred.[29] The board of education nonetheless settled on this vague and inclusive, if inaccurate, compromise.

Or consider New Jersey's effort to revise its history standards in early 2002. The revised standards added new references to the evils of slavery, obscure slavery opponents Sarah Grimke and Theodore Dwight Weld, the Holocaust, and present-day Iraq. To make room for this material, the standards dropped references to George Washington, Thomas Jefferson, Benjamin Franklin, the pilgrims of Massachusetts Bay, and the Mayflower. When attacked for excluding the Founding Fathers, the head of New Jersey's Division of Academic and Career Standards responded, "We don't intentionally exclude names. But how long should the list of names be? Who do we include or not include?"[30] That decision was implicitly to be left up to each individual teacher, effectively derailing the original mission of content standards. After an outcry from traditionalists, the Founding Fathers were added to the revised standards, along with Abraham Lincoln, Franklin Roosevelt, and Martin Luther King.[31]

Conclusion

The most conspicuous result of successful multicultural efforts—those launched by "mainstream" minorities on safe constitutional ground in the areas of social science and the humanities—has been to encourage policymakers to adopt a studied ambiguity when crafting standards for high-stakes accountability. Historian Diane Ravitch has concluded that only fourteen states have strong U.S. history standards, whereas more than half have weak standards or none at all.[32] The result is history and literary standards that have no obvious meaning, besides a sense of grandiose ambition, even in states with standards widely regarded as exemplary. A simple comparison of history standards to math standards in various states helps make clear just how relatively vague history standards often are. Take, for example, Pennsylvania's grade six history standard: "Identify and explain how individuals and groups made significant political and cultural contributions to world history (for Africa, Asia, Europe, the Americas)."[33] Or consider New York's standard for grades one through five: "Students should know the roots of American culture, its development from many different traditions, and the ways many people from a variety of groups and backgrounds played a role in creating it."[34] It is not clear what these statements mean, what teachers are expected to teach, or what students are expected to know. The standards are vacuous aspirations carefully shorn of substantive significance.

Such ambiguity is the norm rather than the exception. In Texas, a state widely regarded as a national exemplar for its standards, students in grades nine through twelve are to understand "how people from various groups, including racial, ethnic, and religious groups, adapt to life in the United States and contribute to our national identity."[35] Sixth graders in Oklahoma, another state hailed for its standards, are asked to "analyze selected cultures which have affected our history" with the corollary that they should be able to "compare and contrast common characteristics of culture, such as language, customs, shelter, diet, traditional occupations, belief systems, and folk traditions."[36]

This is not to say that there are no states with clear, specific, and meaningful standards. Indiana and Kansas, for instance, have been commended for the clarity and general excellence of their content requirements.[37] It may be worth noting, of course, that both states are more than 85 percent white and among the most racially homogeneous states in the nation. The multicultural tensions that exist elsewhere are milder in states like these. The reduced influence of minority groups enables public officials to stand more readily by specific standards without fear they are courting trouble.

The politics of multicultural conflict under accountability are straightforward. The majority discourse enjoys only vague support, whereas the discrete ethnic, religious, and racial interests are mobilized and advocate for particular concessions. If the original document is majoritarian, it gets watered down. If it is pursued in a collaborative fashion, it typically comes out watery or with too much objectionable material—in which case it can trigger a majority backlash. The process eventually teeters toward a vague, fence-straddling compromise yielding hollow standards that sound promising but are subject to an enormous range of interpretation. In practice, such ambiguity undermines test validity, leaves much of the substance of what students need to know to the whims of test-designers, and undermines the notion that standards provide clear direction as to what students are expected to master.

Consequently, it becomes increasingly easy for public officials to focus testing on the relatively uncontroversial areas of reading, mathematics, and science, while marginalizing the role of testing in subjects such as history and literature. A pernicious cycle is possible, with reduced testing leading to diminished emphasis on the humanities and social sciences. The challenge is that useful standards must be coherent, reasonable, and concrete, but that the checks and balances of the American system, with plentiful veto points and permeable democracy, tend to promote grandiose ambiguity. Whether policymakers can find a way to resist this temptation may go far toward determining the status of liberal education in twenty-first-century schools.

10

"Trust Us," They Explained: Racial Distrust and School Reform

In December 2002, the nation engaged in a brief but wrenching discussion about the cultural and political legacy of the civil rights era. The proximate cause was Senate Majority Leader Trent Lott's remarks at the hundredth birthday party for Senator Strom Thurmond, suggesting that the country would have been better off had Thurmond prevailed in his 1948 Dixiecrat presidential bid.[1] The episode pressed hot-button issues of race, resurrected uncomfortable questions for conservatives and Republicans, and concluded with Republican senators replacing Lott as majority leader and committing themselves to a more "inclusive" agenda.

The incident provided an important window into the racial distrust that has persistently attended modern conservatism. Especially significant was Lott's last-ditch reversal of longstanding opposition to affirmative action and race-based preferences. In abandoning his commitment to colorblind conservatism, Lott variously managed to imply that his prior convictions had been misconstrued or shaped by ignorance, or marked a broader need for conservatives to rethink race-based policies. In mounting this flailing defense, Lott fed the perception that the only sincere efforts to remedy racial inequities are those rooted in Great Society prescriptions, and that market-based or colorblind approaches are rooted in ignorance, malice, or a desire to camouflage a hidden agenda.

Lott's plight illuminated the challenge that hampers efforts to reimagine Great Society–era social policy, even in an era when many on both left and right see a legacy that has included an urban underclass and a generation of failing urban schools and social services. It also made clear the degree to which the moral legitimacy of contemporary conservatism depends on the credibility of its commitment to equalizing opportunity and empowering every citizen to make the most of his or her talents. That universality of opportunity is critical if conservatives are to hold a morally coherent and defensible position as they embrace low taxes and limited government and reject efforts to equalize outcomes.

Questions about conservative racism or disregard for blacks strike at the very heart of the opportunity premise and raise the specter that conservative principles are inconsistent with efforts to democratize opportunity. The problem for conservative reformers is that black distrust of their motives is not altogether unwarranted. The legislation and court decisions of the civil rights era culminated more than a century of ardent and arduous African-American efforts to win access to wider educational opportunities. During that time, black Americans had few allies, and what little support they did receive came predominantly from the left.

African-American distrust of conservatives has been significant in ways that extend beyond the facts of the moment. In debates over urban policy and equal opportunity, black Americans play a privileged role. Given the circumstances of America's racial history, black leaders are accorded a singularly powerful voice in discussions of social equity and opportunity. In recent decades, the plight of the black community has often served as the barometer by which the nation's commitment to opportunity is measured.

Nowhere is the black-conservative schism more significant than in the case of schooling. Education is where the conservative commitment to equal opportunity meets its acid test, and where efforts to redress social inequities must ultimately be won. In the postindustrial economy, schooling plays a dominant symbolic and substantive role in debates about social equity and equal opportunity. African-American distrust of conservatives, combined with the left's embrace of civil rights legislation and affirmative action, has led to a longstanding alliance among African-Americans, teachers' unions, and the public school establishment. The result has been a tacit agreement in which the left avoids blaming schools for education problems, promotes bureaucracy and teacher protections as a response to failing urban schools, and cloaks the educational status quo in the rhetoric of civil rights.

Conservatives must address urban poverty and racial inequity, but they cannot do so by wishing away political reality, and they should not do so by crumbling before it. Rather, they must understand the reasons that blacks regard them so warily and address that skepticism in a principled fashion.

The Aftermath of 1964

Modern attitudes on race and public policy can be traced to the 1960s, when Lyndon Johnson signed, in quick succession, the Civil Rights Act (CRA) and the Voting Rights Act (VRA) in 1964 and 1965, while Republican Barry Goldwater embraced a "states' rights" platform in the 1964 presidential campaign—a stance that Southerners interpreted as aiding their efforts to resist federal civil rights legislation.

As late as 1962, Americans were evenly divided on whether the Republican or Democratic party was more supportive of racial equality. In fact, the vast majority of Republicans in both the House and Senate endorsed Johnson's efforts on civil rights; the opposition was led by southern Democrats.

In the aftermath of Johnson's decision to aggressively push the CRA and VRA and of Goldwater's campaign, public attitudes rapidly and radically changed. By 1964, surveys found that the Democrats enjoyed roughly a fifty percentage-point lead when the American public as a whole was asked whether the Democrats or Republicans were more "sympathetic to blacks." Beginning in 1964, the white South began a massive migration from the Democratic to the Republican column. The loss of the "solid South" sloughed from the Democratic Party its conservative and hawkish wing, enabling its activist wing to embrace a domestic policy agenda sensitive to the claims of racial minorities, unions, the academic elite, feminists, and the countercultural left.

Thus was framed the narrative of the next three decades, with the Republican Party positioned as the defender of middle America and conventional values, and the Democratic Party as the guardian of the marginalized and the disadvantaged. In that period, African-Americans cemented their ties to the left as the Democrats became the standard-bearers for affirmative action, race-based set-asides, and expanded social welfare programs. Meanwhile, some Republican candidates did have occasion to employ racially tinged appeals to court white voters, especially in southern races.

That distrust became embedded in the culture of the black community. J. C. Watts, former chairman of the House Republican Conference and the only black Republican on Capitol Hill for eight years, often related that his own father wondered how Watts could be a Republican, and would remark, "A black man voting for the Republicans makes about as much sense as a chicken voting for Colonel Sanders."[3] In 2000, the most recent year for which the information is available, the Joint Center for Political and Economic Studies reported that of the 9,040 black elected officials across the country, just 50 were Republican.[4] In 2004, just 10 percent of blacks identified themselves as Republicans.[5] Since the 1980s, 80 percent or more of blacks have consistently self-identified as Democrats.[6]

Opportunity Conservatism and the Educational Challenge

As discussed earlier in "Seeking the Mantle of 'Opportunity,'" the issue of racial equity looms so large due to the nature of contemporary conservatism. From the New Deal to the early 1960s, the Republican Party was dominated by a midwestern, fiscally prudent, localist conservatism that rejected any government role in proactively extending opportunity. In 1964, however, a radically different conservatism came to the fore, championed by GOP presidential nominee Barry Goldwater. While this new conservatism would prove politically potent, it would be squeezed between its implicit promise to broaden opportunity in an unequal society and its hostility toward activist government.

Goldwater conservatism did not end with his defeat in 1964. It reappeared in 1980 with Ronald Reagan, who argued that Democrats had abandoned equality of opportunity for a doctrine of equality of results. In doing so, they abandoned shared American values, and this shift was to blame for the nation's stagnant economy and general malaise. Reagan could promise to roll back government and still broaden opportunity for the disadvantaged because he inverted the Great Society storyline in which the government was the protector of opportunity by recasting the government as "self-interested bureaucrats," and federal programs as weeds choking the paths of social and economic opportunity. The Reagan-influenced shift to "opportunity" conservatism became unmistakable in the early 1980s, when a group of conservative and mostly young Republican congressmen, including Newt Gingrich and Trent Lott, unabashedly argued that Reaganite reforms would do more than the welfare state to democratize opportunity.

In the 1980s, after more than a century spent trying to kick down the doors to the nation's schools, the African-American community had finally triumphed in its long effort to gain access to the education system. In a bitter twist, this was the moment when a Reagan commission issued its 1983 report, *A Nation at Risk*, and the public awoke to the troubled condition of the nation's schools—especially its urban schools.[7] The report spurred divergent calls for improvement. The teachers' unions and their allies embraced prescriptions focused on teacher pay, participatory governance, professionalism, heightened licensure barriers, and curriculum and pedagogy. The conservative response featured accountability, core curricula, teacher-testing, and nascent efforts to promote choice-based arrangements—with accountability and school choice the two most prominent strands. While questions of accountability are compelling in their own right, political tensions of this essay will focus upon the issue of choice-based reform.

In promoting school choice, conservatives endorsed policies that would make it easier for families to exit the schools to which African-Americans had only recently gained access. While there were compelling policy reasons behind this stance, the conservative proposals were seen as potentially serving to undo the "access" agenda for which the African-American community and its allies had long fought. Choice-based reform held special appeal because it squared the "opportunity" circle—it married conservative antipathy toward activist government to a proactive commitment to increase social equity. Whereas Reagan's earlier choice rhetoric had focused on appealing to disaffected Catholics, by the late 1980s, Republicans began a tentative effort to use school choice as a way to neutralize the party's weakness on education and the fairness issue and to reach out to the black community. The 1988 Republican platform supported federal school vouchers as a way to "empower [low-income families] to choose quality schooling."[8]

Conservative efforts to portray vouchers and charter schooling as a way to help African-American and urban youths trapped in inferior schools did little to broaden Republican support among these groups, despite growing support among African-Americans and urban residents for aggressive measures to improve schooling. Throughout the 1990s, Democratic leaders were successful in depicting the conservative commitment to equal opportunity as half-hearted or hollow. Even in 2000, when Republican presidential nominee George W. Bush promoted a doctrine of "compassionate conservatism," criticized conservatives who wanted government to "get out of the way," promoted his gubernatorial record of appointing minorities and addressing minority concerns, and ran with the strong endorsement of General Colin Powell, he claimed just 9 percent of the black vote.[9] In 2004, after the passage of No Child Left Behind and a diligent effort to broaden the Republican base, Bush still only received 14 percent of the black vote.[10]

A Natural Reform Alliance

There is a natural alliance between the African-American community and education reformers, both right and left, who are willing to embrace structural measures designed to address the root causes of mediocrity. Both are frustrated with schools that are inflexible, inefficient, and resistant to demands for improvement. Both are tired of half-hearted "reforms" that do not require educators to take responsibility for student learning, remove ineffective teachers, reward effective educators, or help schools to tap locally available talent and entrepreneurial energy.

These shared interests bind the African-American community and school reformers and make their relationship fundamentally unlike those between reformers and teachers' unions, education schools, or professional education associations. The education establishment has strong material incentives to oppose accountability, managerial flexibility, performance-based pay, the overhaul of teacher licensure, or choice-based reform because such changes promise to undermine the political influence of education interest groups, end their privileged position, reduce their revenue, and threaten their philosophical notions of how schools should be run. As a result, these constituencies have reason to make excuses for current performance and to oversell modest concessions.

Neither urban residents nor members of the black community are under any such compunction. African-Americans are consistently more critical of school performance than the general population. While a majority of the general population rates its local public schools as good or excellent, most black adults routinely rate them as fair or poor. The most negative segment of the black population is twenty-six- to thirty-five-year-olds—those who do not share the affective attachment of their elders to the public system. Less than a third of blacks believe that their schools are improving, and younger and low-income blacks are especially likely to report that they are getting worse.[11] In 2002, 56 percent of African-American parents gave their public schools a "C" grade or lower, and the most frequently cited problem in local schools was lack of discipline.[12] While majorities of suburban and rural residents gave their local schools an "A" or a "B" in 2002, less than a third of urban residents did so.[13] Black America's Political Action Committee (BAMPAC) president Alvin Williams has observed, "African Americans are becoming increasingly frustrated with the public school system and its failure, in many cases, to provide a quality education for their children."[14]

The new generation of African-American leadership coming to the fore is less concerned about conventional questions of "access" or "integration" than it is about school quality and what aids black children. This generation is less attached to the old alliances, more willing to criticize the failure of social welfare and race-conscious policies, and more receptive to new policy prescriptions. Many of these leaders regard the emphasis on integration as having undermined school communities, hurt educational quality, and aggravated middle-class flight. In fact, there is little evidence that ongoing efforts to promote desegregation have done much systematically to improve the conditions or achievement of black students. John Chubb and Tom Loveless noted in 2002 that testing data showed a continuing "racial gap in achievement."[15] Christopher Jencks and Meredith Phillips noted that in the late 1990s, "the typical American black still score[d] below 75 percent of American whites on most standardized tests," and acknowledged, "It is true that the [racial] gap shrinks only a little when black and white children attend the same schools."[16] These inequities translate to the labor force. Princeton economist Alan Krueger and his colleagues have noted, "The relative earnings of black workers have declined since the mid-1970s—on the heels of a period (1940–1970) in which the wage gap narrowed substantially."[17]

Given this status quo and the lack of evidence of improvement, it should not surprise us that majorities of African-Americans consistently tell pollsters they support school choice and other radical school reforms. In 2004, the Joint Center for Political and Economic Studies, a left-leaning think tank that focuses on issues that concern the black community, reported that 48 percent of African-Americans supported school vouchers.[18] Other surveys have frequently reported figures of 60 percent or more.[19]

Understanding Black Distrust

Despite these figures, groups like the Congressional Black Caucus and the NAACP remain solidly opposed to vouchers, and African-American voters continue overwhelmingly to support liberal Democrats. The Joint Center for Political and Economic Studies reports that 69 percent of black elected officials oppose vouchers.[20]

Moreover, when one interviews urban African-American parents and leaders about education, suspicion of conservative motives is palpable. This is especially true among the community leadership. Though fed up with mediocre urban schools, African-Americans are reluctant to abandon their traditional allies to align with market-oriented, generally conservative voucher proponents with suspect motives. As one member of the NAACP leadership in Milwaukee remarked to me regarding the city's voucher program, "These Republican types, the ones in business and the suburbs, never used to care about black children. Now they do? I don't buy it. They're after something."[21]

David Bositis, senior political analyst at the Joint Center for Political and Economic Studies, has noted that many older African-Americans "believe that school vouchers would represent a transfer of public money to subsidize those white parents who prefer that their children attend all-white schools." Blacks will be inherently distrustful of conservative overtures, he believes, because conservatives have historically "cared so little about the lives of black Americans."[22] There is a deep-rooted suspicion among the older generation of leaders that today's charter laws, tax credit programs, and voucher programs are Trojan horses, designed to attract African-American support for programs that will later be rewritten in ways advantageous to white, suburban families and corporate interests.

This resistance to conservative overtures has confounded more than a few proponents of school choice, who express exasperation that African-Americans would continue to support elected officials who stand by policies that show little evidence of working. Choice proponents point out that their proposals primarily benefit minority children trapped in poor urban schools. As one ardent choice organizer said to me,

> We're breaking our pick trying to offer solutions to these families, and the numbers show that the people we help are really satisfied. But the unions and their friends just sweep in and tell the papers that we're racists, without offering anything that will help, and a lot of people believe them. Sometimes you just want to rent a bunch of billboards that tell the community . . . "We're the ones who are on your side." And you wonder why they don't see it.[23]

The seeming puzzle disappears upon closer examination. The calculation is eminently sensible from a black perspective, as leadership entails making nuanced calculations about alliances and future outcomes that individual voters need not address.

Two points are critical. First, choice proponents too often regard the desirability of vouchers as fully and firmly settled. They are not.[24] Trying to generalize from existing experiments and programs to a large-scale choice system poses several daunting challenges regarding such factors as what new schools would look like, the constancy of peer effects, whether disciplinary norms could be replicated, and so on. Choice proponents should not regard skeptics as necessarily being apologists or dupes.

The second, larger issue is that voucher and charter programs today consistently promote equity and increase racial integration, but that is largely because these programs are designed to prohibit discriminatory practices and offer advantage to poor children. Skeptics may reasonably fear that this is merely a tactic of the moment, and that choice proponents are secretly itching to discard redistributive strictures and program constraints once the programs are safely up and running. Such concerns are entirely legitimate. In fact, while voters are unlikely to concern themselves with such complex possibilities, leaders who did not consider them would be remiss.

Concerns over evidence and design features are buttressed by other attachments the African-American community has forged to public schools. In urban centers, political control of the school system is a source of jobs, political power, and community pride. Urban schools are leading employers, and African-American community leaders fear for their influence over jobs and system operations.

Black elected officials, civil rights leaders, and community activists do not control any institutions at the national or state level. What black leaders in urban areas do control are the institutions of municipal government, along with the influence, jobs, revenues, and symbolically potent platform those institutions represent. The largest and most visible of these are public schools. Measures that undercut the ability of black leaders to control urban schools routinely encounter fierce opposition—whether the mechanism is school choice, state takeover, privatization, or anything else. Efforts to reduce local control are often viewed through an explicit racial lens. Often forgotten in discussions of Milwaukee's voucher experience is the fact that the entire debate was sidelined for about five months in 1998, when the governor called for a possible state takeover of Milwaukee schools. The city's African-American community attacked the proposal as an effort by upstate Republicans to seize control of a mostly black system. Democratic state representative Johnnie Morris-Tatum offered a typical riposte, commenting, "We don't need lily-white faces telling us what to do."[25] In fact, the most recent figures available from the Equal Employment Opportunity Commission show that African-Americans constitute 21.8 percent of full-time city government employees—a figure that is almost twice the black percentage of the general population.[26] Harvard professor Gary Orfield has noted that cutting urban budgets or municipal systems inevitably "means cutting into the black middle class since city government tends to hire much larger proportions of blacks than other large employers."[27]

A New Day

The presumption that the American left is the defender of African-American interests has ensured it near-uniform black electoral support in return for a commitment to affirmative action and conventional civil rights legislation. However, in return for the left's support on explicitly race-conscious policies, the civil rights leadership and black elected officials have accepted policy constraints demanded by their allies in the municipal employees' unions and the cultural left. The black leadership tacitly agreed not to blame urban problems on ineffective bureaucracies, uninspired public employees, a breakdown in discipline or civil society, or poorly designed social policies.

In place of such critiques, which had been much in evidence before the 1960s, black leaders held their allies blameless by tracing nearly all community ills to racial discrimination, poverty, and insufficient government spending. These complaints provided common cause with other constituencies of the left—permitting black leaders to lobby shoulder-to-shoulder with their allies for more spending, set-asides, and government programs—while avoiding the uncomfortable silences that would arise if black leaders asked why urban public institutions were the sites of such profound failure.

Those black leaders who have challenged this tacit arrangement have been quickly tarred as subversives and apologists. Howard Fuller, former Milwaukee school superintendent and school choice advocate, has wryly noted, "If you support something that so-called conservative people support, you're duped. If you support something in this country that so-called liberal people support, you're brilliant."[28]

A significant element of the black community traces many of its continuing problems to arrangements that cannot be redressed without confronting the vested interests of the municipal employees' unions and the professional civil liberties lobby, and this is crucial to effectively reshaping Great Society–era social policy. The fact that bad educators cannot be fired nor good ones rewarded, that educators have not been held accountable for student learning, that school discipline is undermined by a sprawling regime of procedural rights, that special education legalisms inhibit sensible allocation of resources—these are all the products of policies and contractual agreements sought by the allies of black America. And recognizing the problems caused by these constraints does not even begin to address the cases of outright corruption or malfeasance on the part of these allies, such as the larceny that has wracked major urban teachers' unions or the construction scandals that have plagued cities such as Cleveland and Los Angeles.

A new generation of black leadership has come of age in an era when doors are now open to the most talented members of their community—but when those who want to return to that community to aid others in turn often find themselves stifled by regulation, red tape, avaricious interests, and lethargic bureaucracies. Young black leaders in organizations like the Black Alliance for Educational Opportunities are willing to entertain the notion that their alliance with the teachers' unions, the civil liberties lobby, and the professional education constituencies is a bad deal—they can see that access, integration, and money don't help black children if schools are dysfunctional, undisciplined bureaucracies whose performance depends on the intrinsic motivation of educators.

Acknowledging that longstanding allies are part of the problem, however, will require black leaders to sever ties and walk away from their base of political and institutional support. There is little (read: no) likelihood that significant elements of the black leadership will do this unless they believe they have a viable alternative. Openness to change does not mean that black leaders are willing to put their faith in allies who were late to the dance or whose motives are in doubt.

"Trust us" is not an adequate answer to such concerns. Reformers who wish to convince the African-American community to abandon its old alliances must forcefully address fears that it will be abandoned by its new allies halfway through the journey. This requires more than symbolism or protestations that one's heart is pure, but should not be thought to suggest that reformers ought to kowtow to Al Sharpton or embrace race-conscious policy prescriptions. Working respectfully with the African-American community does not mean abandoning colorblind values or principled policy preferences.

In fact, transparent pandering and mimicry of the left's positions may undermine the black leaders who are seeking to mount a more profound critique of twentieth-century welfarism and the culture of victimhood.

Rather than offering a different way to redress festering social problems, such appeals suggest that the left was correct all along—raising the question of why African-Americans should flee their longstanding allies for these Johnny-come-latelies and, more importantly, damaging the credibility of daring black leaders who suggest that the old answers are not the right answers.

The rarely acknowledged truth is that African-Americans and conservatives approach school reform in very different ways. Unlike conservative reformers, who are often inclined to school choice on theoretical or normative grounds, African-American urban parents and community leaders tend to approach school reform in the same pragmatic fashion that a drowning man approaches a life preserver. Frequently, conservative views of choice are informed by either an abiding faith in the efficiency and fairness of markets or a concern with trying to protect social and ideational behavior from the embrace of spreading government. Both impulses take the desirability of choice-based arrangements as a given. Blacks and urbanites, on the other hand, are generally looking for a way to receive better services and take better care of their children. In fact, polls show they are amenable to nearly any potentially promising reform.

Suburbanites and middle-class urban residents see the common-sense benefits of markets daily in their choice of groceries, gas stations, and dry cleaners. In impoverished neighborhoods, for a variety of reasons, markets have not historically provided the same conveniences, choices, or efficiencies. To be blunt, urban residents generally do not have very positive personal experiences with markets. Disorganized and impoverished communities generally boast little that illustrates the potential benefits of a functioning market. The Boston Consulting Group has found that the "urban core is dramatically underserved. Unmet consumer demand ranges from 25 percent in some inner-city areas to as high as 60 percent in others . . . [and] retail competition in the inner city is minimal or nonexistent."[29] Pricewaterhouse Coopers has reported, "In general, inner-city residents have less access to shopping center and food stores than do their suburban counterparts. Shoppers in the inner city typically pay higher prices for goods and services and have fewer products to choose from."[30]

Observing the imperfections of urban political economies is not an indictment of choice-based reform, but it does explain why urban

African-Americans might be sympathetic to school choice without becoming ardent supporters. While reformers can design school choice to serve urban interests and avoid potential perils, it is not certain that they will do so. In fact, choice arrangements can be used—and have been used in recent decades—to facilitate efforts by whites to avoid minority populations.

What Then?

Winning minority support requires reformers to explain how black interests are shortchanged by their current allies and why accountability, flexibility, responsibility, choice, and merit will improve schooling and democratize opportunity. Rather than bemoaning the lack of trust, it makes sense to take small and careful steps together. Common action, shared effort, and reliability build trust. If conservatives and blacks take some steps and see that neither group intends to cut and run, it will be easier to take larger and more ambitious steps. The challenge is to start with measures that are less threatening and less reliant on sustained good will, ones which don't require as great a leap of faith and whose potential fallout isn't as negative. Clearly, asking urban black leaders to open up one of the few major institutions they control, to put substantial numbers of black jobs at risk, and to give up the fruits of bitter legal battles all on the good faith of longtime opponents does not fit the bill.

Would-be reformers will benefit if they augment choice-based efforts with intermediate steps that will advance accountability, weaken the education monopoly, improve school quality, and create a context in which choice-based reforms are more likely to function as intended. The appeal of these steps is that they do not demand the faith required by radical choice. What are examples of such steps?

One popular approach has been promoting accountability systems that hold schools and educators responsible for student learning. At the heart of the 2002 No Child Left Behind Act (NCLB), such accountability has the potential to serve as a lever to ensure that essential skills are being taught to the worst-served children. While the particular system of accountability embraced by NCLB raises real concerns, as I discuss later in "On Leaving No Child Behind," the commitment to the principle of "tough-minded accountability" is important. By assessing student performance and holding educators and schools accountable for results, high-stakes systems can harness the self-interest of teachers and administrators to concrete improvement. While such accountability systems inevitably include trade-offs, they provide a powerful lever to ensure that the educators of minority or poor children can no longer excuse incompetence or overlook failing teachers or schools.

Another approach is to reshape the teaching profession radically by making it easier for adults to pursue teaching jobs, and for schools to terminate ineffective practitioners or reward effective ones. A third course is to enable nontraditional candidates to pursue positions of educational leadership, to make it easier to remove ineffective principals, and to permit schools or school systems to more readily hold educational leaders accountable and reward them on the basis of performance.

A fourth tack would be to address the legal and procedural morass that constitutes so much of special education and results in defensive posturing on the part of school officials, difficulties enforcing school discipline, and an often-reflexive allocation of educational dollars. A final approach could include working to increase access to public choice and to the supplemental services promised under the provisions of NCLB. This might include helping to launch and support parental information centers, providing resources to support transportation, providing technical and legal resources to small supplemental service providers, and so on.

While these steps will not satisfy the most ardent voucher supporters, they will advance their goals in important ways. They will enhance parental choice, increase accountability for student learning, and make schools more flexible and performance-oriented. At the same time, they will weaken the education cartel and begin to challenge the privileged positions of the schools of education and the status quo education constituencies.

Finally, such changes will provide a concrete agenda on which serious school reformers of all races may find common ground. Absent the verbal pyrotechnics associated with school vouchers, such an approach may also have the virtue of helping the African-American leadership to more readily see where their traditional allies have forsaken common cause for self-interested ends.

11

School Vouchers and Suburbanites

Proponents of school vouchers, charter schooling, and school choice have been on a roll: The Supreme Court ruled in *Zelman v. Simmons-Harris* that vouchers are constitutional; a congressionally backed voucher program in the nation's capital has joined several other similar programs; No Child Left Behind called for a dramatic expansion in school choice; and charter school enrollment is approaching one million students.[1] For all of these successes, however, it's possible that this seemingly triumphal march could be heading for a cliff.

Proponents of school choice today find themselves in much the same position as that inhabited by the social-engineering left after President Lyndon B. Johnson's sweep a generation ago. Their ideas ascendant, they stand on the side of social justice, have strong allies and spokespersons, and are winning prominent legal battles. Yet amidst the fruits of victory, something is missing: full approval from the mass of the American middle class.

Like the architects of LBJ's Great Society, voucherites express puzzlement as to why many suburbanites don't share their enthusiasm for school choice. Increasingly, I find myself sitting in meetings of would-be reformers where voucher advocates quietly berate white suburban families for a callous disregard for poor, minority children. Conservative school choice proponents nod along as compelling advocates for the urban underclass like Howard Fuller, Robert Aguirre, and Floyd Flake voice frustration with suburban whites, then join in lambasting white suburbanites for being insufficiently interested in helping free minority children from troubled urban schools.

That's no way to win a policy fight. Thirty years ago, the Great Society's champions berated and nagged middle-class America smack into the arms of the opposition. Enthralled by their own virtue and the elegance of their domestic policy prescriptions, Great Society liberals forgot about simple democratic notions like self-interest, concern about unintended consequences, and the public's natural aversion to risk. They tried to guilt-trip the public into supporting their bold reforms. But showing the caution and good sense typical of a democratic majority, voters eventually opted for Republicans and moderate Democrats who were less likely to belittle their reservations.

Conservative advocates for school vouchers risk repeating this mistake. The dominant wings of the voucher movement are free-marketers on the one hand, and urban minorities tired of waiting for public school improvement on the other. As discussed in "'Trust Us,' They Explained," the result has been a sometimes awkward marriage that has permitted conservatives to claim the potent language of civil rights and tempted Republicans into believing they could make political inroads with black and Latino voters.

What these advocates have overlooked is the resistance to vouchers and other choice plans among suburban homeowners. While vouchers routinely win the support of 70 percent or more of urban populations, support levels are barely half that in the suburbs, even in favorably worded polls.[2] This resistance has made voucher proponents increasingly frustrated. Are suburbanites just too naive and timid to see the problems with today's inefficient school monopolies? Or do they not care about issues of equity and equal opportunity?

It's time for choice proponents to recognize that suburban resistance to school choice is entirely rational, based largely on self-interest, and unlikely to go away. Otherwise the political clumsiness of voucherites could eventually create an unfortunate suburban backlash against school choice—in much the same way that Lyndon Johnson's Great Society programs suffered through a devastating boomerang in public opinion during the late 1970s and 1980s.

Imagine a hard-working couple, the Grays, who own four season tickets on the forty-yard line for the local pro football team. They invested lots of money and sweat in obtaining the seats, and now use them to share a special experience with their two children. The Grays value these hard-won tickets highly.

Now imagine that the Grays show up one Sunday to find that the stadium has adopted a first-come, first-served seating pattern. What do you predict their reaction is likely to be? Will they smile and say, "Oh, then that's all right!" after the stadium management explains, slowly and in few words, that the old system had produced inequitable results for the poor? Seems unlikely, doesn't it?

Local school quality affects family life in ways great and small. It controls the need to invest in private schooling, shapes social circles and the culture of the neighborhood, determines whether young families envision their neighborhood as a way station or a place to set down roots, and directly influences property values and the wealth of local residents. Parents who have sacrificed to purchase an expensive, heavily taxed home in a better school district have often done so largely because it confers a ticket to the local classrooms for their children. From the perspective of these parents, school choice proponents are essentially suggesting that their tickets be torn up.

This is true in a couple of ways. In their purest form, school vouchers allow the family to receive the public funds earmarked for a child's schooling and to use those funds to send their child to any public or private school. Such an arrangement eliminates the formal link between neighborhood and school assignment. While no school choice arrangement has been implemented in this fashion, even muted choice arrangements weaken the link between residence and school, introduce the likelihood that residential location will be a less effective means for ensuring the composition of a student's school population, and raise the possibility that high-quality teachers may be more readily lured away by new specialty schools.

School choice has much to commend it. In the long run, I believe it would render American schooling more vibrant, rigorous, and efficient. It's important to recognize, however, the real and disruptive distributional consequences of choice-based reform. While these may be viewed as socially desirable by egalitarian reformers, they present an imposing political problem in a nation where suburbanite homeowners dominate the electoral landscape. Those who own homes in districts with good schools risk losing tens or even hundreds of thousands of dollars in home equity.[3] These parents worry they may no longer be able to assure their children access to the educational services they've already purchased. They may find that local schools no longer get the first crack at the best teachers, or provide as uniformly desirable a peer group.

These are not small concerns. One can be troubled by the inequities of our existing system without pulling the rug out from under suburban families who have worked hard to get their children into decent schools. It is a simple reality that these families are unlikely to look benignly upon measures that might undercut the educational security they have struggled to achieve. This is why cities with troubled public school systems, like Cleveland, Milwaukee, Philadelphia, Dayton, and Washington, D.C., have embraced choice or charter schooling, while suburban communities with more successful schools have remained skeptical.

Let's stipulate that homeowners in good suburban districts will often start out with reservations about school reforms that hand all parents fully paid vouchers, negating the sacrifices they made to get their children into functional schools. Like it or not, this sprawling bloc of educated and influential voters will prove pivotal to the fate of choice-based reforms. Even copious amounts of morally superior nagging won't change their minds.

What are the implications for voucher proponents? Quite simply, the concerns of these suburbanites need to be addressed rather than dismissed. Specifically, efforts must be made to provide suburban parents with incentives, compensations, or limits on possible ill effects of publicly funded school choice. This can help ameliorate fear and opposition.

One approach would be to convince suburban voters that even their "better" schools are much worse than they think, and that the system-wide benefits from choice will create a rising tide that lifts all schools. There is much evidence that suburban public schools, while not dysfunctional, could be much more effective and could benefit from competition. But such an effort would have to confront public skepticism. It risks being undercut if overly rosy instant benefits are promised and not delivered.

A second approach would be compromising to mitigate possible negative side effects of choice plans. A favorite strategy so far has been to limit the area affected by school choice to urban districts, so as to immunize suburban voters from the change. The Milwaukee and Cleveland voucher programs stipulate that city students can only use their vouchers to attend suburban schools if the suburban districts approve (which they rarely do).[4] Establishment of charter schools has also been limited in suburban communities. Reformers have used gradual changes and half-measures, like choice among existing public schools only, to acclimate parents to the idea that the longstanding link between where you live and the schools your children attend is gradually dissolving. Of course (as will come up later in "On Leaving No Child Behind"), such a course threatens to undermine the import of choice-based reform. Such limitations may leave students with few real options to escape failing schools.

A third approach has barely been considered. This would involve appealing to the reasoned self-interest of suburban parents by sweetening the potential of choice to address their hopes and needs. School choice laws might explicitly encourage new schools to provide options hitherto unavailable even to suburban parents—like alternative daily school schedules or annual calendars, or advanced courses that are currently not available or oversubscribed.

A more radical appeal to self-interest might involve using financial compensation to mitigate, or even undo, perceived negative effects of school choice. Homeowners who feel that the state has constricted their property rights through publicly funded school choice might be offered a tax deduction for the amount of assessed value a home loses in the aftermath of choice-based reform. Permitting homeowners to write this deduction off against current income over a period of time would temper their concerns. This would be analogous to authorities compensating the Grays for nullifying their stadium tickets.

For school choice supporters, self-righteous indignation and sanctimonious declarations of love "for the children" are not the ticket to winning popular support. As it did for the architects of the Great Society, that path leads to a refined, self-satisfied, irrelevance in a nation steered by a healthy respect for self-interest and common sense. Whether educational choice succeeds is ultimately in the hands of America's suburban middle class. Choice advocates had better start talking straight to the soccer moms and NASCAR dads—with respect, reason, and rational incentives.

12

The Voice of the People

In a nation that daily can contrast the gridlocked, embittered partisanship of Washington, D.C., with the booming productivity of the private sector, it is probably not a surprise that there is a growing body of sentiment holding that an excess of democracy is hampering school improvement. Appalled by our inability to significantly improve urban schools, prominent professors and policymakers have suggested that—at least in urban districts—we replace locally elected school boards with boards appointed by state officials or the mayor.

Tom Glass of the University of Memphis, Ken Wong of Vanderbilt University, and Paul Hill of the University of Washington are among the eminent education scholars who have recently suggested that elected boards, at least in the case of large urban districts, are no longer workable. Meanwhile, mayors like Anthony Williams of Washington, Tom Menino of Boston, Michael Bloomberg of New York, and Jane Campbell of Cleveland have argued that only direct mayoral control can make real improvement possible.

Critics fear that elected boards attract members who are not focused on academic performance and who permit personal agendas to crowd out questions of teaching and learning. Further, they charge, elected school boards give noneducators too much control over educational decisions, foster system instability, and too often stray from policy and oversight and into micromanagement. Appointed boards, these critics suggest, would be more professional, less prone to petty politics, more focused on student achievement, and less distracted by personal concerns.

In the past decade, elected boards have been eliminated in several large districts. Between 1988 and 2003, the Education Commission of the States reported that almost fifty elected and appointed boards were replaced in nineteen states. Seven of the twenty-five school districts with more than a hundred thousand students—New York, Chicago, Philadelphia, Detroit, Baltimore, Baltimore County, and Prince George's County, Maryland—have boards that were appointed following a state or mayoral takeover.[1]

Elected boards remain the norm, however, even in the largest districts. As of 2002, 72 percent of the nation's twenty-five largest districts had elected boards. Nationally, about 96 percent of districts had elected boards.[2]

Less-than-Convincing Critiques

Despite the publicity that surrounds embarrassing board conflicts, there is no research to make the case that appointed boards systematically outperform elected boards or produce better schools or better learning. It is not at all clear that appointed officials consistently do a better job than elected officials of weighing competing interests, providing oversight, or tending to the marginalized—no matter how hard the occasional headline may make that to believe.

Anecdotes abound, but no hard data exist demonstrating the benefits of mayoral or state control. In other fields, the evidence on the advantages of appointed versus elected overseers is actually quite mixed. For example, research suggests that appointed judges are generally less partisan than elected judges,[3] but that appointed utility commissions do a worse job of keeping residential rates down than do elected commissioners.[4] Why might self-interested, bickering elected officials do as well as their appointed peers? It's really quite simple. While elected officials are always pushed to worry about their own interests and the concerns of their constituents—this is, after all, what makes democratic institutions so notoriously inefficient and frustrating—appointed officials tend to get quietly "captured" over time by interest groups.

Histories of regulatory commissions charged with overseeing everything from air travel to trains to telecommunications have found that too often the regulated industry winds up exerting tremendous influence over the regulators.[5] This was apparent in the revelations that the Securities and Exchange Commission moved tepidly to address the chicanery, fraud, and questionable accounting that ran rampant on Wall Street in the late 1990s.

Remember, too, that early experiences with mayoral control are not typical of broad-brush reform. These reforms have been championed by atypical mayors who wanted control over schooling and were willing to throw their political capital behind their school systems. It is by no means clear whether their scattered successes would be replicated under the next mayor—or under mayors in other districts who are less focused on education.

Unlike elected board members, appointed monitors have no independent base of authority. They are not motivated by electoral pressure and are not responsible for addressing the demands of the constituents. Without the prodding of these unpleasant requirements, it is easy for appointees to become complaisant. This may not happen initially—especially under the watchful eye of an enthusiastic mayor and attuned media—but it becomes increasingly likely with time.

Two Arguments for Democratic Control

Two cases can be made for elected school boards, which we can refer to as the "strong" case and the "weak" case. Both depend on questioning certain assumptions about school governance—beliefs that underlie the call for appointed boards.

The heart of the case for appointed boards is this: If we want school districts to pursue a single, clear goal and readily assess performance toward that goal through outcome measures (as is the case with most publicly owned for-profit firms), then elected boards are an inefficient and largely unnecessary encumbrance. But if we question the assumption that schools should pursue a single, clear goal, or that bottom-line performance can be readily assessed through outcomes, then we can make a strong case for elected boards.

Even if we do not question the single-goal assumption, malfeasance at companies like Enron, WorldCom, Tyco, and Sunbeam has shown how an absence of board-monitoring can permit management to take shortcuts and adopt unethical practices that advance management's own interest at the expense of employees and customers.[6] The weak case for elected boards, then, is that over the long haul, and despite their often disappointing performance, they are more likely than appointed boards to address administrative malfeasance or to have their failure to do so made public.

Let's begin by considering the weak case.

The "Weak" Case: Skeptical Safeguards

Few would disagree that the most effective boards focus on student achievement, do not micromanage, maintain professional relations among themselves and with the administration, and are fiscally disciplined. What this means in practice, however, and how priorities and issues of equity should be adjudicated or weighted, are questions without easy answers.

Particularly in troubled communities, there is concern that elected members too often violate the norms of effective boards. The problem with such critiques is that, in many cases, these "violators" are addressing real concerns. Personal conflicts, interagency squabbles, or accusations of micromanagement often reflect tensions about inequities in resource distribution or performance or real disagreement about the school system's direction. Appointed officials, unconcerned with their political prospects or constituent support, might not raise a fuss over these matters, but they would create a more tranquil system only by ignoring important issues.

In corporate America, we have learned that collegial boards—which are nominally elected but generally handpicked by the sitting board and by management—are often reluctant to ask hard questions, and we have seen the price of that deference. The corporate revelations of recent years remind us that intramural cooperation can come at the expense of oversight and at a cost to the little guy. In fact, corporate reforms in the past year have tried to increase the likelihood that corporate boards will include skeptical outsiders who will not yield too rapidly to the wishes of the management team.[7]

The American political system assumes that good intentions aren't enough; the best way to defend the public interest is to have citizens keep a watchful and self-interested eye on their elected officials.

Appointed bodies, on the other hand, place their faith in the judgment of the appointer and the expertise and honor of the appointee. Sometimes, and in some places, this approach can prove very effective. As a systemic reform, however, the danger is that—after a few years of avid public attention—the appointment process can readily settle into a quiet arrangement in which the appointer rewards friends and placates powerful interests. All this can play out without the inconvenient meddling of voters or community groups.

No matter how thoughtful the present mayor or how well-intended the current appointees, this presents unavoidable long-term concerns. They are not insuperable and may be preferable to the alternative, but they should be faced.

The "Strong" Case: Setting Public Priorities

Despite our commitment to accountability systems focused on academic achievement, it is not clear that we have settled on an organizing purpose for schools akin to the profit motive in the private sector. The "strong" case for democratic governance becomes relevant if, indeed, we are hesitant to fully embrace such a model.

While we believe that accountability systems measure school performance, we also have a long tradition of expecting educators to provide music and art instruction, encourage physical health, teach children shared social norms, ensure that children who have special needs or are disadvantaged are adequately provided for, keep an eye out for abused children, provide specialized services, and so on. It's not clear that many of these roles can be assessed using existing accountability systems.

Decisions in each of these areas can be sensitive and linked to local values that may vary from one place to the next, making state-level guidance problematic and suggesting a role for local deliberation. Moreover, deciding how to distribute these services fairly and equitably is a difficult call—one that is less a management than a policy decision. Appointed officials do not have the inclination to wrestle with competing priorities and equitable distribution and have not been democratically granted the authority to do so.

While there are obvious grounds for questioning the effectiveness of elect-ed boards, we have historically elected public school boards for a reason. In education, more than in most areas of public policy, there is far-reaching dis-agreement. Rather than simply disagreeing about the size, scope, or location of public services (as in health care or highways), we dispute the very nature of the service. As we discussed in "Inclusive Ambiguity," there is disagreement about what content should be taught in history or literature. Even aside from questions about educational effectiveness, there are cultural dimensions to debates over whether immigrant children should be immersed in English or taught primarily in their first language. Given such disagreement, it may make sense to separate educational governance from general municipal government, where such concerns either will be marginalized or will crowd out less ideologically charged issues of local policy.

We look to democratic bodies for many things—to ensure that differ-ent voices get heard, that the marginalized have someone to appeal to, that different concerns get weighed—and the record suggests that appointed officials have little appetite for such responsibilities. If we want educators to fill roles under the existing accountability regime, and we intend to let communities determine what the schools will pro-vide and how to provide it, there is really no good substitute for the teeth-grinding, frustrating option of democratic control.

This does not mean, however, that we have to accept the degree of inef-ficiency and incompetence that characterizes some elected boards today.

A Democratic Model of Reform

It may be that the problems with board governance are a product not of too much democracy, but of too little. Candidates for board seats have few resources or support for explaining their views or critiquing their oppo-nents. They compete for largely unappealing positions, have little chance to negotiate or discuss matters in a nonconfrontational forum, and, because of low voter turnout, are only marginally accountable in the political process.

In a turn that will strike many observers as ridiculous, I am suggesting that school board elections are not political *enough*—that the lack of adver-tising, party affiliations, and policy positions that characterize most candidacies make it difficult for the voters to express clear preferences or hold their representatives accountable. One result is that mobilized constituencies—especially public employees' unions—disproportionately influence many board elections. Moreover, the long hours, poor or no pay, and general unattractiveness of board service make it harder to lure many busy, ambitious, and competent community leaders who might otherwise be enticed to serve.

In a 2002 study of more than eight hundred school districts that I conducted for the National School Boards Association, only about 10 percent of districts listed a board candidate's party affiliation on the ballot, and less than half always held elections on the same day as national or state elections.[8] The lack of candidate party affiliation and the timing of elections were intended by progressive reformers to render board elections apolitical and ensure that everyone focused on what would best serve the schools.

What these reforms have actually done, however, is suppressed turnout and kept most voters from having a clear idea of what any candidate supports or opposes. The absence of party labels makes it more difficult for voters to tell candidates apart or know what they support. The lack of party politics also prevents state and local political parties from using their infrastructure and resources to help promote candidates or explain candidate positions. This incoherence makes it much harder for reformers to organize slates of like-minded candidates or for the public to hold identifiable candidates accountable for their decisions and the consequences. The result is that only members of a few organized groups, especially members of the teachers' and school employees' unions, have a clear sense of what candidates believe.

Even in districts with twenty-five thousand or more students, most board members are unpaid, and three-quarters earn less than $10,000 a year for board service.[9] Meanwhile, most board members in large districts report spending ten hours a week or more on board business.[10] Board members typically lack the staff support or resources to monitor the district or collect data on constituent concerns, forcing them to rely on the district administration for information.

Finally, boards operate under stringent "sunshine" laws that leave members with little ability to negotiate, build trust, or find ways to assemble compromises that require tempering impassioned stands. These laws typically make it illegal for more than two or three board members to discuss business in private, requiring that such conversations be formally posted in advance and open to the public. This approach has its problems. As conservative pundit George Will has noted, "In the sweltering Philadelphia summer of 1787, the Constitutional Convention closed the doors and even the windows of Independence Hall so that statesmanship and compromise could flourish without concern for an audience of factions."[11] A hesitancy to compromise makes it difficult for officials to build agreements in which all must lose a little so that the larger community may gain a lot.

In fact, the results of a school board's decisions on policy, executive hires, spending, and programs are visible and measurable. Given this, and because board members are accountable for the consequences of their actions, it is neither necessary nor desirable that mobilized public constituencies scrutinize board deliberations each and every step of the way.

Board members run in depoliticized elections for demanding positions that pay poorly and lack resources or authority. It is little surprise that boards attract gadflies, often lack stability, and permit the personal to squeeze out the professional. A democratic reform strategy would make board elections partisan, hold them on the same day as elections for more prominent state or national offices, increase pay and support for board members, and repeal or restrict sunshine laws.

As much as we malign Congress, state legislatures, or city governments, they are maintained by a core of experienced and ambitious individuals who are concerned about protecting their political futures and serving their constituents. Harnessing this ambition mitigates the worst problems and helps drive notable legislative successes. Without the discipline brought by party organization and electoral accountability, absent professional support, and lacking the leeway to negotiate, even professionalized legislators would be unlikely to produce the occasional successes that they manage. In all likelihood, they would be as paralyzed as school boards.

Real Democratic Control

Am I suggesting, then, that appointed boards pose a threat to schooling? Not at all. Am I suggesting that moving to an appointed board is necessarily a mistake? No. In some districts and at some times, mayoral control or an appointed board may prove beneficial. In fact, in some cases, it might make sense to do away with the appendage of the school board altogether and make the superintendent a conventional mayoral appointee.

But there is little reason to think that the wholesale embrace of appointed boards and mayoral control will provide a systemic answer to the challenges of troubled city schools. If we agree on the narrow objectives schools are to pursue, if we have effective educational leadership and engaged political leadership, and if we trust that there is little likelihood of administrative malfeasance, then appointed boards make sense. In the absence of these conditions, however, appointed boards may be a well-intentioned solution to the wrong problem.

Today's problems with board governance are largely the legacy of a poorly conceived and incoherently executed reform agenda advanced nearly a century ago.[12] The penalties for slapdash or makeshift efforts to remake political structures are large and enduring. Before we decide to reform the governance of public education by removing control from that pesky and troublesome public, let's be sure first to consider the case for trying meaningful democratic control.

PART IV

Finding Teachers and Principals

Introduction

Perhaps no question in school reform is more important than that of how we find, attract, and keep outstanding teachers and educational leaders. Come to think of it, in the twenty-first century, there may be few questions that matter more for our health and well-being as a nation.

Today, nearly all states have pretty intrusive regulations governing who may be considered for a job as a teacher or a principal. In two white papers that raised the hackles of the educational establishment when they were released, I argued that these policies are fundamentally flawed.[1] The two pieces, "Tear Down This Wall" and "A License to Lead?" are published here in the abridged forms that ran in *Education Next*. While one essay deals with teachers and the other with school leaders, the pieces share the presumption that today's attempt to regulate our way to educational quality is mistaken. Both were initially issued by the Progressive Policy Institute—the think tank affiliated with the centrist Democratic Leadership Council. The fact that these broadsides on key struts of the regulatory system were published by PPI, where education policy was directed by Andrew Rotherham, President Bill Clinton's former special assistant for education, gave them an added impact.

"Tear Down This Wall," which called for stripping down most of the barriers that prohibit educated adults from applying for teaching positions, was initially published in 2001. At the time, amid debates over teacher quality and efforts to craft a "Highly Qualified Teacher" provision as part of No Child Left Behind, it attracted considerable attention. It was presented at a White House conference on teaching, endorsed by the editorial page of *USA Today*, and frequently cited by Department of Education officials.[2]

Issued in 2003, "A License to Lead?" contributed to a growing skepticism toward traditional educational leadership—a skepticism brilliantly illuminated in 2005, when Art Levine, the president of the venerable Teachers College at Columbia University, issued a scathing study of educational leadership preparation.[3]

As questions of teacher and administrative licensure continued to gain attention and nontraditional training programs like Teach For America, New Leaders for New Schools, and the New Teacher Project flourished, I found myself pulled into discussions regarding the role and the quality of education schools. Schools of education had long been a favorite target of reformers. As a graduate and former professor at two of the nation's elite education schools, I agreed with many of the criticisms that were being leveled. However, I also found much of the vitriol to be anecdotal, hysterical, and ultimately unconvincing. If we were to talk seriously about reforming professional preparation, making colleges of education piñatas in the culture wars did not get us all that far. Meanwhile, few reformers were subjecting education schools to the kind of systematic, informed analysis that could support policy reforms and bring serious pressure to bear on the status quo.

After all, requiring candidates to complete education-school courses makes sense if teacher- and principal-preparation programs are providing rigorous and indispensable training. If they are not, the calculus changes. Unsurprisingly, champions of these programs insisted on their value. Lacking compelling evidence to the contrary, most policymakers and practitioners were inclined to favor the experts. So, a handful of reform-minded scholars set out to take a harder look at the question. Two groundbreaking analyses by professors David Steiner and David Leal carefully considered these claims with regard to teacher preparation for the 2004 book, *A Qualified Teacher In Every Classroom?* They found little evidence that the requisite preparation either taught essential skills or did much to ensure teacher quality.[4] I pursued the question of principal preparation in 2005, publishing an analysis entitled "Learning to Lead?" that casts a harsh light on the substantive value of most preparation programs. In "Ready to Lead?" published in the *American School Board Journal*, I summarized some of the key findings of that work and discussed what they mean for policymakers, district leaders, and reformers.

Finally, for reasons I discuss more fully in the fourth selection, this entire line of inquiry has led to heated and sometimes personal discussion. It will come as no surprise that criticism of existing rules governing the selection and training of teachers has been regarded by some as an attack on the intentions of those who design, staff, and operate these systems. In truth, more than a few critics have muddied matters by engaging in vituperative and personal attacks on education schools and those who train educators. In "The Predictable, but Unpredictably Personal, Politics of Teacher Licensure," first published in the *Journal of Teacher Education*, I try to put the debate into perspective and make the case for a more reasoned and less personal approach to the issue. While we may never come to consensus on questions like teacher licensure, I believe that the integrity, acuity, and civility of our disagreements are themselves important.

13

Tear Down This Wall

Picture Gerard, a twenty-eight-year-old business consultant who majored in economics at Williams College and graduated with a 3.7 GPA. He has been working for a consulting firm in Stamford, Connecticut, but is looking for a new, more fulfilling position. He has demonstrated strong interpersonal skills and work habits. In addition, though he didn't major in math, he aced several calculus courses in college. Yet if Gerard were to apply through normal channels to teach math at a junior high school in the Hartford public school system, his application wouldn't even be considered. Why? Because he isn't a certified teacher.

Why shouldn't a principal or a faculty hiring committee in the Hartford schools even be allowed to look at Gerard's application and judge his qualifications against those of other candidates? The assumption undergirding the contemporary approach to teacher certification is that public school hiring personnel are either unable or unwilling to gauge the quality of applicants. Our response has been to embrace a bureaucratic solution that handcuffs the capable and incapable alike and supposedly keeps weak teachers out of the classroom. As a result, having discouraged or turned away Gerard and hundreds like him, many large school systems resort to last-minute fill-ins who teach on emergency certificates.

This is not to suggest, even for a moment, that candidates with "real world" experience or high GPAs are necessarily qualified or equipped to become teachers, or that professional preparation for teachers is unimportant. It is only to say that some potential applicants might be more effective teachers than the alternatives who are currently available to public schools.

The central premise underlying teacher certification is that—no matter what his or her qualifications are—anyone who has not completed the specified training is unsuited to enter a classroom and must be prohibited from applying for a job. Presumably, the danger is that, in a moment of weakness, a human resources director or a principal will otherwise mistakenly hire Gerard in lieu of a trained teacher. It is essential to remember a simple truth that is often overlooked: Allowing someone to apply for a job is not the same as guaranteeing him employment. Making applicants eligible for a position simply permits an employer to hire them in the event they are deemed superior to the existing alternatives. The argument against certification is not that unconventional applicants will be good teachers; it is only that they might be. If one believes this, case-by-case judgments are clearly more appropriate than an inflexible bureaucratic rule.

Imagine if colleges and universities refused to hire anyone who lacked a PhD. They would lose the talents and insights of "lay practitioners" like poet Maya Angelou, journalist William Raspberry, or former public officials such as Alan Simpson, Julian Bond, and Al Gore. The artists and writers "in residence" at dozens of public universities would fail to meet the criteria implicit in the public school certification model. Do we really believe that these universities are ill-serving their students by hiring people whom the public schools would consider unqualified?

Competitive Certification

The theory behind certifying or licensing public school teachers is that this process elevates the profession by ensuring that aspiring teachers master a well-documented and broadly accepted body of knowledge and skills important to teaching. Supporters of teacher certification often make analogies to professions like law and medicine, where being an effective professional requires the acquisition of vast knowledge and skills. Licensure in these professions ensures at least minimal competency and boosts the public's confidence in members of the profession.

The problem is that no comparable body of knowledge and skills exists in teaching. Debate rages over the merits of various pedagogical strategies, and even teacher educators and certification proponents have a hard time defining a clear set of concrete skills that make for a good teacher. Yet most aspiring teachers are still forced to run a gauntlet of courses, requirements, and procedures created by accredited training programs that vary dramatically in quality.

This is not to deny that teacher education can provide valuable training. After all, one may think that journalism schools produce better journalists without requiring all journalists to complete a mandatory set of courses before seeking work in the profession. Instead, it is assumed that a candidate's training is factored into the hiring process, along with considerations like aptitude, diligence, and energy.

Clearly some sort of screening process for aspiring teachers is essential; parents and the public rightly expect safeguards for those working with youngsters. What is needed is a competitive certification process that establishes key criteria for entry into the teaching profession, gives public schools greater freedom to hire and fire teachers, and treats teachers like professionals, and their schools like professional institutions, by allowing them to tailor professional development to meet the needs of teachers. Under such a model, aspiring teachers ought to be able to apply for a teaching job if they

- possess a BA or BS degree from a recognized college or university;

- pass a test that demonstrates competency in knowledge or skills essential to what they seek to teach. The definition of "essential" knowledge or skills is obviously a loose one that can be interpreted in myriad ways and rightly should be different for those wishing to teach younger children or older students. The key point is to demand that teachers at least have an appropriate academic knowledge of the material they will be teaching; and

- pass a rigorous criminal background check. States conduct such checks now, but they tend to be compromised by the need to engage simultaneously in related certification paperwork.

Beyond these minimal qualifications, the competitive approach presumes that preparation and training are not only desirable but also essential, as is true in other professions where subtle skills and interpersonal dynamics are essential to effective performance. The questions are where to obtain this training and who should pay for it. Contemporary teacher preparation imposes nearly all of the costs on candidates by forcing them into a system of training that removes key incentives for quality and relevance in teacher preparation. The competitive model instead treats teachers as autonomous professionals able to make informed decisions about developing their skills and expertise. In short, the competitive model would substitute meaningful professional development for what is essentially a guild system funded by levying a significant tuition-based tax on aspiring teachers before permitting them to enter the profession.

The Assumptions of Certification

Over the years, an array of studies has sought to determine whether certified teachers serve students more effectively than uncertified teachers. There are two problems with this line of work. First, the methodological wrangling has often obscured the larger questions and the central assumptions of the certification model. Second, the case for certification is thin whether or not certified teachers boost student achievement more than their uncertified peers. The issue is not whether teacher education improves the performance of graduates, but whether we ought to—as best we are able—bar from teaching those who have not completed an approved preparatory program. Certification systems deny school administrators the ability to take their context or the promise of a particular applicant into account when hiring. Even if certified teachers are generally more effective than uncertified teachers, such a policy makes sense only if we believe that uncertified applicants are uniformly incompetent to teach or that school administrators cannot be trusted to assess their competence.

The allure of certification rests on three implicit assumptions. They are the beliefs that, first, the training one receives while getting certified in a field is so useful that the uncertified will be relatively ill-prepared; second, that certification weeds out unsuitable candidates; and third, that certification makes an occupation more "professional," and therefore more attractive as a career. However, each of these presumptions is problematic in the case of teacher certification.

As a general principle, certification is most effective when the licensing body ensures that aspiring professionals have mastered essential skills or knowledge, and denies a license to inadequate performers. Licensure is most essential when a professional's tasks are critical and when clients may have trouble assessing a provider's qualifications. For instance, licensure is considered particularly appropriate for engineers, doctors, and attorneys because those who design bridges, tend us when we are ill, or defend our rights all perform tasks essential to our well-being and are frequently charged with aiding us at our most vulnerable. Moreover, it can be difficult for members of the public to know whether a bridge is properly designed, whether a doctor is performing appropriately, or whether an attorney is knowledgeable in the law.[1] Licensing is not an assurance that these professionals are talented practitioners, but it does ensure that they have demonstrated an established degree of professional knowledge.

Educators are also charged with a crucial task. However, the oversight challenge is very different in education, where we have not established a specific, measurable body of skills or knowledge that teachers must master. Education "experts" themselves argue that teaching is so complex that it can be difficult to judge a good teacher outside of a specific classroom context. This makes it difficult, if not impossible, to determine abstractly which aspirants possess satisfactory "teaching skills." Meanwhile, there is widespread agreement that colleagues, supervisors, and families have at least a proximate ability to gauge whether a teacher is effective. Given these circumstances, it is unclear how standardized licensing helps to safeguard teacher quality.

Such a conclusion does not require refuting the claims of teacher-educators or the supporters of certification. It actually follows if one simply accepts their claims. Professional educators themselves have thus far been unable to explain in any concrete sense what makes a teacher competent or what teachers need to know and be able to do.

Consider the widely praised standards that the National Board for Professional Teaching Standards (NBPTS) has painstakingly constructed in twenty-seven distinct fields, which proponents of certification have hailed as a breakthrough in quality control. The areas where the NBPTS ought to have had the easiest time creating straightforward standards are high school math and science teaching, where there is widespread consensus as to what teachers are supposed to do. Even in these areas, however, the NBPTS's "exemplary" standards are so broad and vague as to make concrete judgments of competence nearly impossible. For instance, to receive National Board certification to teach high school math, teachers are to demonstrate mastery of eleven standards, including commitment to students and their learning, the art of teaching, reflection, and growth, and reasoning and thinking mathematically. The board tries to clarify these standards by explaining, for instance, that "commitment" is interpreted as meaning that "accomplished mathematics teachers value and acknowledge the individuality and worth of each student, believe that all students can learn," and so on.[2] Mastering the "art of teaching" is taken to mean that teachers "stimulate and facilitate student learning by using a wide range of formats and procedures." While these are certainly admirable sentiments, nowhere in the National Board's rarified standards is it clear how we are to gauge just what constitutes "competence" in these tasks.[3] The result, unsurprisingly, is that the board has been assailed for the capricious way in which the standards are being interpreted and applied.[4] Despite the best of intentions in the drafting of the Interstate New Teacher Assessment and Support Consortium (INTASC) standards, which Mary Diez discusses, a cursory read makes clear that they are plagued by the same ambiguities evident in the NBPTS standards.[5]

For another prominent example, consider education professors Gerald Grant and Christine E. Murray's award-winning 1999 book, *Teaching in America*. They identify five "essential [teaching] acts" that can be analyzed and taught: listening with care; motivating the student; modeling caring by hearing and responding to the pain of others and by creating a sense of security in their classrooms; evaluating by clarifying, coaching, advising, and deciding on an appropriate challenge for this boy or that girl; and reflecting and renewing. How one is to teach these five "essential acts," much less determine whether a teacher has satisfactorily mastered them, are questions that Grant and Murray never address.[6]

If clear standards of professional competence do not exist, we typically (and appropriately) hesitate to prohibit some individuals from practicing a profession. This is not to say that we think incompetence is acceptable in such a profession—only that we recognize licensing as an ineffective and potentially pernicious way to control quality. While licensure could protect community members (including children) from exposure to "bad" entrepreneurs or journalists, we do not prohibit some people from seeking to start businesses or work for a newspaper. Instead, we trust that potential investors or employers are the best judges of who ought to be supported or hired. If aspiring writers or entrepreneurs are unsuccessful, we trust that they will eventually be persuaded to find a line of work for which they are better suited. This free-flowing process fosters diversity and ensures that unconventional workers are given a chance to succeed.

Even in professions with clear knowledge- or performance-based benchmarks for certification, such as law or medicine, licensure is useful primarily as a way of establishing minimal competence. A medical or a law license is not imagined to ensure competence in ambiguous, subtle skills like comforting a patient or swaying a jury—skills analogous to the interpersonal relations thought crucial to teaching. Basing certification on such traits is difficult, because we may disagree about what they entail or how they can be assessed devoid of context. The skills that teacher-educators deem most important—listening, caring, motivating—are not susceptible to standardized quality control. Emphasis on these qualities is the norm in professions like marketing, journalism, consulting, or policy-making, where a subtle blend of people skills, knowledge, and relevant expertise is required. In professions like these, where there are a number of ways for practitioners to excel but difficult to know in advance how any particular practitioner will perform, the most sensible way to find talent is to allow aspirants to seek work, and to permit employers to screen on a variety of criteria—such as education, experience, and references.

A Dubious Screen

While certification can serve to screen out aspirants who fail to meet a minimal performance standard, our current system is not designed to do so. Generally speaking, schools of education are not selective, flunk out few if any students for inadequate performance, and see that many of their teacher-education graduates receive teacher licenses—the licensing exams are simple, and standards for passage are generally so low that the Education Trust concluded they exclude only the "weakest of the weak" from classrooms.[7]

More than 1,300 institutions provide the training required for licensure. While defenders of the current approach to certification often focus on the certification programs at elite institutions, the top twenty-five education schools train less than 5 percent of the two hundred thousand new graduates produced by teacher programs each year.[8] It is the regional colleges, such as Illinois State University, Cal State–Hayward, and Southwest Texas State University—not the Stanfords and the Ohio States—that train and license the vast majority of teachers. The value of certification turns not on the quality of elite programs, but on that of regional colleges.

Teacher-preparation programs neither screen out nor weed out weak candidates. Even at elite schools, such as UCLA or the University of North Carolina, where admissions rates are about 5 percent for medical school and 25 percent for law school, the master of education programs (which include those seeking postgraduate training for teacher certification) accept more than half of their applicants. Moreover, education-school officials often make it clear that they do not see their mission as weeding out students during their course of study. Explained one such official, "We're here to develop teachers, not to screen people out. For the most part, everyone who enters the program is going to complete it, unless they decide that teaching's not for them."[9]

The Costs of Certification

Especially for anyone who didn't complete a teacher-training program as an undergraduate, the costs of certification can be significant. It is not unusual for postgraduate teacher-training programs to require a full-time commitment of sixteen or even twenty-four months, or a part-time commitment that can stretch to three years or more. The cost of training and the loss of salary due to time spent out of the workforce can easily reduce a teacher's real compensation during the first five years by 25 percent or more.[10]

These barriers make other professions relatively more attractive, so that potentially talented teachers who are unsure about their interest are less likely to try teaching. Whereas candidates can readily try journalism, consulting, or marketing for a year, they must make an extensive commitment before they can try public school teaching. The result is that many who might make fine teachers never enter the profession. There is disturbing evidence that certification may especially dissuade accomplished minority candidates—who have a number of attractive career options and who are often less well-situated to absorb the costs of teacher preparation—from entering teaching.

This would pose no real problem if we were blessed with a surplus of good teachers. In such a case, we might scoff "good riddance" to those dissuaded from teaching. However, we have a desperate need for competent teachers. Moreover, rather than a lack of commitment to teaching, a reluctance to pursue certification may indicate that individuals have attractive alternatives. It is the most talented and hardest-working individuals who have the most career options and who sacrifice the most by entering a profession where compensation is unlinked to performance, and where opportunities for advancement are few. They may wish to teach but be unwilling to forgo work for a year, sit through poorly regarded courses, or jump through procedural hoops. It is candidates with fewer attractive options who will find the tedious but intellectually undemanding requirements of certification less problematic. In fact, by suppressing the supply of teachers, certification provides teachers with enhanced job security. Coupled with a compensation scale that rewards seniority rather than performance, certification may well make the vocation more attractive to graduates seeking a less demanding line of work. In this way, certification can actually harm the public's perception of teaching as a profession—the very opposite of what certification proponents wish to do.

Creative Destruction

In a world without certification as we know it, districts and schools would have more flexibility to ensure that their new teachers are prepared, inducted, and supervised in a manner appropriate to the challenges at hand. Because aspiring teachers would no longer have to attend formal teacher-preparation programs in order to teach, they would be free to make professional decisions about training, in the same manner as business-school or journalism-school students. Weaker teacher-preparation programs would likely fall by the wayside. The fact that schools of education could no longer rely on a captive body of aspiring teachers would expose them to the cleansing winds of competition. Schools would have to contribute value—by providing teacher-training, services, or research that creates demand and attracts support—or face significant cutbacks. Teacher-preparation programs would find it in their own self-interest to ensure that their graduates were knowledgeable and skilled, as this would help graduates win desirable jobs amid increased competition, making preparatory institutions more attractive.

Under a competitive certification system, little is likely to change in many of our high-performing suburban districts, where officials are inundated with applicants and are unlikely to tamper with a formula that is "working." In such districts, except in rare cases, we would expect administrators to continue to cherry-pick from the nation's top teacher-education graduates. It is in the less desirable and more troubled systems, the nation's urban and rural school districts, that administrators currently have tremendous difficulty finding sufficient numbers of certified teachers. This is doubly true in the areas of math and science education. It is in these districts and subjects, where critics have fretted about the numbers of long-term substitutes and "burnt-out" veterans, that the wave of new teachers will most likely be recruited and welcomed. While many of the resultant applicants will no doubt be deemed unprepared or unsuited for the jobs they pursue, there are few urban or rural principals who would not welcome the chance to pick and choose from their ranks.

Critics may fear that the elimination of licensure requirements will mean the end of teacher preparation and professional development. Such concern is unfounded. First, allowing uncertified individuals to become teachers does not mean that they must be viewed as "completed" professionals. Such a mindset is one of the vestiges of our current system, which is erected on a premise that all teachers are certified and therefore competent. Here, a better model might be medicine or law, where entering professionals begin their careers with a trial period (serving as a hospital resident or as a junior partner in a law firm, for instance) during which their full panoply of skills is developed and monitored. Beginning teachers might serve on a probationary basis, receiving substantial monitoring and counseling. However, legal and contractual language ought to make it much simpler to terminate ineffective teachers or to mandate that they engage in support activities designed to improve their performance.

Second, moving to competitive certification does not mean doing away with professional teacher-education programs. Many applicants attend journalism school or business school, even though such training is not officially required, because it may make graduates more effective and can help them find better employment more readily. Likewise, aspiring teachers would presumably continue to attend those teacher-training programs thought to enhance their employability. This change would introduce some much-needed market pressure in this area, as schools would be forced to compete for students based on the usefulness of their course offerings.

Giving districts more leeway to hire promising candidates does not mean they will always make good decisions. Some ineffective teachers will inevitably continue to be hired. However, if entry to the profession is eased, it is appropriate that exit be eased as well. If administrators are to have more leeway to make hiring decisions, they also must be given more leeway to fire—and they must be held accountable for both sets of decisions.

At the end of the day, the individuals best equipped to assess the qualifications of prospective teachers are the principals who will be responsible for them. These same principals ought to have the strongest incentive to see that teachers are effective. If we believe that the administrators charged with managing and supervising schools either are unequipped to evaluate prospective teachers or are unwilling to do so, teacher certification will not suffice to protect our children from such profound systemic dysfunction. If we trust administrators, then certification is unnecessary and entails significant costs. If we don't trust administrators, let us address that issue directly and not rely on the hollow promise of flimsy parchment barriers.

Regardless, it is past time to acknowledge fully the nuanced, multifaceted, and professional nature of teaching. We must move beyond a system that restricts professional entry with ambiguous procedural barriers arising from an inability to clearly define the skills, knowledge, or training essential to good teaching.

14

A License to Lead?

In the early 1990s, IBM had fallen on hard times. The leader of the personal-computing revolution was losing billions of dollars a year and looking for a new CEO. Observers were aghast when the board of directors recruited Lou Gerstner, CEO of RJR Nabisco and veteran of the food and tobacco industries. Critics insisted that his lack of experience running a technology concern would leave him at a "huge disadvantage," wrote Doug Garr in a 1999 book about Gerstner's tenure, because the computer business "moved at a faster pace than other industries; competition came from . . . fanatics who thrived in the often quirky and murky world of digital chaos."[1] It was believed that managers in the high-tech field needed both business savvy and technical skills. Gerstner was seen as woefully unprepared.

By the late 1990s, IBM was again a highly profitable technological innovator. Gerstner was hailed for engineering, as the subtitle to Garr's account, *IBM Redux*, put it, "the business turnaround of the decade."[2] Might another CEO, especially one with more experience in technology, have done better? Possibly. Were the concerns about Gerstner's lack of experience valid? Sure. However, the larger lesson is that Gerstner provided what IBM needed—a CEO "who could penetrate the corporate culture and change the company's insular way of thinking and operating."[3]

Consider Meg Whitman. Formerly a brand manager at Procter & Gamble with an MBA from the Harvard Business School, Whitman was hired in 1998 to lead eBay, the ubiquitous Internet auctioneer. Concerns over Whitman's lack of familiarity with the Internet were initially widespread, but her marketing experience proved invaluable as eBay became one of the few web pioneers actually to turn a profit, and Whitman was named one of the nation's most influential business leaders by *Time* magazine and CNN.[4]

Similarly, when Ben & Jerry's, the quirky Vermont ice cream company, found itself forced to bring in professional management in order to cope with rapid growth, employees and loyal customers were worried that outsiders focused on the bottom line would prove incompatible with the company's socially conscious philosophy. Marketing executive Walt Freese, formerly of Celestial Seasonings, was brought in as the new chief marketing officer and then became CEO in 2004. With zero experience in the ice cream industry or the corporate culture of Ben & Jerry's, Freese launched a successful effort to expand the franchise network while embarking on an initiative to address global warming.[5]

Gerstner, Whitman, and Freese aren't even unusual examples; businesses often turn to leaders from outside their industries. Recruiting outsiders has become more common in K–12 education as well, at least at the superintendent level. Urban school districts from Philadelphia to Los Angeles have hired candidates from outside education to lead their schools. Nonetheless, the overwhelming majority of superintendents, school district officials, and school principals rise through the ranks the traditional way—first as teachers, then as assistant principals and principals, then up to the district office. Many of them make fine leaders. But the fact is that the traditional route to K–12 school management is not serving the nation well. The public school system suffers from a lack of effective managers at both the school and the district level. In 2002, Paul Houston, executive director of the American Association of School Administrators, said, "Five years ago, the pool of good superintendents was fairly shallow, and I thought it was as bad as it could get. I was not nearly pessimistic enough. It's gotten worse."[6] In turn, 60 percent of superintendents told Public Agenda in 2001 that they had had to "take what you can get" when hiring principals.[7] The problem is not a lack of warm bodies, but an artificial shortage of individuals with the skills, training, and knowledge to lead modern schools and school systems.

The shortage is artificial in the sense that state laws needlessly limit the supply of principals and superintendents. More than forty states require would-be principals or superintendents to acquire a license in school administration in order to apply for a job. Typically, attaining licensure as a principal requires three or more years of K–12 teaching experience, completion of a graduate degree in educational administration, and an internship. In several states, candidates are also required to pass the School Leaders Licensure Assessment, an exam designed to check whether the applicants hold professionally sanctioned values and attitudes. The licensing of superintendents involves similar requirements, though states are more likely to issue waivers if a school board requests one. The problem is that these licensure rules constrain the pool of potential applicants when there is no evidence that they produce more effective school managers.

Changing Demands

In today's reform environment, school leaders must be able to leverage technology, devise performance-based evaluation systems, recruit top-notch staff, draw upon data and research when making decisions, and motivate their teachers and students to meet state and federally mandated goals. If the past performance of traditional school administrators gives any indication, it is unclear that teaching experience or education-school coursework provides candidates with the unique combination of technical and interpersonal skills these tasks demand. Inasmuch as private sector, nonprofit, and governmental managers outside of K–12 schooling face many of these same challenges in their work, there is no reason why talented individuals from these sectors should not also be considered for positions as school principals and district administrators.

It is time for a straightforward, two-point standard governing the licensure of school administrators. Applicants for principalships, superintendencies, and other management positions should be expected to demonstrate the following qualifications:

- A college degree and evidence of personal integrity, including passing a criminal background check.

- Possession of the knowledge and skills essential to lead schools and school systems, as defined by those selecting the leader.

While schools and school districts might seek candidates with formal qualifications or credentials, such as teaching experience, a graduate degree in educational administration, or even an MBA, the lack of such credentials would not prevent someone from applying for a position. School districts would be free to consider a range of candidates, rather than only those with the requisite teaching experience and graduate degree.

This approach is similar to the deregulatory strategy many states use to solve their shortages of high-quality teachers and to attract more mid-career professionals to teaching. However, school management positions are even riper for deregulation than classroom teaching. Teachers spend most of their time working independently in self-contained classrooms. By contrast, school managers operate as part of a team and hold more amorphous responsibilities. Not every administrator needs to possess the full range of skills required to run a school or school system. While it may be important for some members of the leadership team to know good teaching when they see it, others may bring complementary skills that can be transferred to an educational setting. It is the team taken together that needs to hold the full complement of skills.

Deregulating the recruitment and training of school managers is especially crucial at a time when the K–12 education system is moving toward using standards, testing, accountability, and choice as its chief reform strategies. To thrive in this new environment, school leaders will need a background in fields where accountability for performance is a part of their everyday working lives. The ability to build effective teams, set goals and motivate individuals toward meeting them, and create a sense of purpose and mission in the schools is now even more urgent. Given these new demands, it is imperative that school boards not be unduly constrained by state regulations that dictate whom they may consider for school management positions.

Instead of recruiting effective leaders from other fields, public schools opt to pull an enormous share of principals and superintendents from the ranks of the nation's gym teachers. In 1999–2000, 34 percent of the nation's principals had been coaches or athletic directors.[8] What uniquely equips a high school coach rather than a director of a tutoring program to lead an elementary school? It might be that coaches are used to managing and motivating teams in a competitive setting and enforcing basic discipline, but this gives lie to the notion, popular among experts on educational lead-ership, that principals and superintendents must be "instructional leaders."

Recruiting leaders from other fields would yield a range of benefits—including some for school administrators themselves. Presently, educa-tional leaders enjoy little respect. While high-ranking military personnel and members of urban mayoral administrations often find themselves with plum offers from the private sector when they leave those fields, few school managers are seen as qualified to do much else. Prying open the channels between leadership in education and other fields would help reverse the tendency to ghettoize school administrators. This would force school systems to pay a fair rate for managerial talent and would create new opportunities for administrators to command the support and respect enjoyed by their counterparts in other sectors.

The new crop of managers would also demand the same tools and responsibilities that they enjoyed in other fields. School leaders who are not given the right to hire and fire teachers, reward and sanction person-nel, or allocate resources cannot be held fully responsible for the results. The first to benefit from these changes would be the thousands of hard-working principals and superintendents who have grown frustrated with their inability to run their organizations effectively. This new agenda is not an attack on school administrators. It is a commitment to professionalize their chosen field.

Closing the Door to Talent

As we discussed in the last chapter, the burden of proof regarding licen-sure should rest on those who embrace it because it *prohibits* those who don't meet the guidelines from applying for work. This makes sense only if we are certain that someone who has not taught and has not com-pleted a university-based program in school administration *cannot* be an effective principal or superintendent. If we're not certain, if we just believe that former teachers will *generally* make better principals, then licensure is problematic.

The traditional approach has fostered a leadership culture that is ill-suited to contemporary management challenges and ill-equipped to implement new technologies, and that produces principals reluctant to be held accountable for student learning. Of principals surveyed in 2003, 45 percent thought it a "bad idea" to "hold principals accountable for student standardized test scores at the building level."[9] We need principals who welcome responsibility for student learning, whether they have come from the classroom or not.

Licensure is a crude device, best suited to ensuring that the clearly incompetent cannot prey on the public. It is especially well-suited to professions like medicine or law, where practitioners are often independent and their quality of work is difficult for clients to gauge. Principals and super-intendents, by contrast, work in a highly visible context—within a large public organization where their performance is increasingly monitored by state officials, local activists, businesspeople, journalistic outlets, and others.

The problem with requiring school managers to earn a license is that the work of a principal or superintendent is typically shaped by that person's immediate context. Job requirements evolve over time and differ from one milieu to the next. Leadership in other lines of work has much the same quality. This is why we cannot imagine licensing business or political leaders, and why the MBA is *not* a license, but a credential that employers value as they see fit. Even in higher education, where formal credentials are required for an individual to become a professor, additional credentials are not necessary to become a dean or president. In fact, as fundraising and running a multimillion-dollar institution have become the chief responsibilities of an academic presidency, more and more universities are looking to nontraditional candidates.

Three fundamentally flawed assumptions underlie the existing approach to licensure:

Only Former Teachers Can Lead, Especially at the Principal Level. This notion begins with the claim that only a former teacher can provide "instructional leadership." The belief that principals need to have taught rests on two articles of faith: that only former teachers can monitor classroom personnel or mentor teachers. Both claims are of dubious merit.

The first may have been plausible when administrators could judge a teacher's effectiveness only by observing classes and monitoring parental complaints. Today, however, there is a wealth of information on achievement, and entrepreneurial managers are finding ways to gather data on other facets of teacher performance. In addition, an effective principal can use master teachers to evaluate their peers, as an increasing number of schools are doing.

The claim that principals must be mentors is equally problematic. In very small schools or systems where no one else is available to work with teachers on curricular or instructional issues, administrators play this role. But in larger schools, where most students are to be found, principals and superintendents lead teams that include a variety of individuals with different strengths. Administrators who use their teams wisely can provide more useful assistance than overstretched leaders drawing only on personal knowledge. A growing number of nonteachers have performed competently as district superintendents or charter school principals. Doctors, lawyers, engineers, and other professionals routinely work in organizations led by individuals from other fields. Are teachers alone so iconoclastic or fragile that they can work only for one of their own?

In fact, the skills that characterize effective teachers may actually hinder their performance as managers. Though experts in educational leadership argue that principals and superintendents—especially those in troubled venues—must be proactive risk-takers who engage in "creative insubordination," research has found that "teachers tend to be reluctant risk takers."[10] A 2003 Public Agenda survey found that barely one in five teachers thought linking teachers' salaries to their effectiveness would help motivate them or reward high-performers, while more than 60 percent worried it would lead to jealousy. Even though 78 percent reported that at least a few teachers at their schools were "simply going through the motions," just 23 percent thought unions should make it easier for administrators "to fire incompetent teachers."[11]

Even professional managers express profound anxiety about tasks like delivering negative evaluations and terminating employees. It is not much of a stretch to suggest that teachers reluctant to link rewards to student performance or unwilling to support steps to purge ineffective colleagues may be ill-suited to some unpleasant but crucial managerial tasks. The years that principals or superintendents spent as teachers immersed in classroom culture may leave them hesitant to take the harsh steps that performance-based leadership sometimes requires.

Quality Control. One argument for licensure is that it screens out incompetent aspirants. But earning a master's or doctorate in educational leadership does no such thing. Even elite programs impose shockingly little quality control. Education schools do not make it possible to examine admissions data specific to their administration and leadership programs, but we can garner a rough idea of selectivity by comparing overall admissions data from colleges of education with those from graduate business schools.

A few examples from the 2004 *U.S. News & World Report* rankings of graduate programs may help to illustrate the point. Pennsylvania State University's thirty-third-ranked business school accepted 24 percent of its applicants, and admitted students had a mean score of 650 on their Graduate Management Admission Tests (GMATs). Meanwhile, the university's school of education, which housed the nation's sixth-ranked educational administration program, accepted 48 percent of its *doctoral* applicants, and the admitted students had a mean verbal score of 480 on their Graduate Record Examinations (GRE). Ohio State University's business school, ranked nineteenth, accepted 25 percent of its applicants while the university's education school, home to the nation's second-ranked administration program, accepted 44 percent of doctoral applicants. The thirteenth-ranked University of Michigan–Ann Arbor business school accepted 19 percent of its MBA applicants, while the education school (with the ninth-ranked administration program) accepted 37 percent of its doctoral applicants.[12]

Professionalism. Today, due in large part to licensure, educational administration is a subspecialization of the sprawling field of leadership and management. Experts on educational leadership dismiss the existing canon of management theory and practice, instead offering their own "educationally unique" formulations of leadership. Prominent thinkers, such as Thomas Sergiovanni in *Leadership for the Schoolhouse*, argue that "corporate" models of leadership cannot work in education. Such simpleminded dichotomies are mistaken. There is no one style of "corporate" leadership; nor is there a unique "educational leadership."[13]

The result is training that does not expose educators to the body of thought that conventionally trained executives deem essential. Major publishers produce lists of "educational administration" texts that number hundreds of books, though they publish nothing similar on managing pharmaceutical firms, retirement communities, or fire departments. The absence of crosspollination leaves school administration a lightly regarded backwater.

Surveying some of the titles pitched to education administrators illustrates the problem. Widely used in administrative training are books like *Leading for Diversity: How School Leaders Promote Positive Interethnic Relations*; *Caring Enough to Lead: How Reflective Thought Leads to Moral Leadership*; and *Leadership and the Force of Love: Six Keys to Motivating with Love*. These volumes never explain why conventional management wisdom and analysis are inappropriate for schooling.

The Costs of the Status Quo

Another drawback to licensure is that it makes it more costly to seek a management position in education, making other professions relatively more attractive. If the hurdles screened out the incompetent or ill-suited, that would be one thing. However, there is no evidence and little reason to believe that one's willingness to pay tuition for lightly regarded courses taught during evenings, weekends, and summers says much about one's aptitude or suitability for leadership. Willingness to bear such burdens may reflect a lack of interest in teaching, a lack of attractive alternatives, or a hunger for a position of authority just as readily as a commitment to learning.

It is simply not the case, as proponents of licensure argue, that school management positions are so challenging that nobody wants them. Recent years have witnessed the creation of several programs that train aspiring nontraditional principals and school district officials. In 2005, the KIPP (Knowledge Is Power Program) Foundation's principal academy had 250 applicants for only eight slots.[14] Similarly, the Broad Foundation's Urban Superintendents Academy received 162 applications for twenty-two slots in 2004.[15]

The most motivated candidates may be the least willing to sit through poorly regarded courses or suffer procedural hurdles. In fact, an extraordinary number of entrepreneurs pursue charter school management positions—despite the obstacles, uncertainty, and reduced compensation—because they are unwilling to wait the requisite number of years before being permitted to seek a position in a conventional district school.

Tried but Not True

Present reform efforts fall into two camps. One is represented by the efforts of the Interstate School Leaders Licensure Consortium (ISLLC) to define "standards" for educational administration and stiffen the requirements for licensure. The idea is to improve the training of potential principals and superintendents—a worthy goal, but one whose effect would be to further narrow the field of candidates.

Formed in the 1990s, ISLLC is a coalition of administrator organizations (like the National Association of Elementary School Principals), education unions, education schools, and other education client groups. In line with what these groups have long advocated, the ISLLC standards assess individual beliefs rather than knowledge or skills.[16] The six standards assert that school administrators should "promote student success" by doing things like "facilitating . . . a vision of learning," "collaborating . . . with community members," and "influencing the larger political, . . . legal, and cultural context."[17] These sentiments are pleasing primarily to those who embrace the ISLLC's notion of "diversity," endorse constructivist pedagogy, and believe school leaders ought to wield political and legal levers to advance "social justice."

The problems are made clear by the ISLLC School Leaders Licensure Assessment, which several states now use to assess the competence of candidates for principalships. While the exam's designers claim that it is "grounded in research,"[18] the exam does not assess legal, budgetary, management, research, curricular, or pedagogical knowledge; it determines little more than fidelity to ISLLC values. As the ISLLC's chairman, Ohio State University professor Joseph Murphy, concedes, "[The exam] is a statement of values about where the profession should be"—or at least where it should be according to Murphy and his allies.[19]

Of the sample situations and questions in the online preparation materials, not one asks a candidate to exhibit an understanding of scholarly research, legal statute, or budgetary concepts.[20] One sample vignette asks candidates to determine what is "in the best interest of the particular student" in a case where a high school senior failing a class asks the principal if he can drop the class, even though permitting the student to do so is "contrary to school policy." In the example, the principal permits the student to drop the class, and test-takers are then asked to explain whether this decision served the student's "best interest." Endorsing the principal's action earns the test-taker a perfect score, while those who recommend denying the request are marked down. ISLLC's public materials indicate that graders would give a score of zero to the following candidate response:

> The principal's action is wrong. . . . Much more is learned in high school than academics. Students must learn that there are consequences for their actions. . . . If this student is allowed to graduate, the lesson he will learn is that he does not have to accept the consequences of his actions.[21]

The other reform strategy pursued by large urban districts from New York to San Diego is to recruit celebrity superintendents from other professions, such as Joel Klein, the Clinton administration's antitrust official, who is now serving as chancellor of the New York City schools. There is nothing wrong with pursuing high-profile nontraditional superintendents. Such hires have imported a number of promising executives into the schools and challenged shopworn assumptions. However, searches for nontraditional leaders too often devolve into quixotic quests for "white knights."

Most nontraditional superintendents are hired not on the basis of a reasoned assessment of their skills, but because they are considered forceful individuals. The fascination with "leadership" that can be readily transferred from one field to the next has sometimes been shockingly simplistic, as with the presumption that military generals would make good superintendents because they run taut organizations, or that attorneys would because they're familiar with law and politics.

American education doesn't need a few dozen superintendents gamely swimming against the tide, but rather tens of thousands of competent superintendents, principals, and administrators working in tandem. The problem with today's efforts is that they are not part of larger efforts to recruit thoughtfully out of an expanded candidate pool, to build and support teams, and to rethink management. Instead, they are too often one-shot prayers in which the district hopes that charisma and personal credibility can jumpstart their moribund institutions.

In the years immediately following World War II, business administration was a minor profession, and business schools were institutions of modest repute, viewed as intellectually suspect stepcousins to university economics departments. As management became more crucial to the postwar economy, the quality of executives improved, and business schools responded to competitive forces. Businesses were forced to discipline their hiring through a new reliance on the bottom line, and business schools became increasingly selective and focused on teaching critical economic, accounting, and quantitative content in a useful and relevant fashion. Today, America's executive workforce is admired across the globe, and its business schools are among the nation's most prestigious educational units. This all transpired without formal licensing; neither business schools nor America are any the worse off because Bill Gates and Michael Dell never obtained an MBA. The world of educational leadership is ripe for a similar revolution.

15

Ready to Lead?

with Andrew Kelly

In seeking to reimagine the American public high school, one barrier has been a shortage of managerial talent. A recent WestEd report on small high schools found effective school leadership to be a crucial factor in driving school improvement. In response, in February 2005, the Gates Foundation announced that it would donate $10 million to New Leaders for New Schools, a nonprofit organization that currently recruits and trains principals for public schools in five cities. The new grant will enable New Leaders to train 127 principals for duty in small high schools and advance the organization's goal of training 550 new principals in the next four years.[1] This is a noteworthy development, but one that might leave other districts wondering where they can turn for the principals they need.

In an era of accountability, when school leaders are expected to demonstrate bottom-line results and use data to drive decisions, the skill and knowledge of principals matter more than ever. Many districts are contemplating reforms that involve decentralization, increased school-site autonomy, charter schooling, or more flexible teacher compensation and hiring, and thousands of principals are getting new opportunities to exercise discretion and operate with previously unimagined leeway. Today, for some of the reasons we discussed in "A License to Lead?" school improvement rests to an unprecedented degree on the quality of school leadership.

An array of thinkers—including Harvard University's Richard Elmore, Ohio State University's Joe Murphy, the National Center on Education and the Economy's Marc Tucker, the Fordham Foundation's Chester Finn, and New Leaders for New Schools's Jon Schnur—has asked whether traditional approaches to preparing and licensing principals are sufficient for this changing world. Principals themselves are among the first to suggest

186

that they could be more effectively prepared for their jobs, with all but 4 percent of practicing principals telling Public Agenda in 2003 that on-the-job experiences or guidance from colleagues had been more helpful in preparing them for their current position than their graduate school studies. In fact, 67 percent of principals reported that "typical leadership programs in graduate schools of education are out of touch with the realities of what it takes to run today's school districts."[2]

Providers of principal preparation have called for new approaches to designing and delivering preparation. Leaders of the University Council for Educational Administration have asserted that "we must rethink and revise our practice in several areas."[3] Reforms have included modified education-school programs, new state-run principal academies, and changes in state licensure statutes.

Amidst all this activity, however, surprisingly little attention has been paid to what principals are actually learning in the course of their preparation, or what this means for school district governance and leadership. In 2005, a four-year study conducted by the president of Teachers College, Art Levine, raised the stakes in this debate by harshly assessing the quality of educational administration programs. Drawing on extensive surveys and case studies of administration leadership programs, Levine concluded that "the majority of [educational administration] programs range from inadequate to appalling, even at some of the country's leading universities." Levine reported that the typical course of studies required of principal candidates was largely disconnected from the realities of school management, though his analysis did not attend to the content of these courses themselves. Among Levine's thoughtful solutions: to create an education management degree like the MBA, to eliminate the EdD, and to stop districts from offering pay raises for course credit.[4] Such structural changes are certainly welcome, but Levine's study raises a more fundamental question as to whether the content of preparation courses, in addition to their structure, must be reconceptualized.

In two studies released in 2005, my colleague Andrew Kelly and I examined what principals are learning in the course of their preparation and what that means for their performance in the schoolhouse. One study focused on what content is addressed in the syllabi of administrator-preparation courses, while the second focused upon the content of the most commonly assigned texts.[5] What we found is troubling for school districts seeking principals ready and able to seize the rudder and ride out the new challenges of accountability.

Principal Preparation

We drew a stratified sample of the 496 programs that grant master of education degrees in educational administration. We surveyed fifty-six of these and were eventually able to obtain at least four "core" course syllabi amenable to systematic analysis from thirty-one of the programs, collecting 210 syllabi in all. The syllabi contained 2,424 discrete weeks of classroom instruction.[6]

Our sample was composed in equal parts of elite programs that influence professional thinking and practice, large programs that train the most candidates, and more typical programs that are neither prestigious nor especially large. The elite programs included the *U.S. News & World Report's* 2004 list of top twenty administration programs. The pool of large programs included the leadership-preparation programs with the largest number of MEd degrees, as reported by the National Center for Education Statistics. A third group of programs was randomly drawn from the remaining universe of institutions.

In the study of syllabi, the bottom line was that scant attention was paid to managing with accountability, using data, or making tough personnel decisions. Crucially, we found that just 2.0 percent of 2,424 weeks of instruction addressed accountability in the context of school management or school improvement, and just 4.5 percent included instruction on managing school improvement via the use of data, technology, or empirical research. Of 350 weeks of instruction devoted to personnel management, just 11 mentioned teacher dismissal and 8 teacher compensation. Just 11 percent of weeks of instruction devoted to personnel management paid any attention at all to the recruitment, selection, and hiring of new teachers.[7]

What about data-driven management? Just 11 percent of 2,424 weeks of instruction mentioned statistics, data, or empirical research. Despite the fact that schools today are asked to operate in a world of public school choice, increased decentralization, and community engagement, just 1 percent of weeks of instruction addressed school public relations or small business skills, and less than 1 percent addressed parental or school board relations. Programs devoted a rather limited amount of time—only about 12 percent of course instruction—to "norms and values." These weeks, while only a small part of all instruction, were overwhelmingly hostile to reforms like test-based accountability and school choice.[8]

In general, traditional management practice and lessons learned in sectors outside of schooling attracted little or no attention. Of the fifty most influential living management thinkers, as determined by a 2003 survey of management professionals and scholars, study of just nine was assigned in the 210 courses. Their work was assigned a total of twenty-nine times out of 1,851 assigned readings.[9]

Finally, there is evidence of skepticism regarding efficiency, testing, pay-for-performance, or competition. For instance, while influential management thinkers rarely surfaced, staunch critics of market-based reform and test-based accountability, like Deborah Meier, Linda Darling-Hammond, and Michael Fullan, were among the most frequently assigned authors. Consequently, superintendents and school boards should not be surprised if new principals enter predisposed to be skeptical of educational choice and/or test-based accountability.

Texts

In the companion study, we looked to see what was actually addressed in the textbooks read by principal candidates. We examined eleven of the thirteen most frequently assigned nonlegal texts to determine the frequency with which they addressed various management concepts like "performance," "evaluation," "culture," "accountability," "efficiency," and "termination." We found that "performance" and/or "achievement" were the most commonly cited terms, appearing forty-four times per one hundred pages. The next most commonly mentioned terms were "evaluation," at thirty-eight times per one hundred pages, and "culture," at twenty-nine. Referred to least frequently among the terms examined were "efficiency," "accountability," and "termination" or "dismissal," all of which were cited fewer than six times per one hundred pages.[10]

Accountability was mentioned only about five times per one hundred pages, and, on the whole, the texts were neutral or slightly critical in their treatment of this crucial concept. About 57 percent of mentions were neutral and 23 percent negative, and about 20 percent were either positive or offered instruction on how to manage with accountability.[11]

Teacher termination and dismissal were referred to only three times per one hundred pages of text. The term "efficiency" appeared six times per one hundred pages and was mentioned in a positive light about 38 percent of the time and neutrally 49 percent of the time. As with accountability, few mentions offered prescriptions for enhancing or pursuing efficiency.[12]

What's the Bottom Line?

In light of our findings, there are four lessons for educational leaders and reformers. First, don't presume that new principals are familiar with important skills like using data, managing with accountability, or recruiting, hiring, evaluating, or terminating personnel. These topics don't receive much attention in the courses or the readings future principals encounter while pursuing graduate studies in educational administration. Yet these are skills that aspiring principals have had little opportunity or need to cultivate while in the classroom. Similarly, it's unlikely they received much concrete mastery working as assistant principals under principals who themselves never had much opportunity to master or embrace these skills. After all, Public Agenda reports that about half of current principals are still fundamentally opposed to the notion that principals be judged based upon measured student performance, and only 16 percent of superintendents deem their principals "excellent" when it comes to making thoughtful recommendations on teacher tenure.[13]

Second, don't assume that new principals have a practical sense of what management practices like accountability and decentralization entail. It's likely that they have had little or no practice constructing balanced scorecards, bottom-lining program costs, devising new performance metrics, or reengineering school operations. Don't even assume that they know where to look when they need guidance or suggestion. Not having read authors or encountered concepts from outside the world of educational administration, they may not know where to start seeking ideas or references.

Third, don't assume that principals have been exposed to management practice in settings outside the schoolhouse. In many other fields, individuals circulate through a variety of organizations on their way to managerial roles. In schooling, of course, future principals start as classroom teachers, complete their administrative credential, and then serve as assistant principals. While this usually ensures that they have exposure to multiple schools (and often to multiple school districts), it also means that they have little or no exposure to organizations other than public schools. Such exposure can introduce them to new ideas, show them how managers in other settings address common challenges, and foster nontraditional thinking.

Finally, don't be surprised if new principals are particularly unenthusiastic about reforms like accountability and school choice, or are unprepared to market their schools, compete for students, or engage in entrepreneurial leadership. For some board and district officials, this state of affairs may not cause much concern. For boards eager to embrace school choice or charter schooling, however, the lack of attention devoted by preparation programs to small business skills may be a real impediment. Similarly, the hostility of these programs to reforms like school choice and test-based accountability suggests that new principals may be unreliable field captains for such initiatives.

What Districts Should Do

What does all of this mean for school boards and district leaders? We think it recommends at least five courses of action.

Expose principals to ideas from outside the schoolhouse. First, given what principals are not learning during their preparation, it is unreasonable to expect them to know how to use accountability data to focus on results, diagnose weaknesses, identify inefficiencies, operate in a choice-based environment, or manage firmly without micromanaging. It is not enough to tell principals, "This is what we expect." Rather, districts should provide principals with workable examples of what high-quality data analysis looks like, what a good marketing plan is, how they can monitor teachers without falling back on intimidation or red tape, and so on. Part of this process is exposing principals to ideas from outside the schoolhouse and to different kinds of organizational environments.

Provide workshops and arrange collaborations. Building on the previous recommendation is the need to provide mentoring and developments that address the ground left uncovered during formal preparation. Workshops can expose principals to management skills and concepts that—while common-place outside education—they may not have encountered on their jobs or in their training. This might entail bringing principals together to read unfa-miliar works, or to study with professors whose expertise is in public- or private-sector management rather than in educational administration. It might entail establishing monthly seminars focused upon nontraditional readings, for which principals receive professional development credit or release time. For instance, principals could benefit immensely from exposure to books like Peter Drucker's *Innovation and Entrepreneurship*, management expert Jim Collins's *Good to Great* or *Built to Last*, Harvard Business School professor Clay Christensen's *The Innovator's Dilemma*, busi-ness writer Michael Lewis's *Moneyball* or *The New New Thing*, or any num-ber of other provocative and accessible studies of management. The point is not to suggest that these books contain some secret formula, or to pro-mote new silver bullets, management orthodoxies, or buzz words, but to expose principals to perspectives that may spark new ways of thinking about their work.

It's also worth pursuing collaborations that offer principals a chance to observe and interact with managerial peers in other organizations. This might mean freeing up administrative time after the end of the school year, but still on the eleven-month calendar, and arranging a two- or three-week program with local firms or public-sector agencies. For some districts, espe-cially those without appropriate local partners, it might be worth exploring more formal arrangements or programs coordinated through business schools or schools of public management. For example, Britain's National College for School Leadership has partnered with a national business group (Business in the Community) to create the Partners in Leadership Program. The program pairs "head teachers," the British equivalent of principals, with senior business leaders across the country, and facilitates interaction between the partners by arranging six sit-down meetings each year and planning regional conferences featuring industry experts and veteran head teachers. Since its launch in 1998, the program has brokered nearly 6,500 education-business partnerships.[14]

Emphasize goals for accountability, evaluation, and decentralization that are straightforward and readily managed. As with anything else, there are managerial schemes of varying complexity and sophistication— and the experts will happily explain why the more nuanced models are typically the best bet. That may be true, in theory. However, so long as districts are working to tackle merit pay, site-based budgeting, or data analysis with unprepared principals, elegant design should probably take a backseat to workability and simplicity, as well as clear expectations and routine assessment of leadership performance.

Create opportunities to exploit the skills of veteran principals. The truth is that our most effective principals today routinely rely upon experience, street smarts, district contacts, and personal charisma to compensate for incomplete preparation and a limited toolbox of management skills. For instance, 45 percent of school principals have told Public Agenda that they "feel like [their] hands are tied by the way things are done in the school system" and that they "must work around the system" to get things done.[15] Too often, entrepreneurial principals who seek to start new programs or gain flexibility are marginalized by central district officials who regard them as malcontents, troublemakers, and iconoclasts. Instead, district leaders need to respect these veterans and find ways to make them more available as mentors and instructors.

Bring nontraditional principals into school systems. Finally, programs to bring nontraditional principals into school systems, like New Leaders for New Schools, should be seen as a mechanism for attracting candidates whose experiences and strengths are in short supply. District officials may be understandably cautious about such candidates. It's vital to recognize, however, that these candidates can bring expertise in leading with data or accountability, leveraging technology, or managing personnel that traditional candidates have not learned in educational administration programs or the classroom. An infusion of such principals who can pioneer new routines and mentor their peers can provide workable examples of entrepreneurial leadership and help transform school management.

Bad management is costly. It fosters faculty resentment and backlash by encouraging small-minded leadership, unnecessary rulemaking, and defensive practices that squeeze creativity and initiative. This all smacks of the pathologies that marked early industrial oversight and early twentieth-century "scientific management," rather than the more flexible model of public accountability developed in recent decades. Poor leadership also threatens to undermine support for the kinds of reform that can transform schools into environments where administrators and teachers are valued, rewarded for their efforts, and given the latitude to make a difference. Challenging schools with accountability and competition is the right thing to do, but schools need leaders equal to that challenge. Policymakers, district leaders, and reformers must accept the responsibility to help secure those leaders—or else their bold demands will ring hollow.

16

The Predictable, but Unpredictably Personal, Politics of Teacher Licensure

The debates over teacher licensure have long reflected a grace, decorum, and rhetorical nuance more appropriate to the final weeks of a partisan political contest than to a substantive policy debate. Perplexingly, given the utterly unexceptional nature of the politics of the issue, the debate has turned into an often venomous dispute focused largely on the intricacies of data interpretation.

The clash between those who would defend licensure and toughen the preparation requirements it entails (the "professionalizers," in their preferred parlance) and those who would downsize much of the accreditation and licensure apparatus ("common-sense reformers," in my preferred argot) has often entailed policy disputes taking on a personal dimension. This may, in part, be due to the reality that there is relatively little reliable information on the value or effects of teacher licensure and preparation. In what is probably the most balanced survey of the research on teacher preparation and licensure, the Education Commission of the States (ECS) found in 2003 that just ninety-two out of more than five hundred studies met the minimal professional standard of basing conclusions on "systematic observation rather than . . . opinion," and that the evidence on seven of eight key questions examined was nonexistent or inconclusive.[1]

My introduction to the personal nature of the discourse came in 2001, when, as an assistant professor of education at the University of Virginia, I wrote a policy brief entitled, *Tear Down This Wall: The Case for a Radical Overhaul of Teacher Certification* for the Progressive Policy Institute. (This is the full version of the abridged piece you read in chapter 13.) The paper was unveiled at a National Press Club event in fall

2001, at which the executive director of the American Association of Colleges of Teacher Education (AACTE) dryly remarked,

> For his own best interest, I urge [Mr. Hess] to consult with his dean about his call to end the exorbitant monetary costs [of teacher preparation] . . . Hopefully, he will have alternatives to present . . . regarding other ways to pay the salaries of assistant professors, absent the student tuition dollars those prospective teacher candidates generate.

He concluded, "Finally, I urge Mr. Hess to withdraw this paper."[2]

On another occasion, in an editorial in the very journal where this essay appeared, the editor described my work, variously, as "replete with melodramatic mixed metaphors," "patronizing," and imbued with "deeply disturbing irony."[3]

Now, I make no claims to being neutral in the debate over teacher licensure or to being a disinterested observer of the attendant politics. Nonetheless, while critical of licensure and the "professionalization" agenda, I have always happily conceded that "teacher education can be beneficial, that education courses can provide valuable training, [and] that there are many effective teacher educators."[4] Ultimately, debates about teacher licensure and preparation should turn not on the merits or motives of particular actors, but on how to construct a system that fosters excellence.

The politics of teacher licensure and "professionalization" are neither complicated nor surprising. Those institutions, organizations, and individuals who have helped construct existing arrangements and licensing systems see their handiwork as sensibly ordered, if imperfect, with improvement requiring primarily the application of higher standards, additional expertise, more fieldwork and partnering with schools, and more resources.[5] On the other hand, those who would strip down much of the existing licensure apparatus—few of whom have any station or influence in the teacher-preparation community—regard such efforts as tinkering that leaves established gatekeepers unchallenged, dissuades talent from entering the field, stifles challenges to the reigning orthodoxy, and inflates the cost of educational provision.[6] These critics would pursue new structural arrangements that allow aspiring educators to bypass traditional preparation institutions, and thus diminish the influence of existing stakeholders. To varying degrees, members of these two camps disagree about the skills and knowledge that aspiring teachers need, how to cultivate good teaching, what effect various licensing provisions have on the quality of applicants, or what the evidence says on these questions. Such conflicts are an unexceptional element of the American firmament—and can be found in disputes about issues ranging from land-use policy and telecommunications to sugar and tobacco subsidies.

Quite naturally, the defenders of credentialing and licensure are largely housed in the teacher-preparation institutions, professional associations, and state agencies that have shaped the existing regime. Meanwhile, the critics of mandatory preparation are largely outside these entities and frustrated by their sense that they lack influence within the status quo. In such conflicts, the established interests typically enjoy enormous advantages over their critics, as they are professionally organized, aided by coordinating institutions, and motivated by a commitment to the arrangements they have helped to construct. Of course, such "establishments" also present something of a sitting target, as their members are called upon to justify existing arrangements while their critics are free to issue critiques without bearing a similar burden. This exposed position has led to sustained skirmishing between the two camps, with outside critics like Chester Finn, Michael Podgursky, and Kate Walsh offering pointed critiques, and the professional teacher-education community dismissing these critics as gadflies or "conservative scholars . . . [who] think that teacher preparation is a waste of time . . . [and who] have not been informed by the latest research."[7]

The impasse is understandable. Teacher educators, preparation institutions, professional associations, and state licensing officials have worked hard, only to see their motives, expertise, and station challenged by those who would have many aspiring teachers bypass longstanding arrangements or skirt established institutions of teacher preparation. Having devoted their careers to teacher preparation, they naturally regard attacks on their handiwork, proposals for radical models of alternative certification, or calls to dismantle the licensure process as hostile and unfounded. As David Berliner has noted, in typically forthright prose, "Because we teacher educators are not the fools we are sometimes portrayed to be, we fight for certain standards in our teacher education programs."[8] Critics view these same efforts by teacher-educators and see—rather than a commitment to quality—defensive ploys to maintain an outdated franchise, stifle dissenting voices, and avoid competition or external accountability. Who is correct? It depends on where one stands.

Formalizing Teacher Preparation

Disputes about how to improve teaching achieved a new national prominence during the passage of No Child Left Behind, as policymakers sought to ensure all children access to "highly qualified" teachers. NCLB marked the most ambitious federal intervention into deciding who is prepared to teach, yet legislators neatly ducked the substantial questions by largely deferring to state officials on how to define "highly qualified" teachers and how to identify them. In the end, this studied ambiguity provided a comfortable refuge for legislators while raising the salience of the longstanding debate.

This ongoing debate is not new. Its roots can be traced back to the early nineteenth century, when locally elected citizen school boards or superintendents issued teaching licenses, and states established "normal" schools to train women teachers. During the course of the late nineteenth and twentieth centuries, these normal schools evolved into teachers' colleges, then state colleges, then regional state universities—all the while remaining the primary site of teacher preparation.

In the late nineteenth and early twentieth centuries, a loose-knit national network of professors, administrators, and state officials sought to standardize existing, erratic arrangements. Between about 1890 and 1940, these "professionalizers" succeeded in formalizing licensure at the state level, while increasingly linking it to the completion of "accredited" preparation programs predominantly staffed by "professionalizers" and sympathetic faculty. By 1937, forty-one states had systems in which all teacher licenses were state-issued, with most requiring teachers to complete approved preparation programs at colleges or universities.[9]

After World War II, the National Education Association (then still a professional association) and allied organizations established the National

Commission on Teacher Education and Professional Standards (TEPS). In 1952, TEPS, along with AACTE and the National Association of State Directors of Education (NASDE), founded the National Council for the Accreditation of Teacher Education (NCATE) to accredit teacher-preparation programs.

Today, these same organizations are the institutional voices of teacher-educators and teacher-training institutions. Their investment in the existing regime of teacher preparation has been predictable and appropriate. After all, in the world of teacher preparation, only these organizations possessed the wherewithal to promote policy, monitor institutions, or fulfill the quasi-official gatekeeping function demanded by statute.

During the 1980s, *A Nation at Risk* fueled concerns about the quality of teacher preparation, giving rise to heated debates about how to attract and retain good teachers. One reasonable response to this challenge was to seek to specify new guidelines that would toughen up the existing licensure and preparation system. Most famously, this was the tack of the reports by the Carnegie Task Force and the Holmes Group, which trumpeted the need for more required training, more funding for teacher preparation and teacher salaries, more integrated subject-matter training, higher standards, and a tiered career ladder.[10] Borne of these efforts was the National Council for Teaching and America's Future (NCTAF), which soon became the self-professed champion of "professionalization."

Aside from considerations of its substantive merit, the "professionalization" agenda proved politically useful for the teacher-preparation community. It provided a common, professionally endorsed, widely acceptable platform for governors, university presidents, and education-school deans that called for channeling more resources to teacher preparation and boosting the field's prestige.

Strikingly, the recommendations did little to assuage critics concerned about the culture of teacher preparation or opposed to having these programs serve as gatekeepers to the profession. In fact, over time, efforts to increase student time in preparation programs and institute new professional requirements actually aggravated the concerns of such critics.

Meanwhile, critics of teacher preparation embraced alternative certification programs pioneered during the 1980s in New Jersey, Texas, and elsewhere, and Teach for America (TFA), launched in 1990. Whatever their merits, these programs meant critics now had concrete proposals to tout and were no longer relegated merely to sniping at traditional arrangements.

Critics of the established regime could now selectively cite these reforms when claiming that traditional licensure was unnecessary, ineffective, or an obstacle to recruiting talented candidates. However, in adopting this course, critics risked signaling that any given alternative they hailed was the new and improved "one best" approach. Finessing that challenge—finding a way to replace prescriptions in place with a flexible model rather than an alternative "answer"—remains a prominent challenge as disputants grapple in the wake of NCLB.

Debating Teacher Licensure

Over time, the institutions, associations, and regulators that helped systematize teacher education and licensure came to constitute a teacher-preparation "establishment." Among the most prominent of these players today are AACTE, NCATE, NASDE, NCTAF, the Association for the Supervision of Curriculum and Development (ASCD), and the Interstate New Teacher Assessment and Support Consortium (INTASC). One can concede the admirable intentions and judgment of these groups and yet recognize that their role in constructing, ordering, and implementing existing arrangements creates an institutional preference for policies that steer candidates into teacher preparation, raise the prestige of teacher-educators, and extend the mandated period of training.

Critics can grant goodwill and nonetheless regard the handiwork of these organizations as problematic, destructive, and in need of radical change. In particular, many critics are concerned that leading voices in teacher preparation—including John Goodlad, Linda Darling-Hammond, Nel Noddings, Marilyn Cochran-Smith, and Gloria Ladson-Billings—have unapologetically argued that teacher education is inescapably about promoting particular moral and social values. As Cochran-Smith, former president of the American Educational Research Association (AERA) and editor of the *Journal of Teacher Education*, has argued, "Education (and teacher education) are social institutions that pose moral, ethical, social, philosophical, and ideological questions. It is wrong headed—and

dangerous—to treat these question as if they were value neutral and ideology free."[11] Ladson-Billings, another AERA president, has said her personal vision of good teaching is promoting an "anti-racist, anti-sexist,
anti-homophobic . . . anti-oppressive social justice pedagogy," despite her
acknowledgment that such teaching will inevitably entail "unpopular and
politically dangerous curriculum and pedagogical decisions."[12]

Obviously, these thinkers and their colleagues have an absolute pre-
rogative to promote norms and values as they see fit. However, it's important to recognize that when standards based upon these values become
requirements that aspiring teachers must master, or when teacher-colleges
embodying these views are empowered to determine who is qualified to
teach, those who disagree with the norms will take issue with existing
requirements. When teacher-educators with strong normative beliefs are
deputized as gatekeepers to the profession, as is the reality of teacher
licensure, the stakes surrounding their convictions grow exponentially.

The norms and values of the dominant voices in teacher preparation,
quite naturally, are embedded in NCATE bylaws, AACTE resolutions, and
ASCD publications. The resulting norms and policies attract criticism
both from those critics of teacher licensure and preparation who are critical of the values privileged within the world of teacher education, and
from institutional critics who recognize the utility of teacher preparation
but question the value of measures that prohibit potentially effective candidates from entering teaching.

These two critiques of teacher licensure—one a cultural critique of
the philosophical orientation of teacher preparation and the other an
argument for paring back its regulatory role—are intellectually distinct,
though they often become intertwined in the course of debate. The
cultural critique questions the intrinsic worth of teacher-preparation programs. The institutional critique asks—regardless of their merits—
whether these programs should be deputized by the state as quasi-official
gatekeepers, as in medicine or engineering, or whether they should play
a less formal role, as in journalism or business management.

Despite the assertion that "deregulators" wish to "dismantl[e] teacher
education institutions,"[13] calls for deregulation and fevered critiques of
education schools are not inextricably linked or even necessarily congru-
ent. It is true that those who criticize the "professional education" culture

have often suggested, or given the impression, that they would like to see education schools abolished.[14] However, the institutional critique merely posits that, given the nature of teaching and the current "science of pedagogy," *mandatory* preparation is an undesirable screen that deters talented candidates and stifles initiative without yielding offsetting benefits. Nowhere in this second school of thought is there the suggestion that teacher-preparation programs should be dismantled or even forced to change. In fact, "common-sense" reformers urge policymakers to give preparation programs more freedom, with the measure of their success the performance of their graduates.[15]

A Vigorous, but Less Personal, Debate

As a political scientist, what I have found most remarkable about the politics of teacher licensure is the vitriol and assumption of ill intention on both sides. Deciding how to regulate the preparation of educators who will teach in schools funded by public revenues and attended by the community's children is clearly grounds for debate that involves both educators and the larger public. We should expect the question to be contentious, as it is fraught with important values and has real consequences for educators, those who prepare teachers, and the general public. However, it should be possible to debate the questions pointedly without resorting to personal invective, attacks on one another's motives, or recitations of research that make little effort to separate good scholarship from bad. A worthy debate would embrace logical argument, be open to lessons learned outside of K–12 schooling, and pay careful attention to the quality of research used to buttress competing claims. Open debate about both ends and means is part and parcel of making public policy in a democratic regime.

It is no surprise that those associated with teacher preparation regard what they are doing as constructive and believe those currently in the sector are the best equipped to improve it. Similarly, it is unsurprising that those outside the sector, uncertain of the competence of the current gatekeepers, or more skeptical of professional expertise and good intentions, would seek to reduce the influence of the traditional preparers and programs. There are no conspiracies here.

These disparate points of view are the normal, healthy result of the different experiences, worldviews, and incentives of the disputants. The splits are not going to go away, cannot be "worked out," and cannot be cogitated into some kind of "consensus." However, the fact that disagreement is predictable and healthy does not mean that the manner in which we have conducted the debate has been either.

What is not typical or predictable is the bitterness and hyperbole that characterize the debate. Unhelpful and often offensive are the charges leveled by some self-styled defenders of teachers and the education community that those critical of teacher licensure are part of an alliance of "marketeers"[16] who seek to turn children and schools "into sources of profit"[17] and hope to make teachers "dependent on the test-prep materials . . . [provided via] contracts with McGraw-Hill et al."[18]

At the same time, there is an unfortunate tradition of personal, inappropriate, and often abusive criticism aimed at teacher-educators and colleges of education. Such critics have charged that "there is a built-in institutional vapidity in ed schools"[19] and fume that "faculties at ordinary ed schools . . . merely pretend to be learned . . . they do not look for, and do not achieve insight into their fatal flaws—arrogance, overweening pride, hypocrisy, [and] ineptitude."[20]

In responding to such malicious onslaughts, however, the teacher-preparation community does itself no favors by pretending that sharp critiques are necessarily malicious or illegitimate. Critics should not be deemed out of line for arguing that preparation programs may be undemanding, ideologically biased, or less than rigorous in screening candidates. If we are to have an honest and constructive debate, those wary of licensure or preparation programs must be able to question both institutional arrangements and the culture of teacher preparation without being vilified or excommunicated from the education fraternity. When even reasonable critiques are attacked as inappropriate, critics lose the incentive to self-police, and it becomes difficult for the media, policymakers, or participants to distinguish hysterical critiques from serious ones. However, it is equally incumbent on the critics of licensure that they pose their critiques in a manner that lends itself to reasoned debate, and not as invective-laden caricatures.

I am not suggesting that critics should bite their tongues when they see fit to criticize teacher preparation, teacher-educators, education schools, or arrangements that permit the teacher-education "establishment" to determine who may teach or what skills and habits of thought aspiring teachers must possess. Nor am I suggesting that "professionalizers" are obliged to use milquetoast language in justifying their efforts, touting their preferred reforms, or responding to their critics. Frankly, I am not known for having qualms about strong rhetoric. However, there is a vital distinction between blunt language and ad hominem attack.

Even if one disagrees with the views or practices of many teacher-educators, little is gained by vitriolic attacks on beliefs or intentions. We can disagree on desirable policy and practice without imputing evil motives to our opponents.

It is not merely that the heated epithets are aesthetically unpleasing. No, the larger point is that this kind of vitriol tends to be self-perpetuating. It shuts the door on fruitful debate and understanding and is absorbed by the rising generation of advocates, thinkers, and practitioners. In place of thoughtful disagreements that can be parsed, we create guarded camps that jeer at one another across the divide and make it difficult for reflective members of one camp to engage with the other. In the end, this is neither democratic policy discourse nor even a thinking community—it is tribal politics. And that's not good for any of us.

Perhaps, in this new century, we can make it a point to try to elevate the level of our debate. Does it matter? I think it does. Even those who recognize the might of institutions and incentives, like me, know that rhetoric and norms influence ideas and policy. We have had our era of reckless language and thoughtless insult—let us see if we can't go forward in a discourse marked by sharp disagreements but conducted in a fashion more fitting to the task at hand.

PART V

The Road Ahead

Introduction

The education horizon appears to be brightening, though the track record of school reform may lead the jaded observer to wonder whether this is truly cause for hope or simply one more pleasing mirage. Buffeted by new demands for accountability, higher quality research, and reforms that treat accountability and incentives as more than buzzwords, educators are facing unprecedented pressure to overhaul the way they do business. It is even possible that after decades of tinkering, buck-passing, and tomfoolery, we will make some hard choices and get serious about reform. In a short piece that draws some lessons from a book I edited on the seven-year effort to reform the San Diego City Schools, I offer some thoughts about one of the more famous urban reform efforts in recent years. The piece, "Lessons from San Diego," was first published in *The Education Gadfly* and took a look at some of the challenges and bottom-line lessons illustrated by one of the nation's most ambitious efforts at twenty-first century school reform. The San Diego experience highlighted just how thoroughly existing statutes, contracts, and infrastructure hamper even the most aggressive reform efforts.

The passage of No Child Left Behind and the creation of the Institute of Education Sciences (IES) hold great promise, hinting at a degree of seriousness about accountability and education research that would have been unimaginable just fifteen years ago. NCLB and IES are potentially revolutionary in their willingness to consider the role that tough love should play in school reform. Nonetheless, they are themselves the products of old habits, including a fondness for grand hopes and a desire for the comfort of easy answers. It is true that these concerns are being raised by a new cast of characters with new aims, but many of the same entrenched habits of mind remain.

The creation of IES and the push for rigorous new standards for education research raise worrisome issues of federal overreaching. In "Science and Nonscience," first published in *The Education Gadfly*, I question the excessive faith that too many would-be reformers have placed in particular "scientific" conceptions of education research. While I voice some concerns in the *Gadfly* piece, I want it to be clear that I regard IES as a laudable and vital attempt to grapple with the application of science, research, and expertise to education. In that sense, IES embodies the recognition that great leaps in efficiency and productivity have always been a product of advances in knowledge and technology. Mastering those changes and using them to free up human ability have led to breakthroughs in medicine, manufacturing, military science, and every other sector. The trouble is that adopting new technology is disruptive and frightening, and it produces concentrated costs for those who must adapt and those who are displaced. For this reason, Americans have never been comfortable using technology to reinvent schooling. My ongoing curiosity as to why technology has not transformed schooling the way it has work routines in so many other sectors led me to tackle the question in an essay for *Education Next*.

The funny thing about the piece, "Technical Difficulties," is that I had not intended to write it. I am an editor of *Education Next*, and we had been hoping to arrange a point-counterpoint on the use of technology to reinvent schooling. The problem was that most mainstream experts in education technology were hesitant to pen the kind of tough-minded piece we wanted. Meanwhile, the "free thinkers" we approached resisted talking about unpleasant subjects like efficiency or eliminating jobs. We solicited two pieces from "revolutionary" thinkers, but neither even deigned to mention issues like productivity or cost-effectiveness. In the end, I wrote the piece. You can judge the wisdom of that decision for yourself.

Ultimately, the lessons of San Diego, IES, and technology suggest that even the more promising pillars of the new educational world are more than a little shaky. The most significant and most fascinating example is probably the landmark No Child Left Behind Act, which is pocked by questionable design decisions that pose real challenges to its long-term viability. In "On Leaving No Child Behind," which first appeared in *The*

Public Interest, my colleague Chester Finn and I take a hard look at the politics, design, and implementation of this ambitious legislation.

With this essay we have come full circle in this volume, leaving off where we began. More than anything, the selections have reminded me just how tightly bound are questions of politics, policy, markets, research, and science, and the need for "tough love" reformers to act accordingly.

Will a new generation of reformers prove itself able to surmount these habits of mind, harness the potential of technology, and cull the critical if unpleasant lessons from hard-won experience? Whether this final set of essays depicts the dawn of a new day of school reform or one more false dawn is something that we, together, will decide in the years ahead.

17

Lessons from San Diego

In 1998, San Diego City Schools launched one of the nation's most ambitious efforts at urban school reform. Superintendent Alan Bersin, former U.S. district attorney for Southern California and President Clinton's "border czar," sought to reinvent the teaching and organization of the nation's eighth-largest school district. At the end of the 2004–5 academic year, after a stormy seven years, Bersin departed SDCS to become secretary of education for the state of California. He departed as one of the longest-serving and most battle-scarred of the nation's big-city superintendents.

When he was first hired, Bersin named Tony Alvarado, former superintendent of District #2 in New York City, to serve as head of San Diego's instructional and curricular program. Bersin and Alvarado moved aggressively to promote a strategy of coherent, uniform instruction drawn from Alvarado's work in New York City. That agenda sparked sharp conflict with the San Diego Education Association, reflected in a persistent three-to-two split on the school board.

Bersin's administration enjoyed some visible successes. During his reign, the percentage of San Diego elementary schools scoring at the top rung of the California Academic Performance Index increased by more than a third, the number of schools in the bottom category fell by more than 90 percent, and the racial achievement gap narrowed.[1] More disappointing, however, middle school and high school achievement stubbornly failed to improve, and some observers questioned the rigor of the district's curriculum, Alvarado's approach to teaching, and Bersin's handling of the union.[2]

What have we learned from Bersin's highly visible and often contentious tenure? Drawing on the research presented in my book *Urban School Reform: Lessons from San Diego*, it seems to me that at least five key lessons emerge for would-be reformers.

First, the centralized, "managed instruction" model of improvement depends critically on the presence of a personnel and managerial infrastructure and on high-quality curricula. Alvarado gave unstinting attention to his centerpiece "Institute for Learning" training program for principals and faculty, and to building a corps of "peer coaches" to assist teachers.[3] But his single-minded focus on these activities resulted in a lack of attention to infrastructure and curricula. As a result, the coaches, the institute, and attempts to assign faculty where they were needed most ran afoul of the collective bargaining agreement's provisions on professional development, staffing, and teacher transfers. A balky human resources operation reliant on outdated technology inhibited district efforts to speed up hiring or promote more flexible staffing.

As for curriculum, by 2004, despite seven years of diligent work developing a carefully calibrated professional development model for literacy, the district still had not promulgated a coherent curriculum for reading and English. Consequently, while teachers were using the prescribed methods, there was too little attention to the quality of content. Some critics believe that the absence of a rigorous, clear curriculum helps to explain the district's apparent successes in elementary reading and accompanying failure to produce similar results in the more content-centered middle school and high school grades.[4]

Second, Bersin strengthened his hand in pursuing reform by embracing statewide accountability (and later NCLB) metrics. He welcomed the "imposition" of the California Academic Performance Index, using it to identify troubled schools and target professional development and resources. However, Bersin's reforms on this front never reached their full potential. Moves to transfer or remove staff were stifled by work rules,[5] while a 2002 fiscal crisis sapped funding intended for low-performing schools. The San Diego effort on this front was less a "success" than an example of what it would take to develop a focused strategy for improving chronically troubled schools.

Third, San Diego showed how dramatic efforts to improve high schools might conflict with other popular reform strategies. In 2004, when the district adopted a high school reform model that featured a "portfolio" of smaller, more personal schools, it created tensions with the district's six-year-old emphasis on centralized, managed instruction.[6]

Allowing faculty to modify curricula to fit the mission of "specialized" high schools, giving them a voice in curricular choices, and the resulting inability to standardize content meant that mentor-coaches encountered math, English, or science teachers in a dozen small schools who might teach a dozen different curricula in a dozen ways. Coaches could mentor all of these teachers on pedagogical technique yet encounter great difficulty applying uniform, consistent guidance on instruction or content.

Fourth, relentless political leadership is part and parcel of being an effective district leader. Some thoughtful observers have asked if Bersin's style was unduly confrontational. What such critiques tend to downplay is that an effort to reimagine radically the way a district does business is bound to spark conflict. One could argue that Bersin would have been more apt to forge a cooperative relationship with the local teachers' union had he proceeded more slowly. But even in his unusually extended seven-year term, Bersin didn't accomplish all he had hoped. Moreover, his approach threw a spotlight on board votes and helped him hold together his three-two bloc for nearly seven years.[7] So, we should be skeptical of suggestions that he could have fared much better merely by being kinder and gentler.

Finally, perhaps the most important lesson from San Diego is how limited the prospects are for radical improvement in urban public education in the absence of structural change to personnel systems, technology, accountability, leadership, and compensation. For all their sweat and struggle, Bersin & Co. found their efforts to build the workforce they wanted stymied by statute and contract language. An outdated information system meant the district had to try to build on the fly the tools it needed to enable serious improvements to school accountability, human resource management, and budgeting.[8]

Bersin began his tenure with multiple advantages, including dazzling local and national contacts, personal charisma, a facile mind, polished negotiating skills, impeccable public service credentials, and a deft fundraising touch. If the legacy of his seven-year run is in doubt, the San Diego experience illustrates, above all, that even the boldest attempts to overhaul urban schooling are today undermined by the same institutional and organizational failings that they are intended to address.

18

Science and Nonscience:
The Limits of Scientific Research

American education research has turned a corner. The 2002 creation of the Institute of Education Sciences (IES), the ascendance of accountability, and the demand of the No Child Left Behind Act for "scientifically based research" have radically altered an education research culture that just a few years ago bridled at the "medical model" and too often championed ethnographies, action research, "critical narrative," "discourse analysis," and other approaches that provided parents, practitioners, or policymakers with little useful information.

Together, both NCLB and IES represent a demand that rigorous scientific principles be used to assess programs. This development did not "happen," and it was not an inevitable evolution embraced by the education research community. Rather, it was the consequence of prodigious efforts by proponents like Congressman Michael Castle, reading expert Reid Lyon, and IES head Russ Whitehurst.[1] For their efforts, they have met with fierce resistance from some quarters of the education research community, as well as professional discourtesy, bizarre conspiracy theories, and ad hominem attacks.[2]

The notion that education ought to hold science in the same high regard as medicine and engineering would seem axiomatic. In principle, IES's mission to transform education "into an evidence-based field in which decision makers routinely seek out the best available research and data before adopting programs or practices" is entirely to the good.[3] The changes have focused researchers on questions of validity, reliability, and duplicability, while raising the bar for the investment of federal funds.

Amid this good news, however, lurks the risk that the pendulum will swing too far, that the lure of "scientifically based research" will cause certain methods of study—especially randomized field trials—to be demanded even when ill-suited for the issue at hand.

I am—emphatically—not issuing a plea for "mixed methods," nor expressing concern about the practice of science. Rather, I am raising a more concrete and practical concern: that we risk stifling sensible and promising structural reforms in schooling. This risk is posed when we start to imagine that reforms to personnel, management, or financial systems need to be subjected to these scientific standards. In such cases, a premature or unyielding application of the tenets of "scientific research" could insulate ineffective and dysfunctional arrangements from needed and attainable reform.

How does this danger arise? In large part, it occurs from an imperfect understanding of how the "medical research model" works in medicine, and how and when to import it into education. It's vital to recognize that there are really two kinds of "reforms" in medicine or education—and that the proper role of science and scientifically based research is very different from one to the other. One kind of reform relates to specialized knowledge of how the mind or body works; the other relates to the manner in which we design and operate organizations, governments, and social institutions.

In education, the former category deals with the science of learning and with behaviors and programs that induce it. Such measures include pedagogical and curricular practices, and interventions that relate to the development, knowledge, skills, and mastery of individual students. Relevant approaches would include methods of literacy instruction, bilingual education, sequencing mathematical subjects, and so on. Each of these entails the application of discrete treatments to identifiable subjects under specified conditions in order to achieve specific ends. Such interventions are readily susceptible to field trials, and findings on effectiveness can reasonably be extrapolated to other populations. It is desirable and appropriate that such reforms be subjected to rigorous empirical evaluation (and, whenever possible, to randomized field trials) and that educators be encouraged, even pressed, to use demonstrably superior approaches—and to eschew those lacking such evidence.

The second category of reform entails governance, management, or policy innovations intended to improve organizational effectiveness. It includes such innovations as permitting mayors to appoint school boards, permitting schools to operate free of some regulations, paying employees based on performance, and so on. None of these changes is unique to education. They draw upon a mass of experience gained in other sectors—and their effects are consistent enough and understood well enough across a broad swath of human experience that it's neither useful nor appropriate to use the scientific method to determine whether, for example, initiatives to reward excellence, increase managerial flexibility, or ensure accountability may hold promise in schooling.[4]

Such interventions are rarely precise, do not take place in controlled circumstances, and generally are administered to classes of people rather than discrete clients. Since the results of these structural reforms will be contingent on the context and manner in which they are implemented, even well-designed studies will find it problematic to draw lessons from isolated experiments that trump our broader body of knowledge regarding the use of incentives or markets. Of course, we should welcome inquiry and take new findings into account when reflecting on policy or program design. However, it's vital to remember that a lot is already known about these questions. Whatever the results of small-scale experiments with merit pay or educational competition, this accumulated knowledge ought to weigh more heavily than the findings of one or another context-specific study.

Reforms that address pedagogy, curricula, or teaching practices are fundamentally different from those that seek to change the incentives under which educators operate, how much flexibility they have, or how they are hired, managed, or held accountable—and they should be treated as such. For instance, in medicine, while we deem it appropriate for the Food and Drug Administration (FDA) to monitor and approve drug therapies and treatments, we don't require FDA approval before we permit doctors, hospitals, or health-care firms to change their management practices, compensation strategies, accountability metrics, or work routines.

In truth, charter schooling, accountability systems, school vouchers, alternative certification, and merit pay are not really "educational" innovations in any meaningful sense. They don't rest on conceptions of teaching or learning processes or practices in the way that decisions about literacy or math programs do. They are the results of decisions about how to arrange and deliver services, similar to those made in social welfare, library management, higher education, or private enterprise. Such decisions draw upon our experience across a wide range of human endeavors and organizations. They apply practical wisdom and experience about human behavior from a wealth of sectors. We should welcome research on the effects and efficacy of such reforms and use them in debating and crafting policy. But we also need to understand the limits of science.

The notion that rewarding performance ought to be subject to scientific validation before adoption is akin to suggesting that the National Institutes of Health should determine permissible compensation systems for doctors. If we applied that logic elsewhere in state government, presuming that states should only embark upon reforms whose merits have been "scientifically" validated, we may well never have automated revenue departments, streamlined departments of motor vehicles, or adopted measures to control urban sprawl.

As we seek to build a scientific knowledge base in education, after a century of dawdling, we should be careful not to swing the pendulum so far that we come to regret it. While the elevation of "education science" is laudable, it's important to keep it in perspective. The push for scientific inquiry should not undermine sensible efforts to promote flexibility, competition, efficiency, and accountability. Those who want school reform to track both science and common sense must take care that proper respect for science is accompanied by a similar respect for the limits of science.

19

Technical Difficulties

In 2000, at the height of the technology boom, Maine governor Angus King made a splash by proposing to give laptop computers to all of the state's seventh graders. His stated purpose was to "do something different from what everybody else is doing."[1] Missing from the $50 million proposal, however, was any rationale related to school performance. Seemingly, little thought had been put into how this major investment in new technology would make schools more efficient, produce future savings, or enhance the learning process.

King's proposal was typical of the way in which technologies like the personal computer and the Internet have been used in public education. The tendency has been to sprinkle computers and Internet connections across classrooms in the pleasant hope that teachers will integrate them into their lessons. The purpose is seldom to make teachers more productive or rethink the way in which lessons are delivered.[2] Indeed, PCs often serve as little more than high-priced typewriters, sitting unused in the backs of classrooms for most of the school day.

This state of affairs stands in sharp contrast to how technology is used by business and government enterprises that engage in competition with other manufacturers and service providers. To them, technology is not an end in itself, something to be adopted merely because it exists, but instead a tool for self-improvement. A competitive enterprise adopts new technologies when these enable workers to tackle new problems or to do the same thing as before, but in a cheaper and more efficient fashion. For example, technology investments enabled the U.S. Postal Service, under heavy competitive pressure from United Parcel Service and Federal Express, to trim its workforce by thirty-nine thousand employees between 2001 and 2003. The cuts were made possible not by reducing service, but by substituting technology in areas where people were performing either routine tasks or roles that automated machines could handle more efficiently.

At a broader level, in recent years the nation's one hundred largest companies improved productivity so rapidly that in 2003 it took only nine workers to do what ten workers had done in 2001.[3] And while economists have long recognized that the potential for growth in productivity is more limited in service sector industries, like education, than in manufacturing or retail, even the service sector has witnessed productivity gains of about 1 percent a year during the past three decades.

Public schools, by contrast, have steadily *added* to the ranks of teachers and reduced class sizes, even as they have made ever-larger investments in new technologies. Spending on technology in public schools increased from essentially zero in 1970 to $103.46 per student in 2004, according to *Education Week*.[4] In 1998, there were 12.1 students for every computer connected to the Internet; in only three years, the ratio had dropped by more than half, to 5.4 students per computer, according to the Department of Education.[5] In the past five years alone, the nation spent more than $20 billion linking schools and classrooms to the Internet through the federal E-rate program, with little to show for it in the way of instructional changes or improved outcomes.[6] Between 1997 and 2004, the federal government appropriated more than $4 billion to the states for the purchase of educational technology. Meanwhile, despite these huge new investments in technology, a massive increase in the teacher workforce drove the student-teacher ratio from twenty-two to sixteen students per teacher between 1970 and 2001.[7]

Cultural Bias

Why have public schools so far failed to put all this fancy new technology to good use? One clear reason is that they face no pressure to do so. Organizations like the postal service make effective use of technology because they must keep up with FedEx, UPS, and other delivery services. Competitive enterprises are constantly searching for ways to boost their productivity, hold down their costs, and develop innovative products—because they know that their competitors are always on the lookout for similar advantages. No executive wants to adopt a painful course like downsizing the workforce or imposing wrenching change. They take these steps only when compelled.

Public schools, however, are insulated from the pressures of competition. They thus have no reason to regard technology as a tool to trim their workforce or to rethink the ways in which they deliver education. This problem is compounded by the fact that collective-bargaining agreements between school districts and employees' unions have made using technology to displace workers or reinvent processes extraordinarily difficult.

There is also a bias within the culture of education against ideas that seem too "businesslike." Indeed, the very words "efficiency" and "cost-effectiveness" can set the teeth of parents and educators on edge. Proposals to use technology to downsize the workforce, alter instructional delivery, or improve managerial efficiency are inevitably attacked by education authorities as part of an effort to, in the words of Henry Giroux, "Transform public education . . . [in order] to expand the profits of investors, educate students as consumers, and train young people for the low-paying jobs of the new global marketplace."[8] The notion that the responsible use of public money is the work of some shadowy global conspiracy evinces a fundamental lack of seriousness about educating children.

Traditionalists insist that it is impossible to educate children more efficiently, as there is no way technology can be substituted for anything that educators do. They frequently compare teaching to the arts: Where the act of creation itself is the end product, it can be difficult or impossible to use technology to improve performance. As the late Daniel Patrick Moynihan, legendary U.S. senator, was fond of saying, producing a Mozart quartet two centuries ago required four musicians, four stringed instruments, and, say, thirty-five minutes. Producing the same Mozart quartet today requires the same resources. Despite breathtaking technological advances, productivity has not changed.`

In the case of schooling, however, this analogy is incomplete and ultimately misleading. In the arts, what has changed over two centuries is that through radio, MP3 players, television, and digital media, the number of people able to *hear and appreciate* a given performance has increased dramatically, at an ever-decreasing cost. Improved technology has now made available to the general public what was once the preserve of the elite.

The spread of the Internet and other technological advances has created similar opportunities in education. For instance, during the 2002–3 school year, the Florida Virtual School, a public entity that provides instruction to schools and districts throughout the state, enrolled more than 6,800 students in its seventy-five course offerings. The school provides web-based classes, instruction, and assessments to students in a variety of academic subjects and electives. Like virtual schools operating in fifteen other states, Florida Virtual allows faculty to provide courses to a scattered student population. Programs like Florida Virtual may make it possible to provide some academic instruction more cheaply and more effectively, freeing up resources for other needs.[9]

At the university level, nearly two million students took at least one course online in the fall of 2003. In a national survey of college administrators of nearly one thousand public and private institutions conducted by the Sloan Consortium, 57 percent of the administrators reported that Internet-based courses were already at least equivalent to traditional courses in quality. And a third of those same administrators thought that the web-based courses would be superior to in-class instruction within three years.[10] Such improvements are to be expected among the many colleges and universities now competing for students' distance-learning dollars. However, efforts to use the Internet in an effective manner are few and far between among K–12 public schools.

Technology and Data Management

Used wisely, information technology has the capacity to help schools become dramatically more effective. Data systems that track information on individual students permit teachers to quickly check the performance of individual students on specific tasks. Information technology can also give school-site personnel unprecedented control over budgets and hiring and can increase their flexibility regarding resource allocation. The Learning First Alliance, a consortium that includes the National Education Association and the American Federation of Teachers, has highlighted how this has worked in districts like Long Beach and Chula Vista, California, and Aldine, Texas.[11]

Outside of schooling, a compelling illustration of how accountability and technology can together improve public services comes from the remarkable success that New York City and other cities enjoyed using new tools to combat crime in the 1990s. The New York City Police Department introduced a system called CompStat, short for "comparative statistics," which compiled data from police reports, crime complaints, arrests, and crime patterns. Over time, the system was broadened to include 734 categories of concern, measuring even the incidence of loud parties and of police overtime.[12]

In the first five years after the 1993 introduction of CompStat, the number of homicides in New York City fell from 1,946 to 629—a rate of decrease three times that of the nation as a whole. Similar results were experienced in other cities that implemented the system, from Philadelphia to Los Angeles.[13] Why did the system work? It helped to hold officers accountable, to pinpoint areas of concern, and to provide the information that could help all police focus on using their skills. In New York City, precincts were required to update their crime statistics on a weekly or daily basis, rather than on the monthly or quarterly basis that had traditionally been the norm. New software allowed department officials to precisely map clusters of crimes, correlating them with drug sale sites, areas of gang activity, schools, public housing, and other relevant locations, and to share the information department-wide within seconds.

In K–12 education, by contrast, most districts and schools have managed information the way stores managed inventory in the 1960s. Almost unbelievably in this day and age, the typical district spends forty or more minutes a year per student collecting, processing, and reporting the data required by the U.S. Department of Education under the No Child Left Behind Act.[14] That equates to more than six thousand hours of employee time in a district with ten thousand students. The tremendous delays in processing data and the staff time consumed are the consequence of districts' having personnel fill out written forms and retype data from one software package to another. Simply equipping districts to report data electronically and acquire data from existing databases is a daunting challenge.

When principals or teachers are asked for this information, those that have it available almost inevitably turn to large binders rather than more nimble electronic interfaces. Asked if he could pull some data on teacher absenteeism or staff training costs, one veteran principal in a well-regarded district spluttered, "Do you know what I do if I want substitute teacher data? I have [my secretary] go through the files and tally it up. She keeps a running total on a piece of graph paper for me. . . . If I want to check on a supply order, I call the deputy [superintendent] for services because we're old friends, and I know he'll actually have someone pull it for me."[15]

Modern information technology offers a wealth of straightforward, time-tested ways to make the necessary data widely and instantly available. There is an array of systems, produced by firms like Scantron and IntelliTools, that allow teachers to call up simple graphs detailing the performance of individual students at the push of a button. However, using these systems requires the consistent collection of information on student learning. Assigning paper-based quizzes ensures that almost all of the information on student mastery will be lost, while the software produced by a dozen or more firms is able to quickly read the results from electronically administered tests into an evolving portfolio of data that tracks student learning.

Ultimately, to be useful, this information has to be at people's fingertips. This is an eminently solvable technical challenge. Huge, complicated organizations, from Wal-Mart to the Internal Revenue Service, routinely track productivity figures, costs, and evaluative measures.

Rethinking Teachers' Work

How else can technology support innovation and reinvention in education? Consider that, historically, teachers have been expected to take on a wide range of responsibilities. Each is expected to design lesson plans, lecture, run class discussions, grade essays and exams, mentor colleagues, supervise homeroom, and patrol the cafeteria. Every year our high schools have tens of thousands of teachers giving variations of the same lectures on the Civil War, the digestive system, and the properties of quadratic equations. In fact, the job description of a teacher today is pretty similar to that of a teacher in 1950.

In medicine, by contrast, progress has been marked by specialization. Doctors with different types of training have taken on more precisely defined roles, while less expensive professionals like registered nurses and physical therapists are now performing tasks that don't require a doctor's training. Similarly, sixteen-year-old volunteers using handheld scanners are able to track medical supplies and hospital inventory with a precision that would have been unimaginable in even the best-managed enterprise just two decades ago.

Imagine a hospital with no nurses or physicians' assistants or physical therapists, where doctors performed every task. A slew of additional doctors would be required, each with less time to devote to any particular specialty, and costs would skyrocket.

How can technology enable teachers to specialize in the same manner as, say, doctors, and use their time more productively? Let's consider one classroom example. Teachers know it is useful to have students write on a regular basis. When I taught high school social studies, like so many of my colleagues, I required students to write at least three pages a week commenting on class readings and discussions.

The problem was that, at a minimum, this meant my 150 students would turn in 450 pages a week of writing. A teacher who reads, marks, and comments on each student's weekly work in just five minutes will spend more than twelve hours a week simply providing feedback on such writing assignments. Most of this time isn't spent providing particularly cerebral feedback, but instead flagging obvious grammatical and structural problems and reminding students to write in complete sentences. Meanwhile, teachers also need to prepare for teaching, assess other assignments, assist and advise students, and lead personal lives. The result is often that teachers provide limited feedback, read student work sporadically, or (most commonly) assign less writing than might be ideal.

Once, such compromises were unavoidable. That is no longer the case. Today, for instance, there is essay-grading software, commercially available from companies like Vantage Learning or the Educational Testing Service, which can quickly and efficiently analyze pieces of writing on dimensions such as sentence construction, language, and mechanics. Several of these programs match the scores given by expert human raters more than 90 percent of the time, which is actually *higher* in some cases than the rate of agreement among multiple human readers. How can this be? In most cases, we're not talking about evaluating Proustian prose; we're talking about helping the typical fourth grader learn to write clearly and effectively. Most of the mistakes that students make and most of the feedback they need are pretty predictable.

Clearly, technological tools cannot imitate the full range of skills a teacher brings to reading a student's essay. Technology cannot gauge a student's growth, analytic prowess, possible interests, or unexpected developments. However, assessment software can replicate the routine elements of evaluation, providing more complete feedback on the essentials while freeing up teachers to make fuller use of their expertise. The result is that teachers spend less time on trivia while adding more value. Rather than requiring hundreds of thousands of teachers to spend hundreds of hours a year circling dangling participles or errant commas, the sensible substitution of technology can help ensure high-quality feedback while allowing teachers more time for preparation, instruction, and tutoring.

Human ingenuity is the most expensive commodity in the developed world. People are costly to employ; no well-run organization hires multitudes of bodies when it is possible to hire more selectively and use employees more thoughtfully. This is why efforts to reduce class size are a static, unimaginative, and inefficient way to improve schooling. These efforts presume that teachers need to perform all the duties and tasks now in place; helping them accomplish these tasks more effectively thus requires shrinking the number of students they must teach. However, if the teacher's role were retooled so that scarce resources like time and expertise were used more carefully, teachers could spend more time on the areas where they add value even while working with larger classes of students. If grading essays or examining student performance on weekly quizzes took only half as much time as it currently does, a teacher could work with more students and still have more instructional time for each student in that class.

A Tool, Not a Miracle Cure

The nation continues blithely to operate schools in a fashion that was dated in the 1970s and that today would be deemed irresponsible in a toothpaste factory. Rather than demand that education dollars be invested with particular care, we pour money into technology with little thought to how these tools might be used most sensibly.

The ability to share instantly full information on student perform-ance, school performance, and costs across vast distances permits a focus on results that was simply not feasible until the most recent decade. The technology that makes the easy sharing of information possible is the engine that makes tough-minded accountability, school choice, and visionary leadership a possibility.

Using new technological tools to relieve educators of routine func-tions will help them focus on those roles that add substantial value—enhancing their contribution, making the organization more productive, and thereby increasing both the benefit to the customer and the resources available to reward employees. Reducing rote demands allows people to focus on what they do best and reduces the number of talented workers who need to be hired—which, in turn, allows us to pay employees more.

Ultimately, if leaders lack the tools to increase efficiency, streamline their workforce, or sensibly reallocate resources, they won't. Technology is not a miracle cure. It is a tool. Used wisely, it can help professionals take full advantage of their skills, slash the time spent on rote tasks, and con-centrate resources and effort where they are needed most.

20

On Leaving No Child Behind

with Chester E. Finn Jr.

Passed by Congress in 2001 and signed into law by President George W. Bush one fast year after his inauguration, the No Child Left Behind Act (NCLB) is the most ambitious federal education statute in decades and the administration's signature domestic accomplishment. Whether it will fulfill its grand promise remains very much an open question.

NCLB's sprawling, 1,100-plus pages radically overhaul the federal role in education, rewrite the rules, reassign power, and dramatically increase Washington's role in K–12 schooling, while striving to boost overall pupil achievement, narrow a host of "learning gaps," and assure every student a "highly qualified teacher."[1] The legislation's engine, though, is its historic attempt to impose a results-based accountability regime on public schools across the land.

Given near-universal support for NCLB's commitment to educating all American children and general agreement that schools can and must do better, even the law's harshest critics feel compelled to "support its objectives" before citing concerns about its mechanisms, timetables, regulations, or funding.

Less than three years into implementation of a statute that sets a twelve-year schedule for boosting student achievement to universal "proficiency" (in math and reading, mainly in grades three to eight), it is premature to judge NCLB's efficacy or predict its ultimate fate. After all, it took more than a decade for the machinery of its legislative ancestor, the notably less ambitious Elementary and Secondary Education Act of 1965, to function approximately as Lyndon Johnson and Congress intended. But NCLB has already stirred a furious national debate, its fragile bipartisan consensus is in peril, and it's not too soon to venture preliminary assessments of the workability of some of its key provisions and to suggest needed repairs.

Operationalizing any statute as complex as NCLB brings inevitable headaches. Different agencies and levels of government must learn to work in new ways, officials must take on unfamiliar roles, and educators must alter ingrained routines. As these arrangements are negotiated, a certain amount of confusion is to be expected. Such problems are normal, usually diminish with time and experience, and are mainly of interest to students of government processes. However, some laws also summon more fundamental woes by incorporating perverse incentives, incompatible interests, or unworkable expectations. These do not go away with aspirin and a night's rest. They may, in fact, require surgery. NCLB is afflicted with several such maladies, and there's considerable risk that the public discontent and professional animosity they are engendering will undermine the legislation's many meritorious features.

To grasp why NCLB inspires both accolades and catcalls, not infrequently from the same observers, one should begin by noting that this legislation is both evolutionary *and* revolutionary.

The DNA of NCLB

During the 2000 campaign, both presidential candidates promised aggressive action on education. Texas governor George W. Bush promoted as a national model his state's strong and relatively successful standards-based accountability program, leavened with "charter" schools and other elements of school choice. Vice President Al Gore sounded remarkably similar when he said things like: "Every state and every school district should be required to identify failing schools, and work to turn them around—with strict accountability for results, and strong incentives for success. And if these failing schools don't improve quickly, they should be shut down fairly and fast, and when needed, reopened under a new principal."[2] As we discussed earlier in "Seeking the Mantle of 'Opportunity,'" Gore also favored limited forms of school choice—as had Bill Clinton.

The similarity of the Democratic and Republican positions resulted from both teams' acceptance of the same analysis of what ailed American K–12 education—and how to cure it. This diagnosis hearkens back to 1983's celebrated *A Nation at Risk* report and the Washington-driven remedies urged in its aftermath by George H. W. Bush and Bill Clinton. The former called his plan "America 2000," while the latter termed his "Goals 2000," but few outside the Beltway could spot major differences. Both started with the belief that U.S. schoolchildren were not learning enough, especially when it came to the "three R's," and that this could be set right by inducing states to set explicit academic standards, deploy tests to determine whether and how well students and schools met those standards, and create behaviorist "accountability" mechanisms whereby rewards would come to those that succeeded, and interventions of some sort would befall those that failed. Long before NCLB, governors of both parties had embraced this strategy, and a number of states had acted upon it. Though conservatives and liberals bickered about how far Washington should go in prodding laggard states, by 2000 the federal statute books already contained much prodding, notably a pair of laws that Clinton nudged through Congress weeks before the 1994 GOP takeover.

NCLB can fairly be termed the feisty progeny of those earlier measures. Yet, in other respects, it has no precedent: It creates stern federal directives regarding test use and consequences, puts federal bureaucrats in charge of approving state standards and accountability plans, sets a single nationwide timetable for boosting achievement, and prescribes specific remedies for underperforming schools—and the children in them. In other words, NCLB marks both an evolutionary development and a revolutionary departure from existing policy.

The challenge of making NCLB work is a consequence, in large part, of the mismatch between Washington's educational ambitions and its actual authority over K–12 education. Federal funds amount to barely eight cents of the public school dollar, giving Congress limited fiscal leverage.[3] Constitutional responsibility for education is vested in state capitals; Americans cherish "local control" of public schools; and the formidable lobbying operation of the "education establishment" is known for its ability to keep much from changing beyond modest annual spending increases for an ever-proliferating array of "categorical" programs.

In 2001, George W. Bush rode into the White House touting the results of Texas school reform. Seeking to leap over obstacles that had blocked earlier national efforts to boost pupil achievement, he promoted a more forceful role for the federal government—one that would use

mandated tests and consequences to compel state and school cooperation, while increasing parental choice of schools and granting states more
freedom in spending federal aid. Within days of taking office, he dis-
patched to Capitol Hill a legislative blueprint that drew heavily on his
experience in Austin. From the outset, however, Bush also insisted on
bipartisan support, and his legislative strategists pressed to win that. The
complex law that resulted accordingly drew in ideas from left, right, and
center—often without reconciling their inconsistencies.

After nearly a year of negotiations, administration and congressional
leaders hammered out a bipartisan measure that commanded support not
only from most Republicans, but also from such prominent Democrats as
Massachusetts senator Edward M. Kennedy and California representative
George Miller, the "ranking members" of Congress's two education com-
mittees. The price of that broad support, however, was a radical reshaping
of the original Bush proposal. The compromise bill joined Bush's quality-
focused, results-centered approach to a host of equity-oriented provisions
dealing with matters ranging from the performance of racial groups to the
assignment of teachers, while sharply curbing the White House's school
choice and state-flexibility proposals. Though NCLB is routinely labeled
a "Bush" law—in no small part because the White House spent 2002 and
2003 claiming it as the president's major programmatic domestic policy
achievement, while Democrats spent much of 2003 and 2004 backing
away from it—in fact its provisions are a Rube Goldberg–like assemblage
of administration proposals, "New Democrat" schemes, favorite liberal
ideas of Messrs. Kennedy and Miller, and proposals and cautions introduced by countless other constituencies, all superimposed upon habits,
assumptions, and rules that had accumulated since Lyndon Johnson sat
in the Oval Office. Indeed, this mishmash recalls the phrase that the late
Daniel Patrick Moynihan used to describe LBJ's multifaceted community
action program: "maximum feasible misunderstanding."[4]

NCLB's passage was the high-water mark of bipartisan comity on
domestic matters in the months after 9/11. The water level has been
falling ever since, and the rocks are now clearly visible along the parched
riverbed. Some of the ruckus has been traditional partisan posturing, as
official Washington and the parties struggle to differentiate themselves—
not an easy thing with a law that both Republicans and Democrats backed

in massive numbers and that Bush enthusiastically signed. Some of it, however, arises from the simple (and predictable) fact that Congress didn't get it quite right the first time. Like all major legislation, especially the kind with so many moving parts, NCLB is going to demand repair work by the administration and Congress in the years ahead.

NCLB-Style Accountability

NCLB's accountability engine is driven by two pistons: imposing systematic testing on schools and districts, and then imposing forceful remedies on weak schools, together with immediate relief for their pupils. Yes, the statute contains hundreds of other provisions. But if its two main pistons aren't firing well, this complex engine won't budge the massive barge that is American schooling—much less render it a more agile craft.

On the assessment front, NCLB requires that all public schools annually test all their students in grades three to eight in reading and math, and that every state measure whether its public schools are making "adequate yearly progress" (AYP) toward universal proficiency in those core subjects. (Science will be added in 2007–8.) Each school must annually show steady improvement in every grade and demographic subgroup, including gender, race, disability, and English language status. A school is then judged on the achievement level of each category in which it enrolls a minimum number of students (that minimum being determined by the state, subject to federal approval). If the school fails to "make AYP" in any of those categories in any year, it is deemed "in need of improvement," which subjects it to a cascade of sanctions and interventions that grow more draconian with each additional year of failure.

In the early stages of intervention, NCLB stresses alternatives for the children in these faltering schools. Such measures are also intended, via competitive pressures, to create incentives for the schools to improve. If a federally aided school fails to "make AYP" for two consecutive years, its students are supposed to be offered "public school choice." Under that provision, the local district is to provide each child with a choice of alternative public (and charter) schools that *are* making satisfactory progress. If a school falters for a *third* straight year, its district is supposed to provide pupils with the opportunity to obtain "supplemental educational services"—essentially free after-school tutoring—from diverse providers, including private firms, to be paid for with a portion of the school's federal dollars—not unlike miniature vouchers. If a school fails to make AYP for a fourth year running, it must write a school improvement plan, and after the fifth year it is to be "reconstituted." Various regulations govern how districts are to manage these processes, how states are to oversee districts, and so forth.

On paper, this all proceeds in an orderly and familiar top-down sequence, with federal regulations telling states what to do, states telling districts what to do, and local school systems having the primary obligation to repair their faltering schools (and offer options to their pupils). State education departments are charged with setting standards, creating tests, intervening in districts that themselves fail to "make AYP," and generally overseeing matters. That hierarchy of responsibility—from Washington to state capital to local school system—has been the basic architecture of federal education policy for decades. But it was never intended to support a results-based accountability system, to make effective repairs in faltering schools, or to function in an education environment peppered with novelties like charter schooling, home schooling, and distance learning.

Can this old architecture support a new and greatly expanded federal role? Or is there a basic mismatch between NCLB's ambitions and its machinery?

A Mixed Report Card

Some parts of the law will likely work well and do some good. The great boon of the legislation is the ample sunshine it beams upon student, school, district, and state performance in reading and math. NCLB's testing mandate is already yielding a wealth of valuable achievement data that deepens popular awareness and parental understanding of school effectiveness, fosters prudent choices among schools, equips principals and superintendents to manage their schools better, and arms elected officials to do informed battle with the traditionally secretive public-education establishment.

On the other hand, NCLB's most problematic feature is its imposition of blunt, uniform remedies for perceived institutional failings across varied schools and dissimilar communities. Setting aside the contentious but theoretical question of whether fixing—and liberating kids from—broken schools is a *proper* federal role in K–12 education, we must reckon with the fact that it's damnably difficult to do, at least so long as Washington relies on the selfsame state and local agencies that presided over weak achievement and broken schools now to effect a major transformation of those schools. Put simply, NCLB assumes that the entities that long permitted these schools to fail to educate millions of children will now display the fortitude, ingenuity, and capacity to turn them around. Moreover, key provisions of NCLB depend on state and local agencies to execute policies that clash with their own financial and reputational interests, that complicate or subvert their own systems for attaining similar ends, and that could inadvertently cause successful schools to falter.

This matters. If NCLB is seen to expect the impossible, if it cannot effect the changes that it calls for, if it undermines things that are working reasonably well, and if it forfeits popular support, that failure could erode the commitment to results-based educational accountability and school choice that was beginning to thrive in many states sans federal involvement.

That NCLB's accountability system has some built-in problems is becoming evident even to its authors. Most notably, it is overbearingly prescriptive on some elements of testing and holding schools responsible for results at the micro level, while being so loose on other elements that the entire apparatus is vulnerable to gamesmanship.

For example, the multiple subgroups created by congressional directive and bureaucratic interpretation mean that even generally successful schools can be red-flagged based on simple statistical fluctuation in their test scores—and larger or more diverse schools are at greater risk simply because they have more such subgroups whose scores will fluctuate. Some schools can have forty or more subgroups, yet there is no distinction between a school that failed to make AYP in thirty-five and another that fell short in just one.

The law also imposes a lockstep, twelve-year timeline on all states. Yet this otherwise prescriptive statute is mute regarding what a state's academic standards should look like, laid-back about how high the "proficiency" bar should be set, and agnostic as to which tests are used. In other words, NCLB is breathtakingly explicit about the *processes* of accountability while taking pains to give state officials wide latitude with regard to the *substance* of accountability.

Each state, for example, devises its own "stair-steps" by which achievement rises to universal proficiency by 2014. That means a state can "backload" most of the requisite gains into the final bits of the twelve-year period, not unlike a balloon mortgage, leaving the heaviest lifting to those who will be in office long after the designers of that state's plan have departed the scene. Each state is required to seek approval of its system from bureaucrats at the Department of Education. In practice, this has meant extensive negotiations between state and department officials— with the White House playing an active role. The rules invite finagled timelines, eccentric assumptions about rates of improvement, and passing rates that appear to rise as "cut scores" (the number of questions a student needs to answer correctly in order to pass a test) quietly descend. This arrangement could be termed "flexibility." More realistically, it can be described as freedom for states to flout the spirit of NCLB while nominally complying with its letter. Such a course is likely to grow more seductive as states find increasing numbers of their schools labeled "in need of improvement."

Remedies and Interventions

NCLB's remedy provisions also give cause for concern, beginning with the new options supposedly available to students in low-performing schools. These options are not based on the time-honored, school-choice rationales that parents have the right to direct their children's education, or that a free society ought not compel youngsters to attend one school rather than another. Such precepts withered under the Bush administration's commitment to crafting a bipartisan bill. Rather, the new law's choice provisions arise, first, from the assumption that needy children will more readily attain academic "proficiency" if moved to effective schools or given increased access to competent providers of instruction;

and, second, from the Adam Smithian hunch that weak schools threatened with the loss of pupils will have an incentive to get stronger.

But of course it's not that simple. Given the way that AYP is calculated, NCLB's public school choice provision is apt to punish effective schools that find the room to enroll low-performing students. Such pupils are apt to drag down the receiving schools' overall academic results. This creates little incentive for strong schools to welcome transfers from weak ones.

In any case, districts with many schools "in need of improvement," hence with many youngsters eligible to change schools, are likely to have few sound alternatives to offer. Federal rules say districts must provide eligible students with at least two adequately performing schools. Yet many districts have no such capacity. A large fraction of urban schools "need improvement" and are therefore not viable options under the law. Moving kids among schools also means disrupting bus routes and possibly running afoul of statutes or court orders governing student assignment and racial balance. Rural communities and small towns may have but a single school. As for nondistrict options, most good charter schools already boast waiting lists. And nearby school systems with plenty of high-performing classrooms, often located in the suburbs, are disinclined to accept students from poor inner-city schools. The result: there is simply not enough space in successful schools to provide attractive alternatives for more than a handful of eligible children. Worse, NCLB contains few incentives for states and districts to create more high-performing schools. Nothing in the law suggests that state or district leaders will benefit from taking steps to expand the supply of these schools, nor does it contain sanctions for failing to do so.

As for supplemental services, the compromise that emerged from Congress marked a break with precedent as Democrats assented to (limited) public education dollars flowing to private (nonprofit and for-profit) providers of tutoring services. These can range from national firms such as Sylvan Learning to diverse e-learning organizations to school districts themselves. While constrained in many ways, these "minivouchers" mark a notable step toward ensuring that federal support serves the children for whom it is provided and toward engaging entrepreneurial providers in results-based innovation. A number of school district officials regard supplemental services as a promising tool to help boost student perform-ance, improve outcomes, and help schools to make their AYP targets. These officials prefer providing supplemental services to shifting children among schools, which they view as solving no problems at the sending school while creating new woes at the receiving school.

But NCLB's supplemental services provision brings perversities, too. Most vexing is its assignment of conflicting roles to local districts. With one hand, NCLB makes districts responsible for determining which outside providers may tutor students and the terms on which they will operate. The districts contract with these outside providers, choose among them, and even rent them space in which to tutor. With the other hand, NCLB simul-taneously empowers districts themselves to provide supplemental services to pupils, thus serving simultaneously as both vendor and regulator, both contestant and referee. A district may discourage rival providers from work-ing with its students by delaying the execution of contracts, charging exces-sive rent for the use of facilities, and so on, even as it urges parents to sign up for district-delivered services. (Recall that this is the same district whose own schools failed to "make AYP" for three consecutive years before the supplemental services provision even kicked in.)[5]

One may also doubt whether NCLB's choice mechanisms, besides yielding few viable options for children, are apt to be "felt" by schools or districts in ways that prompt them to improve. Will a school turn itself inside out because it's losing two dozen kids to intradistrict choice, or sev-enty-five of its students sign up for supplemental tutoring from a private vendor? After all, schools that shed pupils suffer few adverse effects and may even see benefits (such as rising scores and less-crowded class-rooms). Moreover, many troubled schools are located in communities that have long offered such education options as magnet schools, open enrollment, interdistrict choice and charter schools. In places like Milwaukee, Philadelphia, Washington, D.C., Houston, Los Angeles, and Boston, district schools have operated for years amid sundry choice pro-grams. If that competition has failed to trigger a dynamic response from traditional public schools, one must ask why NCLB's addition of two more choice programs will dramatically alter the picture.

Politics

In the 2004 election year, NCLB was less a subject of sensible discussion than a handy football. The debate was framed by administration boasts that the law was the crowning achievement of modern school reform, Democratic complaints that it imposed unfunded mandates on hard-pressed states and districts, union claims that its provisions were unreasonable and intrusive, laments among the education professoriate that it relied overmuch on testing and was harmful to children, and state-level grumbling—often voiced by Republicans—about federal micromanagement and overreaching.

By April 2004, twenty-one state legislatures had considered bills or resolutions that criticized the law or sought significant waivers from the Department of Education. Legislative action ranged from requesting additional flexibility and resources to prohibiting the expenditure of state funds for NCLB implementation, or opting out of NCLB altogether. GOP legislators in Arizona and Minnesota introduced bills that would allow those states to reject some NCLB provisions. Vermont's legislature voted to prohibit the use of state funds for NCLB-related programs, while Utah's GOP-controlled House refused to implement parts of NCLB for which it did not receive adequate federal funding. Some districts in Vermont and Connecticut sought to opt out of NCLB and forfeit federal funds, while a Pennsylvania district sued the state to correct "inequities" in the law.[6]

On balance, public opinion remains friendlier toward NCLB than these protests might suggest. Americans have long favored high standards, results-based accountability tied to testing (except, perhaps, when it pinches one's own kid), and the right to choose one's school. But Americans also believe in local control of education and are skittish about heavy-handed federal intervention. Hence, NCLB elicits mixed reactions, with people tending to affirm its goals but worry about its means. The more Americans see the law's specific mechanisms in practice, the more concerns there are. A Public Education Network and *Education Week* poll released in April 2004 found that the percentage of adults who had heard of NCLB increased from 56 percent in 2003 to 75 percent in early 2004. This increasing awareness, however, was coupled with ebbing support. The percentage of voters who favored the law declined slightly from 2003 to 2004, falling from 40 to 36 percent. More significantly, the percentage of voters who opposed the law shot from 8 to 28 percent in that period, with more than half of those reporting that they strongly opposed the law.[7] The bottom line is that NCLB has become a political target, public support is mixed, and the future is uncertain.

The Bush administration has denied this reality or regarded it as a failure of public relations. Meanwhile, the administration has also been needlessly defensive about the adequacy of federal spending to help states and schools offset the costs of complying with NCLB's mandates.

Leading the offensive over funding levels have been prominent Democrats, including, most notably, 2004 Democratic presidential nominee John Kerry. Yet the complaint that NCLB is an "unfunded mandate" is not true. As the Government Accounting Office noted in May 2004, NCLB is not really a "mandate" at all, considering that states willing to forgo its funding can opt out of the entire program. For those that participate, NCLB's true requirements—testing every child, for example—are relatively inexpensive and more than adequately offset by federal education appropriations that nearly doubled between 2001 and 2004, rising from $29.4 billion to $55.7 billion.[8] What may prove costly but is not, in fact, mandatory under NCLB is reforming a state's or city's schools such that more students attain "proficiency." One may fairly term that a moral mandate or a political imperative. It's hard, though, to argue that turning bad schools into good ones is Washington's responsibility—and in many cases the vital ingredient won't be more dollars so much as making better use of monies already being spent.

Making NCLB Work

We assume that NCLB, like other complex new federal laws, will need repairs before it works smoothly. We suggest ten changes, all derived from the belief that NCLB needs incentives sensibly aligned with its objectives and should have enough "play in the joints" that Washington bureaucrats aren't routinely asked to make nuanced decisions regarding district or state practices. Uncle Sam should focus on what students learn, not how schools are run. Washington should resist the urge to prescribe means so long as states, districts, and schools are attaining satisfactory ends. The first five recommendations deal with making NCLB assessment work as intended, and the final five with rendering its remedies more effective.

First, NCLB today is too laid back about the skills and knowledge that young Americans need to acquire and too prescriptive about calendars, state improvement targets, and school sanctions. This is backward. Instead, Washington should offer stricter guidance regarding the essentials that students must master while being notably flexible with regard to how states, districts, and schools produce those results—and how they address failure.

Though NCLB pretends otherwise, the United States already has a reasonable level of nationwide agreement as to what children should learn in reading and mathematics. Federal lawmakers should take advantage of that consensus. There's less regional variation here than in other subjects, little demand for sixth graders in North Carolina to master math skills much different from what sixth graders are expected to know in Vermont or Oregon. Using the National Assessment of Educational Progress (NAEP) as a benchmark, Washington could easily set clear and uniform expectations regarding student mastery in these subjects in grades four, eight, and perhaps twelve. Though some will decry the prospect of a "national curriculum" even in math and reading, most Americans, we are confident, would welcome a single set of academic standards in these most basic of skills rather than inviting states to play games with passing scores and performance targets.

Second, AYP should be gauged based primarily on the academic value schools add (that is, the achievement gains their pupils make)—not, as is the case today, on the aggregate level at which students perform. In essence, under a "value-added" system, a student is tested at the beginning of fourth grade and again at the end of the year. The difference between these scores is the child's one-year achievement gain—the value that his school and teacher added during that year. Measuring a student's overall level of achievement encompasses three things—learning in the current school year, learning in all previous years, and everything else going on in the child's life—of which only the first is relevant to gauging whether schools and educators are performing adequately. Today, neither NAEP nor most state assessments are designed to capture the value that schools are adding. However, this capacity is rapidly developing. Such analyses provide a valuable complement to familiar measures of achievement in relation to fixed standards—a terrific way of gauging teacher and school effectiveness that largely washes out the influence of children's backgrounds and prior attainment. Today's NCLB is hostile to value-added analysis. That should change.

Third, an obvious problem with "value-added" approaches is that schools whose students are already getting high scores have difficulty posting further test gains. The sensible solution is to create a "safe harbor" for high-performing schools. For instance, so long as 90 percent of students are reading at grade level, a school might be deemed adequate whatever its gains in reading scores. This would ensure that schools where students are being demonstrably well-served are not caught in a numbers game.

Fourth, sensible assessment of schools means judging them on how well they are doing their job overall, not whether they can overcome every single vestige of poverty or student circumstance. Schools that do an adequate job of helping pupils master the prescribed content at a reasonable rate are adequate—even if they cannot thereby ensure that every single youngster attains mastery. Where students start so far behind that schools may be reasonably effective in moving them forward, yet unable to close the performance gap on a fixed timetable, it does not follow that such schools should be punished or reconstituted. Rather, states and school districts should be required to provide the tutoring, resources, and other support necessary to ensure that every child has a reasonable shot at attaining the prescribed standards. No federal law can wipe out the effects of family, attitude, innate capacity, mobility, and other such differences and influences—not, at least, unless Congress is prepared to mandate and pay for 24/7 learning environments in the form of year-round residential schools for millions of youngsters. Short of that, lawmakers would do well to recognize the limited leverage of schooling in the lives of children, and the fact that educators can be competent without being Herculean. It may be essential to provide extra assistance or resources to educate children who are particularly disadvantaged—but it's wrong to paste an "inadequate" label on an effective school in which most children are learning steadily, solely because its teachers cannot ensure that every needy child has fully closed the gap with more advantaged peers.

Fifth, NCLB should replace its all-or-nothing AYP calculation with a more flexible approach. One might, for example, distinguish among schools that are making progress overall and in 90 percent or more of their demographic subcategories; those that are making progress overall but in less than 90 percent of categories; and those failing to make acceptable overall progress. Such a triage system would distinguish between those that are almost succeeding and those that are catastrophically inadequate. It would enable states and districts to focus on repairing the latter, and it would bolster the confidence of parents and voters in the NCLB branding system.

Sixth, today's AYP calculation foolishly serves to punish principals who would otherwise accept students transferring from weaker schools. Schools that attract a lot of "choice" students will obviously draw them from lower-performing schools. This may pull down the performance of the receiving school, perhaps causing it to miss AYP. In other words, the law discourages rational principals from opening the door to many students from weak schools via NCLB-mandated public choice. One remedy is to assess schools according to whether they strengthen these students—and not penalize them if pupils do not make heroic achievement gains. A less drastic change: Test all students in the school, but base its AYP calculation only on the performance of pupils who have been there for at least two years.

Seventh, states should revamp their testing cycles to identify targeted schools several months before the next school year starts. Only in that way can remedies be thoughtfully implemented, districts enabled to prepare choice and tutoring programs, or families empowered to make intelligent choices. No doubt this will mean reworking testing systems so student performance can be reported faster. That needn't mean moving assessments into the winter, but retooling operations and investing in information technology—for instance, computer-adaptive testing—so as to shorten dramatically the turnaround time for scores. Alternatively, NCLB sanctions might be based on lagged test scores. For example, a school's status in 2005–6 would be based on the value it added to students in 2003–4. Yet another approach is to hinge a school's status on a several-year aggregate or average performance, thus smoothing the annual fluctuations that can be triggered by a wide array of phenomena, some of them purely statistical.

Eighth, as much attention needs to be paid to the supply of potential alternatives for students (that is, effective schools and viable tutoring providers) as to the demand-related rules by which children gain access to them. Confining a youngster's options to existing public and charter schools within the district means that millions, especially poor kids living in urban America, will have no true options. Hence, the supply needs to be expanded, whether by encouraging more charter schools to open, insisting that neighboring school systems accept interdistrict transfers, or jumpstarting such nondistrict options as cyber-schools, home schools, and even private schools. In particular, this means offering incentives and support to entrepreneurs who wish to provide new schools, classrooms, and tutoring programs.

Ninth, it would make sense to reverse the order in which supplemental services and public school choice are triggered. Districts are more comfortable with the tutoring provision than with public school choice. Moreover, it makes sense to try to help children improve their performance within a school before having them exit it. Providing tutoring before school choice would mean (for example) that a school's students would become eligible for supplemental services if it missed AYP two years in a row, and for an exit ticket if the school missed for a third consecutive year.

Finally, school districts need *either* to function as providers of supplemental services *or* as regulators of other providers—not both. It's never a good idea to allow the fox to guard the henhouse, however noble the fox's intentions. In districts that wish to provide supplemental services themselves, states ought to identify another entity to screen, negotiate with, and oversee all providers, including the district. Some such coordinators may come to operate in dozens or hundreds of districts, permitting them to build expertise in managing and evaluating providers, negotiating contracts, and ensuring service quality.

Great Society Redux

Viewed through one lens, NCLB promotes educational accountability and parental-choice policies long championed by conservative reformers. Seen through a different prism, it marks a radical break with conservative tradition, initiating a massive shift of education authority from the states to Washington, the sort of thing more characteristic of "big-government" Democrats than laissez-faire Republicans. The law's far-reaching provisions will powerfully influence how schooling is delivered across America. Indeed, it recalls the towering promises, ornate implementation challenges, and dashed hopes of the Great Society, albeit with fascinating role reversals.

The Bush administration is playing the part of the Johnson administration, advocating ambitious new federal policies and programs and mounting an elaborate new regulatory regime to force states and communities to do their part to fulfill those ambitions. It justifies these acts by wrapping its policies in the mantle of racial and social justice, arguing for federal intervention to protect poor, black, and brown children from the callous disregard of state leaders and local interests. Now, as forty years ago, a well-meaning president strives to use moral authority—decrying "the soft bigotry of low expectations"[9]—first to prod the Congress, then to press state and local officials to ignore self-interest, realpolitik, and ingrained ways of doing things. In fact, by labeling even sensible criticism of NCLB as "anti-accountability," the administration can appear enchanted by the nobility of its aspirations and blind to realities of human nature, organizational behavior, and common sense. The grand irony, of course, is that for more than three decades, this has been the conservative critique of Great Society legislation.

Another historical parallel: On the heels of the fiftieth anniversary of the *Brown* decision, we may remember an earlier instance in which bold rhetoric was used to justify federal intervention as necessary to ensure educational opportunity for black children. We would also do well to recall, however, that the Eisenhower administration found appeals to justice and fairness—even when combined with the weight of a unanimous Supreme Court—insufficient to meet the challenge. In time, it needed to summon the National Guard even to get black children through the schoolhouse door. In demanding deep, complex changes across tens of thousands of schools, NCLB sets a course that is even more ambitious, yet brings far less power to bear.

No Child Left Behind asks state and local officials to undertake tasks that they view as unnatural, unrealistic, or at odds with their self-interest. Moreover, the "street-level bureaucrats" who bear primary responsibility for NCLB's success are public educators, that is, predominantly members of staunchly Democratic unions, and people who enjoy abiding credibility with parents and voters. Opposition (or passive resistance) on the part of educators could easily gut the promise to "leave no child behind"—and it's hard to think what Washington could do to alter that. Nobody expects the National Guard to administer tests or mount tutoring programs. The Department of Education is unlikely even to withhold federal dollars as "punishment" for noncompliance—and were it to do so, it would likely find the sums too small to prompt much change among unwilling people or obstinate organizations.

Given NCLB's ambitious but awkward construction, the surest way to win the cooperation of these constituencies is through moral authority that rewards cooperation and makes resistance politically unpalatable. This will require continued bipartisanship and sustained support from Democratic as well as GOP leaders. Only Democratic leaders can convince educators and local officials that results-based accountability is a good thing and will not go away. Only voices from the center and left can ensure that NCLB is understood not as a conservative ploy to undermine public schooling, but as a renewed national commitment to equality of opportunity. Just as the moral authority and public approbation of Head Start and the War on Poverty forced Richard Nixon to retain and even bolster those Johnson-era programs, so the fate of NCLB will rest in large part on how future Democratic administrations and congressional leaders view this law's imperatives.

Yet political support is only the beginning. Ambitious federal statutes seldom succeed in changing behavior through good intentions or powerful sentiment. When they work, it's because they are feasible, plausible to everyone, and make measured use of mandates and incentives. Vast programs modeled on extravagant hopes and fleeting dreams of large-scale institutional transformation almost always capsize.

The academic field of implementation studies emerged in the 1960s and '70s, as scholars sought to explain the lackluster results of widely hailed Great Society programs. What these scholars learned was that Washington's money and direction are often no match for real-world complexities or the mixed capacities of local officials charged with translating sentiment into practice.

No Child Left Behind could turn out to be another sobering case in point. Or not. History need not repeat itself. Forty years after the fractured results of LBJ's noble efforts to ensure equal opportunity in American education, we have a chance to do better. Perhaps even federal policymakers could learn from history.

Publication Acknowledgments

"Seeking the Mantle of 'Opportunity': Presidential Politics and the Educational Metaphor" was originally published in *Educational Policy* 1, no. 1 (2002): 72–95. Patrick McGuinn coauthored the piece.

"Retooling K–12 Giving" was originally published in *Philanthropy* 18, no. 5 (2004): 27–33.

"Making Sense of the 'Public' in Public Education" was originally published as a policy report by the Progressive Policy Institute in 2002.

"What Is a 'Public School'? Principles for a New Century" was originally published in *Phi Delta Kappan* 85, no. 6 (2004): 433–39.

"The Case for Being Mean" was originally published in *Educational Leadership* 61, no. 3 (2003): 22–26.

"The Political Challenge of Charter School Regulation" was originally published in *Phi Delta Kappan* 85, no. 6 (2004): 508–12.

"The Work Ahead" was originally published in *Education Next* 1, no. 4 (2001): 8–13.

"Choice Is Not Enough" was published under the title "Vouchers Without Competition" by the *Weekly Standard* on May 10, 2004.

"Inclusive Ambiguity" was originally published in *Educational Policy* 18, no. 1 (2004): 95–115.

"'Trust Us,' They Explained: Racial Distrust and School Reform" was originally published in *American Experiment Quarterly* 6, no. 1 (2003): 27–41.

"School Vouchers and Suburbanites" was originally published in *The American Enterprise*, April/May 2003.

"The Voice of the People" was originally published in the *American School Board Journal* 190, no. 4 (2003): 36–39.

"Tear Down This Wall" was published under the title "Break the Link," in *Education Next* 2, no. 1 (2002): 22–28.

"A License to Lead?" was published under the title "Lifting the Barrier," in *Education Next* 3, no. 4 (2003): 12–19.

"Ready to Lead?" was originally published in the *American School Board Journal* 192, no. 7 (2005): 22–25. Andrew P. Kelly coauthored the piece.

"The Predictable, but Unpredictably Personal, Politics of Teacher Licensure" was originally published in the *Journal of Teacher Education* 56, no. 3 (2005): 192–204.

"Lessons from San Diego" originally appeared in *The Education Gadfly* on April 28, 2005.

"Science and Non-Science: The Limits of Scientific Research" originally appeared in *The Education Gadfly*, February 17, 2005.

"Technical Difficulties" was originally published in *Education Next* 4, no. 4 (2004): 15–19.

"On Leaving No Child Behind" was originally published in *The Public Interest* (Fall 2004): 35–56. Chester Finn Jr. coauthored the piece.

All selections reprinted with permission.

Notes

Introduction

1. Thomas L. Friedman, *The World Is Flat: A Brief History of the 21st Century* (New York: Farrar, Straus and Giroux, 2005).

2. Jay P. Greene and Greg Forster, "Public High School Graduation and College Readiness Rates in the United States," Education Working Paper 3, Center for Civic Innovation, Manhattan Institute, September 2003, 1–11.

3. U.S. Department of Education, National Center for Education Statistics, "The Nation's Report Card: Reading Highlights 2003," http://nces.ed.gov/nationsreport-card/pdf/main2003/2004452.pdf (accessed June 4, 2005).

4. Frederick M. Hess, *Common Sense School Reform* (New York: Palgrave Macmillan, 2004), 23.

5. George Archibald, "NEA Conservatives Seek Family-Planning Change," *Washington Times*, July 4, 2005.

6. John E. Chubb and Terry M. Moe, *Politics, Markets, and America's Schools* (Washington D.C.: Brookings Institution, 1990).

Part 1: Public Leadership and Public Schooling

1. Hess, *Common Sense School Reform*, 213.

2. Vartan Gregorian, "Vartan Gregorian Responds on Behalf of the Annenberg Challenge," *Philanthropy* 19, no. 2 (March/April 2005): 21–22, 25.

3. Linda Nathan, "A Response to Frederick Hess: The Larger Purpose of Public Schools," *Phi Delta Kappan* 85, no. 6 (February 2004): 440–41; Joe Nathan, "A Response to Frederick Hess: Some Questions for Advocates of Public Education," *Phi Delta Kappan* 85, no. 6 (February 2004): 442–45, 450; Ray Bacchetti, "A Response to Frederick Hess: An Ongoing Conversation," *Phi Delta Kappan* 85, no. 6 (February 2004): 446–47; Evans Clinchy, "A Response to Frederick Hess: Reimagining Public Education," *Phi Delta Kappan* 85, no. 6 (February 2004): 448–50; Frederick M. Hess, "A Rejoinder from Frederick Hess: Debating Principles for Public Schooling in a New Century," *Phi Delta Kappan* 85, no. 6 (February 2004): 451–54. All available from

http://www.catholiceducation.org/articles/education/ed0238.html (accessed October 21, 2005).

Chapter 1: Seeking the Mantle of "Opportunity"

1. Harry Kursh, *The United States Office of Education: A Century of Service* (New York: Chilton Books, 1965); Frederick Wirt and Michael Kirst, *The Political Dynamics of American Education* (Berkeley: McCutchan, 2001).

2. Kenneth Thompson, ed., *The Presidency and Education* (Lanham: University Press of America, 1990).

3. David Tyack, *The One Best System: A History of American Urban Education* (Cambridge, Mass.: Harvard University Press, 1974).

4. U.S. Bureau of the Census, *Education of the American Population* (Washington, D.C.: U.S. Bureau of the Census, 1999), table 8.

5. Diane Ravitch, *The Trouble Crusade: American Education 1945–1980* (New York: Basic Books, 1983).

6. Roper Center, *Public Opinion Online*, citing a poll originally released by the Gallup Organization on August 4, 1980 (question identification USGALLUP.1160, Q014), question number 45.

7. *The American Presidency Project*, "1980 Republican Party Platform," http://www.presidency.ucsb.edu/showplatforms.php?platindex=R1980 (accessed November 1, 2005).

8. Survey by *Los Angeles Times*, November 9–13, 1980, iPOLL Databank, The Roper Center for Public Opinion Research, University of Connecticut, http://www.ropercenter.uconn.edu/ipoll.html (accessed September 22, 2005).

9. *The American Presidency Project*, "1984 Republican Party Platform," http://www.presidency.ucsb.edu/showplatforms.php?platindex=R1984 (accessed Novem-ber 1, 2005).

10. Survey by ABC News/*Washington Post*, September 7–11, 1984, iPOLL Databank, The Roper Center for Public Opinion Research, University of Connecticut, http://www.ropercenter.uconn.edu/ipoll.html (accessed September 22, 2005).

11. Survey by Phi Delta Kappa and Gallup Organization, April 10–13, 1987, iPOLL Databank, The Roper Center for Public Opinion Research, University of Connecticut, http://www.ropercenter.uconn.edu/ipoll.html (accessed September 22, 2005).

12. *The American Presidency Project*, "1984 Republican Party Platform."

13. *The American Presidency Project*, "1992 Democratic Party Platform," http://www.presidency.ucsb.edu/showplatforms.php?platindex=D1992 (accessed November 1, 2005).

14. *The American Presidency Project*, "1992 Republican Party Platform," http://www.presidency.ucsb.edu/showplatforms.php?platindex=R1992 (accessed November 30, 2005).

15. Survey by NBC News/*Wall Street Journal*/Hart and Teeter, March 4–7, 1995, iPOLL Databank, The Roper Center for Public Opinion Research, University of Connecticut, http://www.ropercenter.uconn.edu/ipoll.html (accessed September 22, 2005).

16. Survey by *Gallup/CNN/USA Today*, October 30–31, 1996, iPOLL Databank, The Roper Center for Public Opinion Research, University of Connecticut, http://www.ropercenter.uconn.edu/ipoll.html (accessed September 22, 2005).

17. Scott S. Greenberger, "Bush Lays Out First Major Policy Proposal," Cox News Service, July 22, 1999.

18. Edward H. Crane, "Bush Not One to Put End to Clinton Legacy," *Seattle Post-Intelligencer*, August 6, 1999.

Chapter 2: Retooling K–12 Giving

1. Foundation Center, "Distribution of Foundation Grants by Subject Categories, circa 2002," in *Foundation Giving Trends* (2004), http://fdncenter.org/fc_stats/pdf/04_fund_sub/2002/10_02.pdf (accessed June 14, 2004).

2. Dan Fallon (chair, education division, Carnegie Corporation), in conversation with the author, July 8, 2004.

3. *New York Times*, "A Private Gift for Public Education," December 21, 1993.

4. William Celis, "Annenberg to Give Education $500 Million Over Five Years," *New York Times*, December 17, 1993.

5. *Patriot Ledger* (Quincy, Mass.), "Boston Schools to Get $30M Reform Boost," October 29, 1996, 23.

6. Gail Levin, "Grantmakers for Education Newsletter Summer 2004" (Portland, Ore.: Grantmakers for Education, 2004), 3.

7. Michael Casserly (executive director, Council of Great City Schools), in conversation with the author, July 30, 2004.

8. Marci Kanstoroom, "Afterward: Lessons from the Annenberg Challenge," in Raymond Domanico, ed., *Can Philanthropy Fix Our Schools? Appraising Walter Annenberg's $500 Million Gift to Public Education* (Washington, D.C.: Thomas B. Fordham Foundation, 2000).

9. Levin, "Grantmakers for Education," 3.

10. Gregorian, "Vartan Gregorian Responds," 1.

11. Bill Porter (executive director of Grantmakers for Education), in conversation with the author, July 8, 2004.

12. Foundation Center, *Top 50 U.S. Foundations Awarding Grants for Elementary and Secondary Education, Circa 1998* (Washington, D.C.: Foundation Center Statistical Services, 2000).

13. Foundation Center, *Top 50 U.S. Foundations Awarding Grants for Elementary and Secondary Education, Circa 2002* (Washington, D.C.: Foundation Center Statistical Services, 2004); Foundation Center, *Top 50 Recipients of Foundation Grants for Elementary and Secondary Education, Circa 2002* (Washington, D.C.: Foundation Center Statistical Services, 2004).

14. Bruno Manno (senior program associate, Annie E. Casey Foundation), in conversation with the author, July 30, 2004.

15. Chester E. Finn Jr. (president, Thomas B. Fordham Foundation), in conversation with the author, July 13, 2004.

16. Tom Vander Ark, "America's High School Crisis: Policy Reforms That Will Make a Difference," *Education Week*, April 2, 2003.

17. Walton Family Foundation, *2003 Awards* (Bentonville, Ark.: Walton Family Foundation, 2003), 1, http://www.wffhome.com/Grant%20Awards.htm (accessed June 25, 2004).

18. Chester E. Finn and Kelly Amis, "Making it Count: A Guide to High-Impact Education Philanthropy" (Washington, D.C.: Thomas B. Fordham Foundation, 2001), 98.

19. *Business Wire*, "Teacher Advancement Program Foundation Launched as Public 503c3 Charity to Accelerate Teacher Quality Reform Through Public/Private Partnerships; Initial Grants from Milken Family Foundation and the Broad Foundation," April 28, 2005.

20. Julie Blair, "ELC, Milken Foundation Launch Teacher-Quality Program," *Education Week*, May 3, 2000, 26.

21. Norman Draper, "Teacher Pay Plan: Will It Get Results?" *Star Tribune* (Minneapolis), September 19, 2004, 1B; Bill Salisbury, "Teachers are Trying Out Performance Pay System: Schools in Waseca, Minneapolis Opt In," *Saint Paul Pioneer Press* (Minnesota), September 14, 2004.

22. Lew Solmon (senior vice president, Milken Family Foundation), in conversation with the author, July 8, 2004.

23. Broad Foundation, *Grants and Contributions Paid During the Year of 2003*, Form 990 PF, 2003, Foundation Center, http://63.240.2.231//990pf_pdf_archive1/954/954686318/954686318_200312_990PF.pdf (accessed June 23, 2004).

24. Center for National Policy, "New Effort to Upgrade School Leadership Announced: Bipartisan Effort Seeks New Talent for School District Management," CNP Online, November 16, 2001, http://www.cnponline.org/Press%20Releases/PRSchoolsups.htm (accessed July 20, 2004).

25. Newhouse News Service, "Gates Charity Pours Out Wealth," *Cincinnati Post*, March 3, 2002.

26. *Seattle Times*, "Big Bucks Going Back to School: Donors Give with Strings Attached," December 10, 2000.

27. Casserly, conversation.

28. Raymond Domanico, Chester E. Finn Jr., Carol Innerst, Marci Kanstoroom, and Alexander Russo, *Can Philanthropy Fix Our Schools? Appraising Walter Annenberg's $500 Million Gift to Public Education* (Washington, D.C.: Thomas B. Fordham Foundation, 2000), 5.

29. Porter, conversation.

30. Fallon, conversation.

31. Barbara Kibbe, "It Takes Capacity to Build Capacity," *Grantmakers for Education Notebook*, Fall 2003, 3.

32. Huff, conversation.

Chapter 3: Making Sense of the "Public" in Public Education

1. The 2002 *Phi Delta Kappan*/Gallup Poll of the Public's Attitudes toward the Public Schools found that 86 percent of Americans supported the intradistrict school choice option included in the 2001 No Child Left Behind Act. Lowell C. Rose and Alec M. Gallup, "The 34th Annual Phi Delta Kappa/Gallup Poll Of the Public's Attitudes Toward the Public Schools," *Phi Delta Kappan* 84, no. 1 (September 2002): 42. In 2005, there were more than three thousand charter schools operating across the nation, a figure that had grown roughly one thousand percent in the course of the previous decade.

2. A particularly useful volume for this conversation is Stephen Macedo, *Diversity and Distrust: Civic Education in a Multicultural Democracy* (Cambridge, Mass.: Harvard University Press, 2000).

3. Patrick J. Wolf, "School Choice and Civic Values: A Review of the Evidence," paper delivered at the Annual Meetings of the American Political Science Association (Boston, August 2002); David E. Campbell, "Bowling Together: Private Schools, Serving Public Ends," *Education Next*, Fall 2001, 55–61; Patrick J. Wolf, Jay P. Greene, Brett Kleitz, and Kristina Thalhammer, "Private Schooling and Public Tolerance," in *Charters, Vouchers, & Public Education*, ed. Paul E. Peterson and David E. Campbell (Washington, D.C.: Brookings Institution, 2001); Jay P. Greene, "Civic Values in Public and Private Schools," in *Learning from School Choice*, ed. Paul E. Peterson and Bryan C. Hassel (Washington, D.C.: Brookings Institution, 1998). See also the collection of essays in Diane Ravitch and Joseph P. Viteritti, eds., *Making Good Citizens* (New Haven: Yale University, 2002).

4. See, for instance, Jonathan Kozol, *Savage Inequalities: Children in America's Schools* (New York: Crown Publishers, 1991); Gary Orfield and Mindy Kornhaber, eds., *Raising Standards or Raising Barriers?: Inequality and High Stakes Testing in Public Education* (Washington, D.C.: Brookings Institution, 2001); and Carol A. Christensen and Sherman Dorn, "Competing Notions of Social Justice and Contradictions in Special Education Reform," *Journal of Special Education* 31 (1997): 181–98. See also the essays collected in Daniel J. Losen and Gary Orfield, eds., *Racial Inequality in Special Education* (Cambridge, Mass.: Harvard University, 2002), and Mara Sapon Shevin, Jeannie Oakes, and Martin Lipton, *Playing Favorites: Gifted Education and the Disruption of Community* (Albany, N.Y.: State University of New York, 1994).

5. John Dewey, *The Public and Its Problems* (Athens, Ohio: Ohio University Press, reprinted in 1954).

6. See John Stuart Mill, *On Liberty* (New York: W. W. Norton, 1859, reprinted in 1975), and Milton Friedman, *Capitalism and Freedom* (Chicago: University of Chicago, 1962).

7. Of course, many participants in the debate have a vested interest in sustaining and promoting this confusion. For instance, Amy Stuart Wells and her colleagues

have pointed out that the coalition supporting charter schools is composed of disparate elements that may be unable to sustain their partnership in those states where their divergent ambitions become too visible. See Amy Stuart Wells, Cynthia Grutzik, and Sibyll Carnochan, "Underlying Policy Assumptions of Charter School Reform: The Multiple Meanings of a Movement," *Teachers College Record* 100 (1999): 513–35.

8. See Lisa Renze-Rhodes, "More Paying to Attend Choice Public Schools: Washington Twp. Leads State with 89 Cash-Tuition Students at North Central," *Indianapolis Star*, October 19, 2002. Indiana's Washington Township enrolled 106 cash-tuition students during the 2002–3 year, generating an extra $402,800 in family payments and prompting a deputy superintendent to observe, "It becomes part of our miscellaneous revenue."

9. For discussion, see Rob Reich, *Bridging Liberalism and Multiculturalism in American Education* (Chicago: University of Chicago, 2002).

10. See, for instance, Chester E. Finn, Bruno V. Manno, and Gregg Vanourek, *Charter Schools in Action* (Princeton, N.J.: Princeton University, 2000).

11. In fact, this is the logical endpoint for those who make the most impassioned indictment of choice-based reform. This tack has actually been attempted in the course of American history, most notably by the state of Oregon. Oregon made public schooling mandatory early in the twentieth century, essentially outlawing private schooling. The decision was only overturned when the U.S. Supreme Court struck down the statute in its 1925 ruling in *Pierce v. Society of Sisters*. For discussion, see Joseph P. Viteritti, *Choosing Equality: School Choice, the Constitution, and Civil Society* (Washington, D.C.: Brookings Institution, 1999), 129–32.

Chapter 4: What Is a "Public School"? Principles for a New Century

1. James Coleman, "Public Schools, Private Schools, and the Public Interest," *Public Interest*, Summer 1981, 19–30. See also Coleman, "Quality and Equality in American Education," *Phi Delta Kappan*, November 1981, 159–64.

2. See Andrew Coulson, *Market Education: The Unknown History* (New Brunswick: Transaction, 1999); and Douglas Dewey, "An Echo, Not a Choice: School Vouchers Repeat the Error of Public Education," *Policy Review*, November/December 1996, www.policyreview.org/nov96/backup/dewey.html (accessed August 8, 2003).

3. Dewey, *The Public and Its Problems*.

4. An extended discussion of this point can be found in Paul T. Hill, "What Is Public About Public Education?" in *A Primer on America's Schools*, ed. Terry Moe (Stanford, Calif.: Hoover Institution, 2001), 285–316.

5. Frank Smith, "Overselling Literacy," *Phi Delta Kappan*, January 1989, 353–59; Alfie Kohn, *No Contest: The Case Against Competition* (Boston: Houghton Mifflin, 1986); Susan Ohanian, "Capitalism, Calculus, and Conscience," *Phi Delta Kappan*, June 2003, 736–47; Nel Noddings, *Happiness and Education* (Cambridge: Cambridge University

Press, 2004); and Deborah Meier, "Educating a Democracy," in *Will Standards Save Public Education?* eds. Joshua Cohen and Joel Rogers (Boston: Beacon Press, 2000), 3–34.

6. See Viteritti, *Choosing Equality*.

Part 2: Competition and Accountability

1. See, for instance, Myron Lieberman, "Voucher 'Experiments' Don't Test Competition," *School Reform News*, August 1, 2002, http://www.heartland.org/Article.cfm?artId=1028 (accessed June 20, 2005), or Marilyn Cochran-Smith, "Sometimes It's Not About the Money: Teaching and Heart," *Journal of Teacher Education* 54, no. 5 (2003): 371–75.

Chapter 5: The Case for Being Mean

1. Public Agenda, *Questionnaire and Fall Survey Results: National Poll of Parents of Public School Students* (New York: Public Agenda, 2000).

2. U.S. Department of Education, National Center for Education Statistics, "The Nation's Report Card: Reading 2002" (Washington, D.C.: U.S. Department of Education, 2003), www.nces.ed.gov/nationsreportcard/reading/results2003/district-achieve.asp (accessed March 8, 2003).

3. S. B. Holcombe, "High Stakes: School Leaders Weigh In on Testing, Reform, and the Goal of Educating Every American Child," *Education Magazine* 46, no. 1 (2002): 20.

4. Keith Gayler, Naomi Chudowsky, Madlene Hamilton, Nancy Kober, and Margery Yaeger, "State High School Exit Exams: A Maturing Reform" (Washington, D.C.: Center on Education Policy, 2004), 121–34.

5. Irene Hunting (state test administration director, Arizona public schools), in conversation with the author, July 8, 2005.

6. D. H. Bowman, "Turf War Erupts in Arizona over Delaying Graduation Test," *Education Week*, April 4, 2001, 21.

7. Hunting, conversation.

Chapter 6: The Political Challenge of Charter School Regulation

1. Sandra Vergari, ed., *The Charter School Landscape: Politics, Policies, and Prospects* (Pittsburgh: University of Pittsburgh Press, 2002).

2. Joe Nathan, *Charter Schools* (San Francisco: Jossey-Bass, 1996).

3. In various states, chartering bodies include state boards of education, state charter school boards, local school districts, universities, and municipalities. However, because most chartering bodies are public boards, our discussion will focus on these.

4. Center for Education Reform, "Charter Schools Today: Changing the Face of American Education" (Washington, D.C.: Center for Education Reform, 2000), 95.

5. Ibid., 4, 39–56.

6. Ibid., 42–43

7. Macedo, *Diversity and Distrust.*

8. Bruno Manno, "Yellow Flag," *Education Next*, Winter 2003, 21.

Chapter 7: The Work Ahead

1. Milwaukee Public Schools, "About MPS," http://www.milwaukee.k12.wi.us/pages/MPS/Profile (accessed June 18, 2005).

2. American Education Reform Council, "Milwaukee's Public Schools in an Era of Choice," (Milwaukee, Wis.: American Education Reform Council, October 2003), http://www.cse.org/reports/031007choice.pdf (accessed June 14, 2005).

3. Ohio Department of Education, "Enrollment (Head Count) by Grade," http://www.ode.state.oh.US/data/DISTRICT_1993-2005.xls (accessed November 30, 2005).

4. Center for School Finance, "Most Frequently Requested School Finance Data," 2003–4, http://www.ode.state.oh.us/school_finance/simulation_fiscal_analysis/EFM_04.xls (accessed June 18, 2005).

5. National Education Association, "NEA Declares Day of Victory for America's Children," press release, June 11, 1999.

6. Ohio Department of Education, "Scholarship Program Requirements," http://www.ode.state.oh.us/school_options/scholarship/ScholarshipProgramRequirements.asp (accessed October 26, 2005).

7. Milwaukee Parental Choice Program, "MPCP Facts and Figures for 2004–2005, as of February 2005" (Madison, Wis.: Department of Public Instruction, 2005), table 2, http://dpi.wi.gov/sms/doc/mpc04fnf.doc (accessed October 26, 2005).

8. Center for Education Reform, "K–12 Facts," http://www.edreform.com/index.cfm?fuseAction=section&pSectionID=15&cSectionID=97 (accessed October 26, 2005).

9. U.S. Department of Education, National Center for Education Statistics, "The Condition of Education 2004" (Washington, D.C.: U.S. Department of Education, 2004), various tables.

10. Center for Education Reform, "Charter Schools Today," 6.

Chapter 8: Choice Is Not Enough

1. Spencer S. Hsu and V. Dion Haynes, "Voucher Plan Expansion Considered; Senator Weighs Using Schools Outside D.C.," *Washington Post*, June 30, 2005.

2. Jeff Flake, "Congressman Flake: D.C. Parents Deserve the Right to Choose Where Their Kids Go to School," press release, May 9, 2003.

3. Stephen S. Hsu, "How Vouchers Came to D.C.," *Education Next*, Fall 2004, 44.

4. Spencer S. Hsu, "Congress Puts Hold on D.C. School Funds; $10.6 Million Tied to Voucher Program," *Washington Post*, June 24, 2004.

5. Valerie Strauss, "Charter Schools Face Tests in Rush to Get Ready," *Washington Post*, May 4, 1998.

6. Sewell Chan, "Sallie Mae Gives $28 Million to D.C. Charter Schools," *Washington Post*, September 8, 2004.

7. U.S. Census Bureau, *Public Education Finances 2003* (Washington, D.C.: Government Printing Office, March 2005), table 11.

8. For further reading, see Brad M. Barber and Masako N. Darrough, "Product Reliability and Firm Value: The Experience of American and Japanese Automakers, 1973–1992," *Journal of Political Economy* 104, no. 5 (1996): 1084.

9. For further reading, see Caroline M. Hoxby, "Would School Choice Change the Teaching Profession?" *The Journal of Human Resources* 37, no. 4 (2002): 846; Jay P. Greene and Marcus A. Winters, "When Schools Compete: The Effects of Vouchers on Florida Public School Achievement," Education Working Paper no. 2, Manhattan Institute for Policy Research, August 2003.

10. For further reading, see Finn, Manno, and Vanourek, "Charter Schools in Action," and Robert Maranto, "Finishing Touches," *Education Next*, Winter 2001.

Chapter 9: Inclusive Ambiguity

1. Frederick M. Hess, "Reform, Resistance, . . . Retreat? The Predictable Politics of Accountability in Virginia," in *Brookings Papers on Education Policy 2002*, ed. Diane Ravitch (Washington, D.C.: Brookings Institution, 2002); Frederick M. Hess, "Refining or Retreating? High-Stakes Accountability in the States," in *Taking Account of Accountability*, ed. Paul Peterson and Martin West (Washington, D.C.: Brookings Institution, 2003), 69–122.

2. Joseph J. Pedulla, Lisa M. Abrams, George F. Madaus, Michael K. Russel, Miguel A. Ramos, and Jing Miao, *Perceived Effects of State-Mandated Testing Programs on Teaching and Learning: Findings from a National Survey of Teachers* (Boston, Mass.: National Board on Educational Testing and Public Policy, 2003).

3. New York State Education Department, *Learning Standards for Social Studies*, 2003, http://usny.nysed.gov/teachers/nyslearningstandards.html (accessed June 11, 2003).

4. Yehudi O. Webster, *Against the Multicultural Agenda: A Critical Thinking Alternative* (Westport, Conn.: Praeger, 1997), 44.

5. James A. Davis and Tom W. Smith, *General Social Survey* (Chicago: National Opinion Research Center, 2002).

6. "African/African-American Baseline Essays," in PPS Geocultural Baseline Essays Series (Portland, Ore.: Multnomah School District, 1987), http://www.pps.k12.or.us/depts-c/mc-me/essays-5.php (accessed November 1, 2005). See also Erich Martel, "The Egyptian Illusion: Fatal Flaws in One Popular Afrocentric Text," *Washington Post*, February 20, 1994.

7. Irving Klotz, "Multicultural Perspectives in Science Education: One Prescription for Failure," *Phi Delta Kappan* 75, no. 3 (1993), 266.

8. *Edwards v. Aguillard*, 482 U.S. 578 (1987).

9. Jonathan Zimmerman, *Whose America? Culture Wars in the Public Schools* (Cambridge, Mass.: Harvard University Press, 2002), 132.

10. Stephanie Warsmith, "Theory of Evolution Will Face Test in Vote," Akron *Beacon Journal*, December 8, 2002.

11. Associated Press, "Lawmaker Hails Teachers' Union Scrapping of Gay Curriculum," *Associated Press State & Local Wire*, July 8, 2001, retrieved from Lexis-Nexis database.

12. Jason Wermers, "Critics Say SOLs Slight Civil War," *Richmond Times-Dispatch*, March 22, 2001).

13. Paula Caballero and Jessica DeLeon, "Changing the Face of Education: School Districts Must Do More to Teach Students about Hispanics' Contributions to the U.S.," *Fort Worth Star-Telegram*, September 15, 2002.

14. Todd Gitlin, *The Twilight of Common Dreams: Why America is Wracked by Culture Wars* (New York: Metropolitan Books, 1995).

15. Gary Nash and Charlotte Crabtree, eds., *National Standards for World History: Exploring Paths to the Present*, expanded edition (Los Angeles: National Center for History in the Schools, 1994).

16. National History Standards Task Force, *National Standards for United States History* (Los Angeles: National History Standards Task Force, 1994); Nathan Glazer, *We Are All Multiculturalists Now* (Cambridge, Mass.: Harvard University Press, 1997).

17. Lynne Cheney, *Telling the Truth* (New York: Touchstone, 1995).

18. Lynne Cheney, "New History Standards Still Attack Our Heritage," *Wall Street Journal*, May 2, 1996, A14, and John P. Diggins, "History Standards Get It Wrong Again," *New York Times*, May 15, 1996.

19. Clair W. Keller, "Comparing the Original and Revised Standards for History," *The History Teacher* 30, no. 1 (1997): 336.

20. Gary B. Nash, "Early American History and the National History Standards," *William and Mary Quarterly* 54, no. 3 (1997): 600. See also Diane Ravitch and Arthur M. Schlesinger Jr., "The New, Improved History Standards," *Wall Street Journal*, April 3, 1996, and George F. Will, "A Standard for History," *Washington Post*, April 7, 1996, as cited in Clair W. Keller, "Comparing the Original and Revised Standards for History," 320.

21. Jo Thomas, "Revised History Standards Disarm the Explosive Issues," *New York Times*, April 3, 1996.

22. Keller, "Comparing the Original and Revised Standards for History," 312–17.

23. Ibid., 336.

24. Jason Wermers, "Educators Struggle to Revise Standards: What to Include in History, Social Sciences Stirs Trouble," *Richmond Times-Dispatch*, January 22, 2001.

25. Jason Wermers, "Revised Standards Criticized: History Changes Rapped by Second Group," *Richmond Times-Dispatch*, March 12, 2001.

26. Wermers, "Educators Struggle to Revise Standards."

27. Wermers, "Revised Standards Criticized."

28. Jason Wermers, "Panel Suggests Revision: Proposal Adds Armenian Genocide," *Richmond Times-Dispatch*, March 2, 2001.

29. Jason Wermers, "SOL Genocide Plank Deleted: Revised History Standards OK'd," *Richmond Times-Dispatch*, March 24, 2001.

30. Ellen Sorokin, "No Founding Fathers? That's Our New History: Overkill on Political Correctness Seen," *Washington Times*, January 28, 2002.

31. Ellen Sorokin, "Founding Fathers Given New Life in New Jersey: Draft Left Them Out of History Books," *Washington Times*, February 2, 2002.

32. Diane Ravitch, *The Language Police: How Pressure Groups Restrict What Students Learn* (New York: Knopf, 2003).

33. Pennsylvania Department of Education, *Academic Standards for History, 2002,* http://www.pde.state.pa.us/stateboard_ed/cwp/view.asp?a=3&Q=76716&stateboard_edNav=|5467|&pde_internetNav=| (accessed June 11, 2003).

34. New York State Education Department, *Learning Standards for Social Studies*, 1996, http://usny.nysed.gov/teachers/nyslearningstandards.html (accessed June 11, 2003).

35. Texas Education Agency, *Texas Essential Knowledge and Skills for Social Studies: Subchapter C, High School, 1998,* http://www.tea.state.tx.us/rules/tac/chapter113/ch113c.html#113.31 (accessed June 11, 2003).

36. Even traditionalist critics such as the Thomas B. Fordham Foundation have ranked Texas and Oklahoma's history standards as among the ten best in the nation. Thomas B. Fordham Foundation, *The State of State Standards* (Washington, D.C.: Thomas B. Fordham Foundation, 2000). Oklahoma Department of Education, Priority Academic Student Skills: Social Studies, 2002, http://sde.state.ok.us/acrob/pass/socialstudies.pdf (accessed June 11, 2003).

37. The Thomas B. Fordham Foundation has ranked Kansas and Indiana's history standards in the top third nationally. Thomas B. Fordham Foundation, *The State of State Standards.*

Chapter 10: "Trust Us," They Explained

1. Lott's exact words at the December 5, 2002, event were, "When Strom Thurmond ran for president, we [Mississippians] voted for him. We're proud of it. . . . And if the rest of the country had followed our lead, we wouldn't have had all these problems over all these years, either." *Facts on File World News Digest*, "Politics: Lott Criticized for Thurmond Remarks," December 6, 2002, 936D2.

2. Edward G. Carmines and James A. Stimson, *Issue Evolution: Race and the Transformation of American Politics* (Princeton, N.J.: Princeton University Press, 1989), 165.

3. J. C. Watts, "Good, Mad and Ugly: Our Words of the Year," *Daily Oklahoman*, January 4, 1998.

4. David A. Bositis, *Black Elected Officials, A Statistical Summary 2000* (Washington, D.C.: Joint Center for Political and Economic Studies, 2001).

5. Black America's Political Action Committee, "2004 National Survey of African American Registered Voters" (Washington, D.C.: Black America's Political Action Committee, 2004), 6

6. David A. Bositis, *National Opinion Poll: Politics* (Washington, D.C.: Joint Center for Political and Economic Studies, 2002).

7. National Commission on Excellence in Education, *A Nation at Risk: The Imperative for Educational Reform* (Washington, D.C.: Government Printing Office, 1983).

8. 1988 Republican Party Platform, 41, http://www.presidency.ucsb.edu/show-platforms.php?platindex=R1988 (accessed February 12, 2003).

9. *Los Angeles Times*, presidential election 2000 exit poll, based on interviews with 8,132 voters as they exited 140 polling places across the nation on Tuesday, November 7, 2000 (there was an oversample of Californian voters), http://www.pollingreport.com/2000.htm#Exit (accessed November 1, 2005).

10. *Los Angeles Times*, presidential election 2004 exit poll, based on interviews with 5,154 voters (including 3,357 California voters), using self-administered, confidential questionnaires as the voters exited 136 polling places across the nation on November 2, 2004, fieldwork by Schlesinger Associates and Davis Research, http://www.pollingreport.com/2004.htm#Exit (accessed November 1, 2005).

11. This tension can be readily illustrated with poll data. In 1964, for example, 79 percent of respondents to one poll agreed, "We should rely more on individual initiative and ability and not so much on governmental welfare programs." When the same 1964 poll asked respondents to identify what was responsible for holding unsuccessful people back in life, the most common response was not a lack of individual talent or initiative, but a "lack of education and training." Survey by Potomac Associates and Gallup Organization, September 1964, iPOLL Databank, The Roper Center for Public Opinion Research, University of Connecticut, http://www.roper-center.uconn.edu/ipoll.html (accessed September 22, 2005).

12. Joint Center for Political and Economic Studies, *National Opinion Poll: Education.* (Washington, D.C.: Joint Center for Political and Economic Studies, 1998).

13. Black America's Political Action Committee, *2002 National Opinion Poll*, http://www.bampac.org/opinion_polls2002.asp?index=6 (accessed February 14, 2003).

14. Rose C. Lowell and Alec M. Gallup, "The 34th Annual Phi Delta Kappa/Gallup Poll of the Public's Attitudes Toward the Public Schools," *Phi Delta Kappan* 84, no. 1 (2002): 41–56. Ellen Sorokin, "Poll Finds Most Blacks Favor Charter, Private Schools," *Washington Times*, July 19, 2002.

15. John E. Chubb and Tom Loveless, "Bridging the Achievement Gap," in *Bridging the Achievement Gap*, ed. John Chubb and Tom Loveless (Washington, D.C.: Brookings Institution, 2002), 2.

16. Christopher Jencks and Meredith Phillips, "The Black-White Test Score Gap: An Introduction," in *The Black-White Test Score Gap*, ed. Christopher Jencks and Meredith Phillips (Washington, D.C.: Brookings Institution, 1998), 1–2.

17. Michael A. Boozer, Alan B. Krueger, and Shari Wolkon, "Race and School Quality Since *Brown v. Board of Education*," in *Brookings Papers on Economic Activity: Microeconomics*, eds. Martin Neil Baily and Clifford Winston (Washington, D.C.: Brookings Institution, 1992), 270.

18. David A. Bositis, "2004 National Opinion Poll: Politics and the 2004 Election" (Washington, D.C.: Joint Center for Political and Economic Studies, 2004), 9.

19. For instance, polls conducted by the Milton and Rose Friedman Foundation found that over 60 percent and even over 80 percent of African-Americans support school vouchers. See Milton and Rose Friedman Foundation, "National Study Raises Question of Bias in Annual Phi Delta Kappa Poll: Results Show Majority of Americans Support School Vouchers," Rose and Milton Friedman Foundation, August 20, 2004, 1, http://www.friedmanfoundation.org/news/2004-08-20.html (accessed July 9, 2005).

20. Joint Center for Political and Economic Studies database, "Table 7: Would you support a voucher system where parents would get money from the government to send their children to the public, private, or parochial school of their choice?" from section on "Black Elected Officials: Opinions of Black Elected Officials (BEOs) compared to the African-American population," http://www.jointcenter.org/DB/table/NOP/BEO/VOUCHERS.doc (accessed February 11, 2003).

21. Anonymous, in conversation with the author, October 15, 1999.

22. David A. Bositis, "School Vouchers along the Color Line," *New York Times*, August 15, 2001.

23. Anonymous, in conversation with the author, July 22, 2002.

24. Readers are likely to be well acquainted with the work of scholars like Paul Peterson, Caroline Hoxby, Jay Greene, and Terry Moe that suggests the benefits of school choice. This work is certainly valuable and persuasive. However, there is also thoughtful scholarship that could leave a fair-minded reader unconvinced that the merits of choice-based reform are clearly established. See, for instance, Helen F. Ladd, "School Vouchers: A Critical View," *Journal of Economic Perspectives* 16, no. 4 (2002): 3–24, or Derek Neal, "How Vouchers Could Change the Market for Education," *Journal of Economic Perspectives* 16, no. 4 (2002): 25–44.

25. Quoted in Frederick M. Hess, *Revolution at the Margins: The Impact of Competition on Urban School Systems* (Washington, D.C.: Brookings Institution: 2002), 123.

26. Equal Employment Opportunity Commission, *Job Patterns for Minorities and Women in State and Local Government* (Washington, D.C.: Equal Employment Opportunity Commission, 1999), 18.

27. Ibid.

28. Howard Fuller, "A Voice for Choice," as quoted by Fritz S. Steiger in CEO America's electronic newsletter, August 28, 2000.

29. Boston Consulting Group, *The Business Case for Pursuing Retail Opportunities in the Inner City, Initiative for a Competitive Inner City* (Boston: Boston Consulting Group, 1998).

30. Pricewaterhouse Coopers, *The Inner-City Shopper: A Strategic Perspective, Initiative for a Competitive City* (Boston: Pricewaterhouse Coopers, 1999).

Chapter 11: School Vouchers and Suburbanites

1. *Zelman v. Simmons-Harris* 536 U.S. 639 (2002) Docket Number: 00-1751.

2. See Robert Aguirre, "School Choice: The Fears Versus the Truth," in *An Education Agenda: Let Parents Choose Their Children's Schools*, ed. John C. Goodman and Fritz F. Steiger (Dallas, Tex.: National Center for Policy Analysis, 2001). See also Ronald Roach, "Scholars, Policy-Makers Urge Choice as the Way To Education Reform," *Black Issues in Higher Education* 20, no. 8 (June 5, 2003): 8.

3. Thomas J. Nechyba, "Introducing School Choice into Multi-District Public School Systems," in *The Economics of School Choice*, ed. Caroline Hoxby (Chicago, Ill.: University of Chicago Press, 2002).

4. Amy Hetzner, "Open Enrollment Surprises Some Schools; Free to Choose, Parents Aren't Making Decisions that Were Expected," *Milwaukee Journal Sentinel*, February 18, 2001. Erick Trickey, "Crossing the Line; Every Year, Hundreds of Parents Sneak Their Kids into Schools Where They Don't Belong. And Some are Going to Jail," *Cleveland Scene*, October 12, 2000.

Chapter 12: The Voice of the People

1. Glenn Cook, "Leading City Schools: Challenge and Change in Urban Education," *American School Board Journal*, December 2002, special report, 1–2.

2. Frederick M. Hess, "School Boards at the Dawn of the 21st Century: Conditions and Challenges of District Governance" (Alexandria, Va.: National School Boards Association, 2002).

3. See, for instance, Stuart S. Nagel, "Political Party Affiliation and Judges' Decisions," *The American Political Science Review* 55, no. 4 (December 1961): 843-50.

4. See, for instance, Stephen Coate and Timothy Besley, "Elected Versus Appointed Regulators: Theory and Evidence," *Journal of the European Economic Association* 1, no. 5 (2003): 1176–1206.

5. For further reading, see Marver H. Bernstein, "Independent Regulatory Agencies: A Perspective on Their Reform," *Fifth Annual Conference of the Institute of Public Utilities*, Michigan State University, November 4–5, 1971.

6. See Michael K. Schaub, Frank Collins, Oscar Holzmann, and Suzanne H. Lowensohn, "Self Interest vs. Concern for Others: What's the Impact on Management Accountants' Ethical Decisions?" *Strategic Finance*, March 1, 2005.

7. For further reading, see Henry L. Tosi, Wei Shen, and Richard J. Gentry, "Why Outsiders on Boards Can't Solve the Corporate Governance Problem," *Organizational Dynamics*, May 2003.

8. Hess, "School Boards at the Dawn of the 21st Century."

9. Ibid.

10. Ibid.

11. George F. Will, "The Jury Room is No Place for TV," *Washington Post*, January 5, 2003.

12. For further reading, see Jerry Mitchell, "Representation in Government Boards and Commissions," *Public Administration Review* 57, no. 2 (1997): 160–7.

Part 4: Finding Teachers and Principals

1. Frederick M. Hess, "A License to Lead? A New Leadership Agenda for America's Schools," Progressive Policy Institute 21st Century Schools Project, January 2003; and Frederick M. Hess, "Tear Down This Wall: The Case for a Radical Overhaul of Teacher Certification" (Washington, D.C.: Progressive Policy Institute 21st Century Schools Project, November 2001).

2. Patrick Welsh, "System Snubs Qualified Teachers," *USA Today*, Aug 13, 2002.

3. Arthur Levine, "Educating School Leaders" (Washington, D.C.: The Education Schools Project, March 2005).

4. Frederick M. Hess, Andrew J. Rotherham, and Kate Walsh, eds., *A Qualified Teacher in Every Classroom? Appraising Old Answers and New Ideas* (Cambridge, Mass.: Harvard Education Press, 2004).

Chapter 13: Tear Down This Wall

1. Dale Ballou and Michael Podgursky have made this point, explaining, "The case for licensure in medicine rests partly on the premise that consumers cannot make well-informed decisions concerning the quality of medical services. There is a complex body of specialized medical knowledge that medical consumers cannot be expected to know." The same is not true in the case of schooling, since, as we shall shortly see, even professional educators are not sure what teachers need to know or be able to do. See Dale Ballou and Michael Podgursky, "The Case Against Teacher Certification," *The Public Interest*, no. 132 (1998): 17–29.

2. National Board for Professional Teaching Standards, "Early Adolescence/ Mathematics Overview," http://www.nbpts.org/candidates/guide/whichcert/12Early AdolMath2004.html (accessed June 6, 2001).

3. To read about the NBPTS and its standards, visit the board's homepage at www.nbpts.org.

4. For instance, see James Nehring, "Certifiably Strange," *Teacher Magazine* 13, no. 1 (August 2001): 49–51. The article tells the story of a Massachusetts social studies teacher who was denied NBPTS certification because he failed to meet the "Collaboration in Professional Community" standards, even though the teacher had authored four books on teaching and schooling and had helped to launch two successful public schools. For a more systematic and scholarly indictment of the NBPTS's standards and the way they are implemented, see Danielle Dunn Wilcox, "The National Board for Professional Teaching Standards: Can It Live Up to Its Promise?" in *Better Teachers, Better Schools*, ed. Marci Kanstoroom and Chester E. Finn (Washington, D.C.: Thomas Fordham Foundation, 1999).

5. Mary E. Diez, "Teacher Education Programs Are All the Same," in *Dispelling Myths About Teacher Education*, ed. Greta Morine-Dershimer and Gail Huffman-Joley (Washington, D.C.: AACTE, 2000).

6. Gerald Grant and Christine E. Murray, *Teaching in America: The Slow Revolution* (Cambridge, Mass.: Harvard University Press, 1999).

7. See Ruth Mitchell and Patte Barth, "Not Good Enough: A Content Analysis of Teacher Licensing Examinations," *Thinking K–16* 3, no. 1 (Spring 1999), a publication of Education Trust Inc., Washington, D.C.

8. Author's calculation.

9. Anonymous, in conversation with the author, May 13, 2001.

10. Especially for those who did not complete the teacher-training program as undergraduates, the costs can be significant. See American Association of Colleges for Teacher Education, *Alternative Paths to Teaching: A Directory of Post-Baccalaureate Programs* (Washington, D.C.: American Association of Colleges for Teacher Education 2000).

Chapter 14: A License to Lead?

1. Doug Garr, *IBM Redux: Lou Gerstner and the Business Turnaround of the Decade* (New York: HarperInformation, 1999).

2. Ibid.

3. Ibid.

4. For further reading, see Michael S. Malone, "Meet Meg Whitman . . . ," *Wall Street Journal*, March 16, 2005; Patricia Sellers, "eBay's Secret," *Fortune* (Europe) 150, no. 7, November 18, 2004.

5. Over the past four years, the franchise network went from roughly 170 to approximately 300 franchises domestically. Sean Greenwood (public affairs, Ben & Jerry's), personal correspondence, July 27, 2005; Stephanie Thompson, "Player Profile: Ben & Jerry's Puts Freese on Global Warming, Sales; Exec Aims to Drive Sales While Staying True to Mission," *Advertising Age*, August 17, 2001.

6. Del Stover, "Looking for Leaders," *American School Board Journal* 189, no. 12 (December 2002): 38; Paul Houston, "Superintendents for the 21st Century: It's Not Just a Job, It's a Calling," *Phi Delta Kappan* 82, no. 6 (June 2001), 428–33.

7. Public Agenda, *Trying to Stay Ahead of the Game: Superintendents and Principals Talk about School Leadership* (Washington, D.C.: Public Agenda, 2001).

8. U.S. Department of Education, National Center for Education Statistics, *Schools and Staffing Survey 1999–2000* (Washington, D.C.: Government Printing Office, 2002), table 1.11: "Percentage of Public School Principals with Experience in Teaching, Administration, or Other Selected Positions before Becoming Principals, by State and Selected Characteristics, 1999–2000," 27.

9. Steve Farkas, Jean Johnson, and Ann Duffett, *Rolling Up Their Sleeves: Superintendents and Principals Talk About What's Needed to Fix Public Schools* (Washington, D.C.: Public Agenda, 2003).

10. Robert L. Crowson, "Managerial Ethics in Educational Administration: The Rational Choice Approach," *Urban Education* 23, no. 4 (1989), 412.

11. Steve Farkas, Jean Johnson, and Ann Duffett, *Stand by Me: What Teachers Really Think about Unions, Merit Pay and Other Professional Matters* (Washington, D.C.: Public Agenda, 2003).

12. *U.S. News & World Report*, "America's Best Graduate Schools 2004," vol. 134, no. 12 (April 14, 2003): 64, 66; See also expanded edition of the *U.S. News and World Report* special report, "America's Best Graduate Schools" (2004), 51.

13. Thomas Sergiovanni, *Leadership for the Schoolhouse* (San Francisco: Jossey-Bass, 1996), xiv.

14. Steve Mancini (director of public relations, KIPP Foundation), in conversation with the author, July 11, 2005.

15. Joyce Park (program assistant, Broad Foundation), in conversation with the author, July 11, 2005.

16. The states that use the ISLLC standards are Alaska, Connecticut, Delaware, D.C., Hawaii, Illinois, Indiana, Iowa, Kansas, Kentucky, Louisiana, Maryland, Minnesota, Mississippi, Missouri, New Mexico, North Carolina, North Dakota, Ohio, Oklahoma, Rhode Island, Texas, Virginia, and Washington.

17. In full, the standards read: (1) "facilitating the development, articulation, implementation, and stewardship of a vision of learning that is shared and supported by the school community"; (2) "advocating, nurturing, and sustaining a school culture and instructional program conducive to student learning and staff professional growth"; (3) "ensuring the management of the organization, operations, and resources for a safe, efficient, and effective learning environment"; (4) "collaborating with families and community members, responding to diverse community interests and needs, and mobilizing community resources"; (5) "acting with integrity, fairness, and in an ethical manner"; (6) "understanding, responding to, and influencing the larger political, social, economic, legal, and cultural context." Interstate School Leaders Licensure Consortium, "Standards for School Leaders," Council of Chief State School Officers, 1996, http://www.ccsso.org (accessed November 4, 2002).

18. Available online at http://www.ccsso.org/isllc.html.

19. Kate Beem, "Testing Superintendents," *School Administrator*, February 2002, http://www.aasa.org/publications/sa/ (accessed November 8, 2002).

20. Educational Testing Service, *The School Leadership Series Tests at a Glance*, ftp://ftp.ets.org/pub/tandl/SLSTAAG.pdf (accessed November 10, 2002).

21. Ibid, 14. As even Martha McCarthy, chancellor professor of educational leadership at Indiana University and a staunch defender of educational administration programs and licensure, has noted, "It is difficult to envision that responding to a set of vignettes—no matter how skillfully crafted—can confirm that administrative licensure candidates exhibit the desired skills, knowledge, and values for effective school leaders." Martha McCarthy, "Challenges Facing Educational Leadership Programs: Our Future is Now," *Newsletter of the Teaching in Educational Administration Special Interest Group of the American Educational Research Association* 8, no. 1 (2001), 1.

Chapter 15: Ready to Lead?

1. Bill and Melinda Gates Foundation, "New Report: High School Models Show Promise in Increasing Nation's Graduation and College-Readiness Rates," February 15, 2005, http://www.gatesfoundation.org/Education/TransformingHighSchools/Schools/Announcements/Announce-050215.htm (accessed March 13, 2005).

2. Farkas, Johnson, and Duffett, *Rolling Up Their Sleeves.*

3. Michelle Young and Frances Kochan, "UCEA Leaders Respond: Supporting Leadership for America's Schools," in *Better Leaders for America's Schools: Perspectives on the Manifesto*, ed. Thomas J. Lasley (Columbia, Mo.: University Council for Educational Administration, 2004).

4. Levine, *Educating School Leaders.*

5. Frederick M. Hess and Andrew P. Kelly, "Learning to Lead: What Gets Taught in Principal Preparation Programs," Occasional Paper 05-02, Program on Education Policy and Governance (Cambridge, Mass.: Harvard University Press, 2005); Hess and Kelly, "Textbook Leadership? Analysis of Leading Books Used in Principal Preparation," Occasional Paper 05-03, Program on Education Policy and Governance (Cambridge, Mass.: Harvard University Press, 2005).

6. Hess and Kelly, "Learning to Lead."

7. Ibid., 20.

8. Ibid., 27.

9. Ibid., 33.

10. Hess and Kelly, "Textbook Leadership?" 13.

11. Ibid, 15.

12. Ibid, 19–21.

13. Farkas et al., *Rolling Up Their Sleeves.*

14. National College for School Leadership, "One Good Turn," *LDR Magazine*, August 20, 2004.

15. Farkas et al., *Rolling Up Their Sleeves.*

Chapter 16: The Predictable, but Unpredictably Personal, Politics of Teacher Licensure

1. It is worth noting that some prominent "professionalizers" disagree with the thrust of the ECS analysis and argue that the research does, indeed, endorse licensure and preparation. See Linda Darling-Hammond, "Research and Rhetoric on Teacher Certification: A Response to 'Teacher Certification Reconsidered,'" *Education Policy Analysis Archives* 10, no. 36 (2002): 1–54; National Education Association, *Teacher Quality: Moving Forward* (Washington, D.C.: National Education Association, 2004); Michael Allen, *Eight Questions on Teacher Preparation: What Does the Research Say?* (Denver, Colo.: Education Commission of the States, 2003), 3.

2. David Imig, "Remarks," transcript of the National Press Club Discussion Forum on the release of *Tear Down This Wall*, November 27, 2001, 8.

3. Cochran-Smith, "Sometimes It's Not About the Money."

4. Hess, *Tear Down This Wall*, 5.

5. David Berliner, "A Personal Response to Those Who Bash Teacher Education," *Journal of Teacher Education* 51, no. 5 (2000): 358–71; Kenneth A. Sirotnik and Associates, *Renewing Schools and Teacher Education: An Odyssey in Educational Change* (Washington, D.C.: American Association of Colleges for Teacher Education, 2001); Gary Sykes, with Marisa Burian-Fitzgerald, "Cultivating Quality in Teaching: A Brief for Professional Standards," in *A Qualified Teacher in Every Classroom? Appraising Old Answers and New Ideas*, ed. Frederick Hess, Andrew Rotherham, and Kate Walsh (Cambridge, Mass.: Harvard Education Press, 2004); Suzanne Wilson, Linda Darling-Hammond, and Barnett Berry, *A Case of Successful Teaching Policy: Connecticut's Long-Term Efforts to Improve Teaching and Learning* (Seattle, Wash.: University of Washington, 2001); Arthur E. Wise and Jane A. Leibbrand, *A Professional Model of Accountability for Teaching* (Denver, Colo.: Education Commission of the States, 2003).

6. Hess, *Common Sense School Reform*; Marci Kanstoroom and Chester E. Finn Jr., *Better Teachers, Better Schools* (Washington, D.C.: Thomas B. Fordham Foundation, 1999); Michael Podgursky, "Improving Academic Performance in U.S. Public Schools: Why Teacher Licensing Is (Almost) Irrelevant," in *A Qualified Teacher in Every Classroom? Appraising Old Answers and New Ideas*, ed. Frederick Hess, Andrew Rotherham, and Kate Walsh (Cambridge, Mass.: Harvard Education Press, 2004).

7. Arthur E. Wise and Jane A. Leibbrand, "Standards and Teacher Quality," *Phi Delta Kappan* 81, no. 8 (2000): 617.

8. Berliner, "A Personal Response to Those Who Bash Teacher Education."

9. David L. Angus, edited by Jeffery Mirel, *Professionalism and the Public Good: A Brief History of Teacher Certification* (Washington, D.C.: Thomas B. Fordham Foundation, 2001).

10. Carnegie Task Force of Carnegie Corporation of New York, "A Nation Prepared: Teachers for the 21st Century" (New York: Carnegie Corporation of New York, 1986), and the Holmes Group, "Tomorrow's Teachers: A Report of the Holmes Group" (East Lansing: Mich.: The Holmes Group, Inc., 1986).

11. Marilyn Cochran-Smith, "Taking Stock in 2004: Teacher Education in Dangerous Times," *Journal of Teacher Education* 55, no. 1 (2004): 6.

12. Kevin K. Kumashiro, *Against Common Sense: Teaching and Learning Toward Social Justice* (New York: RoutledgeFalmer, 2004), xiv–xvi.

13. Marilyn Cochran-Smith and Mary Kim Fries, "Sticks, Stones, and Ideology: The Discourse of Reform in Teacher Education," *Educational Researcher* 30, no. 8 (2002): 3.

14. Martin J. Rochester, *Class Warfare: Besieged Schools, Bewildered Parents, Betrayed Kids and the Attack on Excellence* (San Francisco: Encounter Books, 2002).

15. James W. Fraser, "A Tenuous Hold," *Education Next* 2, no. 1 (2002): 16–21.

16. Cochran-Smith, "Sometimes It's Not About the Money," 371.

17. Alfie Kohn, *What Does It Mean to Be Well Educated?* (Boston: Beacon Press, 2004), 13.

18. Kathy Emery and Susan Ohanian, *Why Is Corporate America Bashing Our Public Schools?* (Portsmouth, N.H.: Heineman, 2004).

19. Rochester, *Class Warfare*.

20. Martin A. Kozloff, "Insubstantial Pageants," University of North Carolina at Wilmington, 2001, http://people.uncw.edu/kozloffm/pageants.htm (accessed August 21, 2004).

Chapter 17: Lessons from San Diego

1. Daphna Bassok and Margaret E. Raymond, "Performance Trends and the Blueprint for Student Success," in *Urban School Reform: Lessons from San Diego*, ed. Frederick M. Hess (Cambridge, Mass.: Harvard Education Press, 2005), 299–323.

2. Ibid.

3. Amy M. Hightower and Milbrey W. McLaughlin, "Building and Sustaining an Infrastructure for Learning," in *Urban School Reform: Lessons from San Diego*, ed. Frederick M. Hess (Cambridge, Mass.: Harvard Education Press, 2005), 71–92.

4. For further reading, see Jennifer A. O'Day, "Standards-Based Reform and Low-Performing Schools: A Case of Reciprocal Accountability," in *Urban School Reform: Lessons from San Diego*, ed. Frederick M. Hess (Cambridge, Mass.: Harvard Education Press, 2005), 115–38.

5. Joe Williams, "The Labor Management Showdown," in *Urban School Reform: Lessons from San Diego*, ed. Frederick M. Hess (Cambridge, Mass.: Harvard Education Press, 2005), 33–51.

6. Christine Campbell, Michael DeArmond, and Sara Taggart, "Toward a Portfolio of Schools: High School Renewal," in *Urban School Reform: Lessons from San Diego*, ed. Frederick M. Hess (Cambridge, Mass.: Harvard Education Press, 2005), 139–59.

7. Michael D. Usdan, "Board Governance and External Constituencies," in *Urban School Reform: Lessons from San Diego*, ed. Frederick M. Hess (Cambridge, Mass.: Harvard Education Press, 2005): 11–31.

8. Peter A. Robertson, "The Role of Information and Communication Technology in Educational Reform," in *Urban School Reform: Lessons from San Diego*, ed. Frederick M. Hess (Cambridge, Mass.: Harvard Education Press, 2005), 199–221.

Chapter 18: Science and Nonscience

1. For further reading, see Michael Castle, "Delaware Education Community: No Child Left Behind is Closing the Achievement Gap," press release, September 17, 2004, http://www.house.gov/castle/pr_04_nclbhearing.html (accessed January 19, 2005); Alan Farstrup, Cathy Roller, and Reid Lyon, "Reading First," NCLB

Teleconference Series, Plato Learning, February 25, 2003, http://www.plato.com/research/nclb_teleconference.asp (accessed January 14, 2005); Grover (Russ) Whitehurst, mathematics and science initiative presentation, U.S. Department of Education, http://www.ed.gov/rschstat/research/progs/mathscience/whitehurst.html (accessed February 4, 2005).

2. See Kathleen Kennedy Manzo, "Father of 'Whole Language' Rallying Against Reading-Group Speaker," *Education Week*, March 3, 2004, http://www.edweek.org/ew/articles/2004/03/03/25ira.h23.html (accessed February 3, 2005).

3. More information on IES, its mission, and its programs can be found at its website, http://www.ed.gov/about/offices/list/ies/index.html.

4. For further reading, see Michael F. Giangreco and Steven J. Taylor, "Scientifically Based Research and Qualitative Inquiry," *Research & Practice for Persons with Severe Disabilities* 28, no. 3 (2003): 133–37.

Chapter 19: Technical Difficulties

1. Diane Curtis, "A Computer for Every Lap," Edutopia Online, May 13, 2003, www.edutopia.org/php/print.php?id=art_1032&template=printarticle.php (accessed January 12, 2004).

2. For further reading, see Cynthia L. Selfe, "The Humanization of Computers: Forget Technology, Remember Literacy," *The English Journal* 77, no. 6 (October 1988): 69–71.

3. Del Jones and Barbara Hansen, "Companies Do More With Less," *USA Today*, August 13, 2003.

4. *Education Week*, "Technology Spending," November 3, 2004, 17.

5. U.S. Department of Education, National Center for Education Statistics, "Internet Access in U.S. Public Schools and Classrooms 1994–2001," http://nces.ed.gov/pubs2002/internet/4.asp (accessed October 9, 2003).

6. Susan E. Ansell and Jennifer Park, "Tracking Tech Trends," *Education Week*, May 8, 2003, 45.

7. U.S. Department of Education, National Center for Education Statistics, *Digest of Education Statistics 2003* (Washington, D.C.: Government Printing Office, 2004), and *Digest of Education Statistics 1995* (Washington, D.C.: Government Printing Office, 1995).

8. Henry Giroux, "Schools for Sale," in *Education, Inc.: Turning Learning into a Business*, ed. Alfie Kohn and Patrick Shannon (Portsmouth, N.H.: Heinemann, 2001), 106.

9. For more information on the school, visit its website at www.flvs.net.

10. Elaine Allen and Jeff Seaman, "Seizing the Opportunity: The Quality and Extent of Online Education in the United States, 2002 and 2003" (Needham, Mass: The Sloan Consortium, September 2003).

11. Wendy Togneri, "Beyond Islands of Excellence: What Districts Can Do to Improve Instruction and Achievement in All Schools—A Leadership Brief" (Washington, D.C.: Learning First Alliance, 2003).

12. David C. Anderson, "Crime Control by the Numbers," *Ford Foundation Report*, Winter 2001. See also William K. Rashbaum, "Crime-Fighting by Computer: Scope Widens," *New York Times*, March 24, 2002, A43.

13. Raymond Dussault, "Maps and Management: Comstat Evolves," *Government Technology*, April 2000.

14. Elliott Levine, "The Data Trek," *American School Board Journal* 190, no. 9 (2003): 46–48.

15. Anonymous, in conversation with the author, November 12, 2003.

Chapter 20: On Leaving No Child Behind

1. Public Law 107-110, 115 Stat. 1425 (2002).

2. Dave Boyer, "Bush Campaign Says It's in the Bag; Top Strategist Sees 320 Votes; Bill Graham Offers a Boost," *Washington Times*, November 6, 2000, A1.

3. U.S. Department of Education, "10 Facts about K–12 Education Funding," 2005, http://www.ed.gov/about/overview/fed/10facts/index.html (accessed June 7, 2005).

4. Daniel P. Moynihan, *Maximum Feasible Misunderstanding: Community Action in the War on Poverty* (New York: Free Press, 1970).

5. Frederick M. Hess and Chester E. Finn, *Leaving No Child Behind? Options for Kids in Failing Schools* (New York: Palgrave Macmillan, 2004).

6. Molly Walsh, "Four Vt. Schools Opt Out Of Federal Program," *The Burlington Free Press* (Burlington, Vt.), September 22, 2003, A1; Jodi S. Cohen, "2 School Districts Reject Funds; 'No Child' Grants Seen as a Hassle," *Chicago Tribune*, August 15, 2004, C1; Sam Dillon, "Some School Districts Challenge Bush's Signature Education Law," *New York Times*, January 2, 2004, A1.

7. Erik W. Robelen, "Opposition to School Law Growing, Poll Says," *Education Week*, April 7, 2004, http://www.edweek.org/ew/articles/2004/04/07/30pen.h23.html?querystring=No%20Child%20Left%20Behind%20poll (accessed June 4, 2004).

8. U.S. General Accounting Office, "Unfunded Mandates: Analysis of Reform Coverage," GAO-04-637, May 2004, http://www.gao.gov/new.items/d04637.pdf (accessed July 16, 2004).

9. George W. Bush (governor of Texas), education policy speech, Manhattan Institute for Policy Research, New York, October 5, 1999. The full event transcript is at http://www.manhattan-institute.org/html/bush_speech.htm (accessed November 1, 2005).

About the Author

Frederick M. Hess is director of educational policy studies and a resident scholar at the American Enterprise Institute and executive editor of *Education Next*. His many books include *Common Sense School Reform*, *Revolution at the Margins*, *Spinning Wheels*, and *Bringing the Social Sciences Alive*. His work has appeared in numerous journals and publications, including *Urban Affairs Review*, *Social Science Quarterly*, *American Politics Quarterly*, *Teachers College Record*, *Education Week*, *Phi Delta Kappan*, *Educational Leadership*, and *National Review*. Dr. Hess currently serves on the review board for the Broad Prize in Urban Education, as a research associate with the Harvard University Program on Education Policy and Governance, and as a member of the research advisory board for the National Center on Educational Accountability. He is a former high school social studies teacher and professor of education who earned his MEd from the Harvard University Graduate School of Education and his MA and PhD from the Harvard University Department of Government.

Index